Contents

Tele-Visions
An Introduction to Studying Television

WITHDRAWN

Edited by Glen Creeber

For my students.

Television? The word is half Latin and half Greek. No good can come of it.

C.P. Scott.

Television! Teacher, mother, secret lover.

Homer Simpson.

First published in 2006 by the
BRITISH FILM INSTITUTE
21 Stephen Street, London W1T 1LN

The British Film Institute's purpose is to champion moving image culture
in all its richness and diversity across the UK, for the benefit of as wide an
audience as possible, and to create and encourage debate.

Reprinted 2009

Set by Fakenham Photosetting Limited, Fakenham, Norfolk
Printed and bound in Great Britain by Thomson Litho, East Kilbride, Scotland

Cover design: Ketchup
Cover illustration: *24*, Imagine Entertainment/20th Century Fox Television

British Library Cataloguing-in-Publication Data
A catalogue record for this book is available from the British Library

ISBN 1–84457–086–x/978–1–84457–086–7 (pbk)
ISBN 1–84457–085–1/978–1–84457–085–0 (hbk)

Note: selected words and phrases will be set in **bold** in order to draw attention to their importance.

Notes on Contributors

Elan Closs Stephens is Professor of Communications and Creative Industries at the University of Wales, Aberystwyth. She has been a member of the Department of Theatre, Film and Television throughout her academic career and founded the Thomson Foundation Regulatory Compliance Unit in the department. In 1998, she was appointed by the Department of Culture, Media and Sport to chair the Welsh Fourth Channel Authority, S4C, and is now serving her second term trying to apply her regulatory knowledge at first hand. Among her public appointments are Governor of the BFI and Governor of the University of Glamorgan. She is an Honorary Fellow of Trinity College, Carmarthen, and was awarded a CBE in 2001 for services to the Welsh language and broadcasting.

John Corner is Professor in the School of Politics and Communication Studies at the University of Liverpool. His latest book is the edited collection *Media and the Restyling of Politics* (with Dick Pels) (Sage, 2003) and he is currently working with colleagues on a history of the current-affairs programme, *World in Action*. He is an editor of the journal, *Media, Culture and Society*.

Glen Creeber is Senior Lecturer in Film and Television at the University of Wales, Aberystwyth where he currently runs an MA in Television Studies (see www. aber.ac.uk/tfts/ma/tv/). He is the author of *Dennis Potter: Between Two Worlds, A Critical Reassessment* (Macmillan, 1998) and *Serial Television:*

Big Drama on the Small Screen (BFI, 2004). He is also editor of *The Television Genre Book* (BFI, 2001) and *50 Key Television Programmes* (Arnold, 2004). He is currently co-editing a book (with Royston Martin) on digital media culture.

John Ellis is Professor in the Media Arts Department of Royal Holloway, University of London. After teaching Film Studies at the University of Kent until 1982, he set up the independent production company 'Large Door' to make documentaries for Channel 4, and he ran the company until 1999. His previous academic posts were at the Bournemouth Media School (1995–2002) and the University of Bergen, Norway (1989–2000). He is the author of *Visible Fictions* (Routledge, 1982), *Seeing Things: Television in the Age of Uncertainty* (I. B. Tauris, 2000) and numerous articles on television history, documentary and other topics.

Faye Ginsburg is Director of the Center for Media, Culture, and History at New York University where she is also the David B. Kriser Professor of Anthropology and the Co-Director of the Center for Religion and Media. Author and/or editor of four books, most recently *Media Worlds: Anthropology on New Terrain* (co-edited with Lila Abu Lughod and Brian Larkin; University of California Press, 2002), her work focuses on media, social movements, and cultural activism. She has been studying and supporting the development of indigenous media in Australia and elsewhere for over a decade.

John Hartley is Professor and Dean of the Faculty of Creative Industries, Queensland University of Technology, Australia. He is the author of many books and articles on TV studies going back to the 1970s (including *Reading Television* with John Fiske [Routledge, 1978]). His most recent books are *Uses of Television* (Routledge, 1999) and *The Indigenous Public Sphere: The Reporting and Reception of Aboriginal Issues in the Australian Media* (with Alan McKee [Oxford University Press, 2000]).

Matt Hills is a lecturer in the Cardiff School of Journalism, Media and Cultural Studies at Cardiff University. He is the author of *Fan Cultures* (Routledge, 2002) and *The Pleasures of Horror* (Continuum, forthcoming). He has recently contributed work on TV and fandom to edited collections such as *Teen TV* (BFI, 2004) and *The TV Studies Reader* (Routledge, 2004) as well as writing on the subject for journals such as *Mediactive* and *Social Semiotics*.

Jason Jacobs is Senior Lecturer in the School of Arts, Media and Culture, Griffith University, Australia. He is the author of *The Intimate Screen: Early British Television Drama* (Oxford University Press, 2000) and *Body Trauma TV: The New Hospital Dramas* (BFI, 2003) and associate editor of *The Television History Book* edited by Michele Hilmes (BFI, 2003).

Jamie Medhurst is a lecturer in Film and Television Studies at the University of Wales, Aberystwyth. His main teaching and research interests focus on broadcasting history and policy, television historiography, television and national identity and documentary film history. He has published journal articles and chapters in edited volumes on the history of independent television (ITV) in the UK and is currently working on a book on the history of ITV in Wales.

Robin Nelson is Professor and Head of Department of Contemporary Arts, Manchester Metropolitan University. He has broad research interests in the arts and media and his publications on TV drama include *Boys from the Blackstuff: The Making of a TV Drama* (Comedia, 1986) and *TV Drama in Transition: Forms, Values and Cultural Change* (St Martin's Press, 1997).

Kyle Nicholas is Assistant Professor of Communication at Old Dominion University in Norfolk, Virginia where he teaches courses in television and new media. He is the editor of *Open Windows: Remediation Strategies in Global Film Adaptations* (Aalborg University Press, 2005) and has published articles and chapters on telecommunications policy, new media technologies, the evolution of television genre and the development of online communities.

Tom O'Malley is Professor of Media Studies at the University of Wales, Aberystwyth. He has written on press and broadcasting history and policy. He is co-editor of the journal *Media History*. His publications include: *Closedown: The BBC and Government Broadcasting Policy, 1979–92* (Pluto, 1994), with Clive Soley, *Regulating the Press* (Pluto, 2000) and with D. Barlow and P. Mitchell, *The Media in Wales* (University of Wales Press, 2005).

Catrin Prys is a lecturer at the University of Wales, Aberystwyth, teaching through the medium of English and Welsh. She has published on British television drama and has extensively researched the work of Dennis Potter. Her other main research interests revolve around Welsh and European Theatre.

Lorna Roth is Associate Professor and Chairperson at the Department of Communication Studies, Concordia University in Montreal, Quebec, Canada. She has been involved in broadcasting policy development and analysis, and has consulted with First Peoples and multicultural/multiracial groups since the late 1970s. She is the author of *Something New in the Air: The Story of First Peoples Television Broadcasting in Canada* (McGill-Queens University Press, 2005) and *The Colour-Balance Project: Race and Visual Representation* (forthcoming).

Jamie Sexton is a lecturer at the University of Wales, Aberystwyth. He has worked on an Arts and Humanities Research Board-funded project at Cardiff University, studying audiences of cult media, and previously worked at the AHRB Centre for British Film and Television Studies, Birkbeck, researching technological change and aesthetics in British television of the 1960s and 1970s. He is currently co-editing a book with Laura Mulvey, *Experimental British Television*.

Mike Wayne teaches and researches film and television studies at Brunel University. He is the author of *Marxism and Media Studies: Key Concepts and Contemporary Trends* (Pluto, 2003) and the editor of *Understanding Film: Marxist Perspectives* (Pluto, 2005).

Introduction

Father Phil: Hope I'm not barging in.
Carmela: No, no. Just watching TV.

David Chase, *The Sopranos Scriptbook*, 2001: 68.

The dialogue above ironically reflects a general conception about television. 'Just watching TV' is a phrase we have all probably used at one time or another. We are less likely to say 'just watching the theatre' or 'just watching the cinema', but television has become so integrated into our daily and domestic lives that we frequently take it for granted, almost regarding it as just another part of the household furniture. But it is perhaps this everyday acceptance of the small screen that makes the study of television so crucially important. For, although we may have grown increasingly familiar with and indifferent to its ubiquitous glare, its power to construct and determine our view of the world should never be underestimated. Television constantly punctuates, articulates and manipulates the world around us, presenting us with highly constructed and artificial images that inevitably inform and influence our everyday lives and perceptions. Indeed, the potential power of television is so great precisely because we rarely recognise or perceive its internal dynamics at work, so good is it at making itself appear a **natural** and **transparent** 'window on the world'. As Robert C. Allen puts it (1992a: 7):

> Television, like cinema, painting, or photography, does not simply reflect the world in some direct, automatic way. Rather, it constructs representations of the world based on complex sets of conventions – conventions whose operations are largely hidden by their transparency. Like television itself most of the time, these conventions are so familiar in their effects that we don't notice them.

It is perhaps the almost subliminal and habitual nature of the television experience that has prevented the medium being taken seriously for so long. While film critics were soon arguing that *Citizen Kane* (Orson Welles, 1941) was a 'masterpiece' and therefore worthy of academic discussion, it seemed less easy to justify the cultural importance of a television soap opera, a weather forecast or a game show. While film studies could claim that *Citizen Kane* had an 'author' or ('**auteur**') in the form of its director Orson Welles, the mass-produced nature of most television and its highly commercialised context seemed to reduce it to an **industrial** rather than an **artistic** process (see Chapter 1). Indeed, so worthless did television appear to its early practitioners that classic programmes like *Doctor Who* (BBC, 1963–), *Juke Box Jury* (BBC, 1959–67) and *The Avengers* (ITV, 1961–9) were frequently lost or wiped over by television companies who appeared to have no idea of the cultural value of their own products (see Fiddy, 2001). And while *Citizen Kane* lasts a mere 119 minutes, television programmes like soap operas can frequently last decades, generating problems for the potential critic or student. Added to this, before the invention of domestic video recorders in the 1980s it was almost impossible to teach television **textually** (see Chapter 2), programmes (even contemporary ones) were simply not available for repeated analysis.

Many of these problems and artistic anxieties surrounding the study of television have inevitably

The Avengers: some episodes have been lost or wiped over

influenced the way the medium has been academically conceived and discussed. The field is therefore a complex and frequently confusing area of study that needs to be approached with some care and attention if the student is not to be completely overwhelmed by a seemingly endless array of critical issues, methodologies and cultural debates.

The study of television is certainly not easy to define. The major difficulty facing a student new to the field is that television has traditionally been studied in an **inter-disciplinary** manner. This simply means that the subject has generally been made up of a number of different disciplinary approaches – these include Sociology, Politics, Communication Arts, Linguistics, History, Literature, Drama, Media and Film Studies. So, while a Literature department might be interested in analysing the different narrative traditions of particular television programmes, a History department might be more interested in investigating television's institutional, political and historical development. Similarly, a Linguistics department might want to examine the use of language on television while a Sociology department might be more interested in researching the relationship between television and different sections in society.

To complicate matters further there are also those departments that offer **practical** courses in making television programmes, courses that may or may not be accompanied by a **theoretical** dimension or approach. This means that although two departments in the same university may both be running 'television' courses (or even 'television' degrees), what students might study may completely depend on what department they are in and who is teaching them. As Charlotte Brunsdon has put in her article 'What Is the Television of Television Studies?' (1998: 95):

> Television Studies is the relatively recent, aspirationally disciplinary name given to the academic study of television. Modelled by analogy on longer established fields of study, the name suggests that there is an object, 'television', which, in courses named, for example, 'Introduction to Television Studies', is the self-evident object of study using accepted methodologies. This may be increasingly the case, but historically, most of the formative academic research on television was inaugurated in other fields and contexts.

As one might expect, then, these differences in approaching television are reflected in the varied types of academic and journalistic accounts that have helped form this inter-disciplinary field of study. For example, if you were interested in the history of television you might read William Boddy's *Fifties Television: The Industry and Its Critics* (1990). However, if you were more concerned with the interpretations of an actual television programme you might prefer Kim Akass and Janet McCabe's *Reading* Sex and the City (2004). However, if it was television audiences you were interested in then you might pick up David Morley's *Television, Audiences, and Cultural Studies* (1992). Alternatively, if television journalism was more your taste you might choose to read last night's television review in a current newspaper or a collection of television journalism like Clive James's *The Crystal Bucket: Television Criticism from* The Observer*, 1976–79* (1981).

As this suggests, the study of television has followed a rather complex and elaborate route in its gradual formation, a route that has confusingly included a whole manner of different (sometimes even contradictory) styles and methodologies. In order to understand the study of television, then, it is important that a student first acquaints him or herself with a little of the subject's **historical devel-**

opment. For the way television is studied today can only really be understood by charting and explaining the origins and evolution of this relatively new and constantly developing area of academic study. So while it is now generally appreciated that television most certainly needs to be treated seriously, how it should be treated or even what we actually mean by 'television' is still clearly in the process of formation and debate.

STUDYING TELEVISION: A BRIEF HISTORY

> Research is always collaborative, always cumulative: an understanding of prior arguments is essential in order to comprehend new ones.
>
> E. Ann Kaplan 'Feminist Criticism and Television', 1992: 250.

The first generally recognised intellectual movement to study television was a group of German Marxists in the 1930s that went under the broad heading of the '**Frankfurt School**' (see Chapter 3). In exile from Nazi Germany during World War II (originally from Frankfurt, hence their name), this group of theorists (including Max Horkheimer and Theodor Adorno) fled to America where they were shocked by what they saw as the profound commercialisation of the media. For them, the American media (including television) revealed the extreme **commodification** of culture in an industrial capitalist society. They argued that television was simply part of the '**culture industries**' i.e. a form of culture that was as formulaic and standardised as any mass-produced industrial commodity. Consequently, they argued that television was highly ideological and simply worked to promote the interests of Western capitalism (see Adorno, 1991).

Although many of their ideas have since been contested, the Frankfurt School was important in the inter-disciplinary approach it took to the study of television. In particular, it employed a form of research that combined a number of critical methodologies that included the close analysis of the television text, audience and reception studies, ideological analysis and a critique of the political economy of the media/television industries (see Kellner, 2002: 17–21). As such, this type of approach mainly relied on forms of 'qualitative analysis'. Qualitative analysis can be defined as speculative in nature, allowing room for personal interpretation, theoretical issues and subjective conjecture in its investigation of culture. Consequently, qualitative analysis tends to argue that debate and discussion (the type that is not always empirically verifiable) is nonetheless important in the construction of knowledge (see Chapter 2).

However, in the 1940s and 1950s there was a distinct shift in the way that television (and the media in general) was analysed. Many media researchers argued that more 'scientific' methods of analysis were now needed to give greater status to their findings. Paul Lazarsfeld (1948), for example, emphasised 'administrative research' i.e. the systematic gathering of facts by objective means and methods. This type of approach revealed a growing trend in media and television research away from 'qualitative' methods of analysis to more 'quantitative' procedures.

Diametrically opposed to qualitative analysis, quantitative analysis attempts to follow the procedures of the natural sciences, arguing that the only admissible scientific evidence are 'facts', established by enforcing systematic and verifiable methods of research. The 'uses and gratifications' model of media research that first arrived in the 1960s (particularly in America) encouraged this general move towards more 'quantitative' methods in media research, calling for greater procedural rigour in the collection of evidence. Rejecting the conclusions of the Frankfurt School (in contrast, they argued that audiences were a great deal more 'active' in the way that they made sense of television and the media – see Chapter 6), it also rejected their overtly theoretical and speculative findings (see Ruddock, 2002: 70–3).

This general move towards quantitative analysis had a profound influence on the way that television and the media were studied during much of the 1960s. In particular, this shift towards more 'quantitative' forms of research tended to reject all notions

of media theory because its ideological speculations were frequently regarded as empirically unverifiable (see Chapter 2). However, this unfortunately meant that questions of power and politics were often ignored; media researchers being mainly interested in dealing with statistical facts and figures (see Miller, 2002: 1).

It was not until the 1970s that media theory gradually returned to the academic study of the media, critics daring to take a more 'qualitative' approach to the field as a whole. Books and articles began appearing that analysed television in terms of critical theory, using semiotics and other methods to analyse issues of power and ideology (see Chapter 2). Originally developing out of Literary Studies, this approach was also aided by the emergence of Cultural Studies (particularly in Europe) in the 1970s and 1980s, treating television programmes (along with comics, magazines, youth culture, popular music and so on) as important sites of ideological resistance and struggle (see Chapter 3).

The representation of gender, race and class were particularly prominent in such studies: reflecting a growing concern in the cultural significance of the medium as a whole while also allowing the study of television to explore its own historical, generic and theoretical traditions (see Lockett, 2002: 24–7). For example, the interest that feminist television academics took in soap opera revealed an emerging field of study that was beginning to recognise the complex mechanisms by which television is both made and consumed (see Chapter 3). The gradual rise of Film (and later Media) Studies was also important in this respect, breaking new ground in the way that forms of popular culture were now both analysed and assessed (see Chapter 2).

As other disciplines gradually become more involved in the study of television and as television itself grew as a medium in its own right (particularly as its national and global significance became increasingly apparent [see Chapter 9]), so different aspects of television were also placed higher on the critical agenda. In particular, politics and mass communication research greatly emphasised the political and social (both the contemporary and historical)

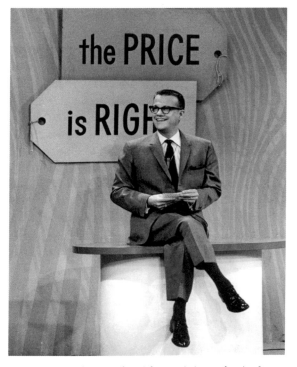

The Price is Right: an industrial or artistic production?

The Cosby Show: cultural studies examined issues such as race on TV

context of the medium. Issues such as globalisation, regulation, commercialisation, viewing practices, social relations and technology were introduced and gradually accepted as important components of the field.

During the 1980s, the rise of **audience studies** particularly brought the methods of sociology (surveys, questionnaires, participant observation and so on) back into the domain of the television researcher who wanted to develop and re-evaluate the potential range of the subject (see Chapter 6). Rather than excluding one form of methodology for another, the study of television seemed to embrace a whole manner of methodologies. Although this was not always a smooth process, the inter-disciplinary nature of the subject was generally becoming more widely acknowledged and accepted within the academy.

Such a complex historical development does perhaps suggest why the study of television (or **'Television Studies'** as it was gradually becoming

known) has such a complex form today. There are now clearly different strands within the field that borrow from and reflect a number of varied methodological schools and traditions. This has been intensified by a gradual breakdown in the conventional boundaries that once existed between the arts and social sciences. This has all meant that 'Television Studies' has grown into a confusing and essentially **pluralistic** field. As John Corner recently put it (2004: 7):

> Developed from such varied sites, with such a range of curricular identities . . . and resourced by different literatures, with areas both of intensive cross-citation but also of mutual ignorance, the default understanding of 'television studies' has to be strongly plural.

It is this plurality of the field that frequently makes 'Television Studies' such a difficult topic for newcomers to the subject to understand. As we have seen, the study of television has gone through a number of academic traditions and schools of thought that have clearly influenced how television is studied today. However, for the purpose of clarity it is possible to break down the contemporary discipline into a number of major academic categories. In particular, we can isolate four related but individual schools of approach that we can broadly title as such:

1. Textual analysis;
2. Audience and reception studies;
3. Institutional analysis;
4. Historical analysis.

Of course, these four major categories are not rigid or concrete forms of knowledge, and various accounts of television may well include a number of these different approaches and methodologies. But an acknowledgment of these four individual methods of study can offer an important form of clarification to those who are initially confused by the subject's inter-disciplinary complexity (see Figure 1).

This, then, is how 'Television Studies' has begun to conceive itself in recent years. Most introductory television textbooks have been arranged along similar inter-disciplinary lines; all generally covering familiar categories that include history, audiences and reception, representation, genre and so on (see 'Annotated Bibliography' below). Such books attempt to do justice to the different and varied approaches that have come to define the field. Although not always agreed on what the 'television' in 'Television Studies' may actually mean, these different forms of analysis provide a general way of approaching the subject within a seemingly coherent

1 TEXTUAL ANALYSIS

This approach to television has its origins in subjects such as Literary and Cultural Studies. It is partly defined by its tendency to analyse actual television programmes, particularly focusing on issues of form, content and representation (for example, the televisual construction of class, race and gender). In terms of methodology it can take a number of critical forms that include semiotics, genre theory, narrative theory, ideological analysis, discourse analysis, feminism, postmodernism and so on. Although undoubtedly 'qualitative' in approach this interest in programmes can also assume slightly more 'quantitative' methodologies such as content analysis (see Chapter 2).

2 AUDIENCE AND RECEPTION STUDIES

This approach generally originated from Sociology and tends to look for more 'verifiable' evidence in its analysis of television. This type of methodology tends to look at the 'extratextual' dimensions that help audiences produce meaning. (While audience analysis tends to concentrate its focus on audience response, reception studies generally look at the way programmes are marketed, distributed and discussed.) In terms of methodology, audience and reception analysis both tend to use elements of ethnography, anthropology and ethnomethodology (observation of routine behaviours), particularly relying on questionnaires, interviews, discussion groups, participant observation and so on. Important fields of audience enquiry have included 'media effects', 'uses and gratifications' research, 'public opinion analysis' and 'fandom' (see Chapter 6).

3 INSTITUTIONAL ANALYSIS

This approach generally originated from politics and mass communication research and takes a more political or socio-economic approach to television as a whole. In particular, it tends to focus on issues of industry, institution, policy and regulation. In terms of methodology, it therefore tends to concentrate much of its focus on the analysis of government legislation and the political nature of the media industries. As such, political and cultural theory may play an important part in its overall assessment of television's role in the production of the private and public sphere (see Chapter 8).

4 HISTORICAL ANALYSIS

Not surprisingly this approach originated from historical studies and tends to focus on the historical development of television. It therefore relies a great deal on archival research, viewing old programmes and analysing and assessing the written archives that TV channels and other public institutions have kept. As one might expect, interviews with past practitioners, government bodies or even past audiences may also provide further areas of research. This type of analysis may therefore employ all the three approaches above to generate and construct knowledge. This may include an historical analysis of its audiences and modes of reception, its social and political context and detailed programme (textual) analysis (see Chapter 7).

Figure 1. Major Approaches in Contemporary 'Television Studies'.

Note: Any 'holistic' approach to television will apply a combination of these methodologies.

methodological context. It is the simple aim of this book to clarify this body of work and to add further coherence to the subject's gradual but inevitable formation.

HOW THIS BOOK IS STRUCTURED

Rather than reducing the historical development of the subject into an overtly reductive form, it is hoped that this book will both explain and do justice to the major trends and debates that have helped to inform and define the study of television to date. I hope its title (*Tele-Visions*) suggests the **inter-disciplinary** nature of the field, emphasising the fact that there are clearly many ways of approaching the subject. This book aims to reflect these different approaches as equally, cohesively and as clearly as possible.

As a general rule (although by no means exact), the book tends to begin with a strong **textual** bias i.e. towards the examination of the programmes themselves in terms of aesthetics, ideology and different forms of genre such as drama and documentary. It then gradually moves towards matters of a more **contextual** nature i.e. towards the investigation of the wider landscape or ecology of television, exploring such issues as history, globalisation, regulation and technology. Of course, many methods and approaches to television will combine both textual and contextual analysis but the distinguishing feature between 'text' and 'context' is still worth making in terms of overall clarity. At all times different modes of methodology will be addressed and the nature and concerns of these varied critical approaches investigated. In this way it is hoped that the inter-disciplinary nature of the field will be foregrounded while both its complementary and contradictory landscape is carefully maintained.

Arguably the first issue that any student new to the subject needs to appreciate is how television differs from other media. The first chapter (**Defining the Medium: TV Form and Aesthetics**) written by John Ellis will explain the experience of watching television and how that influences the forms of programmes (and viewing practices) that it tends to produce. In doing so, it will trace the way in which television has been conceived by academics in the past, explaining and clarifying important notions such as 'flow' and 'segmentation' in the process. That chapter's case study by Catrin Prys (Issues in Television Authorship) will also further investigate the means by which television has tended to be conceived; offering ways to become critically aware of the authorial assumptions so often made by the field as a whole.

Chapter 2 (**Analysing Television: Issues and Methods in Textual Analysis**) will build on this understanding of the medium by exploring the means by which television can be analysed as a textual entity. Written by Glen Creeber, it acknowledges the place of various approaches to the text including semiotics, genre theory, ideological and shot-by-shot analysis. It is hoped that this chapter will provide an important introduction to television as a form of textual research and interpretation. This chapter's case study (Shot-by-Shot Analysis) will explore the general means by which television is usually discussed and textually examined. This introduction to textual analysis will be developed in Chapter 3 (**Decoding Television**: **Issues of Ideology and Discourse**). In particular, it will outline the benefits and problems of using ideology in the analysis of the televisual text, exploring its past traditions and re-evaluating it for the contemporary scene. Its case study written by Mike Wayne (An Ideological Analysis of Sky News) will go on to demonstrate the importance of analysing a 'factual' media text through this type of critical and theoretical framework.

Chapters 4 and 5 will take similar approaches to separate television genres. The first (**Analysing Factual TV: How to Study Television Documentary**) by John Corner will outline the major issues and debates in the study of television documentary. Its case study (Different Documentary Modes: *World in Action*, *Hotel* and *Wife Swap*) will concentrate on the major differences between three important strands of television documentary. Chapter 5 (**Analysing TV Fiction: How to Study Television Drama**) written by Robin Nelson, will follow a similar structure but take the study of television fiction as its focus. Its case study (Modernism and Postmodernism in Television Drama) will then apply this analysis to particular examples, both historical and contemporary.

Chapter 6 (**Television and Its Audience: Issues of Consumption and Reception**) will examine audience research. Written by Matt Hills, the opening section of the chapter will provide an historical overview to the study of the television audience beginning with the post-war polemics of the 'Effects' school of thought through to more recent concerns around issues of ethnography and reception studies. The case study (Fandom and Fan Studies) will concentrate on the more contemporary notion of how 'fans' use television and the means by which that 'fandom' is generated and discussed.

Chapter 7 (**Television and History: Investigating the Past**) will examine history as a means of discussing and introducing the wider context of television as a whole. Written by Jason Jacobs, it will outline the importance of history in understanding many of the more general industrial, institutional, textual and technological developments that have taken place since the medium's conception in the 1930s. As such, it does not aim to give the student *a history* of television, although some of its most important dates and developments will be discussed in the case study (A [Very] Brief History of Television) by Jamie Medhurst.

Chapter 8 (**Television and Regulation: Examining Institutional Structures**) will concentrate on the economic and institutional context of television, who owns what and how the industry is governed and regulated. Written by Elan Closs Stephens, it will examine how governments have consistently intervened in the business of television in an attempt to regulate, monitor and even govern control of the television industry. The pros and cons of such intervention will be assessed, exploring the way governments have consistently attempted to exert influence over the very content, form and distribution of the medium. Issues that will be further explored in the case study (The BBC and the State) by Tom O'Malley.

Chapter 9 (**Television and Globalisation: National and International Concerns**) will take the topic of television onto a more 'international' scale. Written by John Hartley, it will particularly explore the subject of television as a global form. Critics of globalisation frequently accuse television of playing a crucial role in 'cultural homogenisation', often arguing that the influence of television is destroying crucial aspects of national culture and identity. This chapter will examine this claim, exploring, in particular, the cultural dominance of Anglo-American television. However, in the case study (Indigenous Television) by Faye Ginsburg and Lorna Roth will also examine the way television can be used to *resist* certain strands of cultural domination.

The final chapter (**Post TV?: The Future of Television**) will concentrate on the way the medium has changed and developed in recent years and the possible changes likely in the future. Written by Kyle Nicholas, it focuses on the arrival of cable, satellite and digital technology and the emergence of new technologies such as the Internet. Finally, the case study (Television and Convergence) by Jamie Sexton concentrates on the possible 'meltdown' between television, the computer and cyberspace.

Whatever the chapter in question, I hope that there is always a clear sense throughout this volume that Television Studies is a complex and constantly *evolving* area of study. I simply hope that its structure and organisation will help to bring a real clarity to the study of television that – because of its inter-disciplinary nature – may sometimes have been lacking in the past. The book does not expect to cover every aspect or detail of Television Studies, but it is hoped there is enough here to provide a good general introduction to some of the subject's main issues and debates while also introducing and clarifying many of its major methodologies and frequently contradictory schools of thought.

STUDYING TELEVISION: AN OVERVIEW

In a further attempt to clarify television's complex and intricate historical formation, this introduction will end with an annotated bibliography that attempts to offer a brief overview of contemporary Television Studies. While it is clearly not crucial that a student familiarise him or herself with *every* textbook listed, it is nonetheless important that they begin to see the subject not as a static or solid entity but as a dynamic and constantly evolving field of study continually in the process of formation and re-formation. Rather than take the place of these texts, it is hoped that this book will encourage students to go back and revisit the origins of the subject (see below).

ANNOTATED BIBLIOGRAPHY

Please note that the bibliography below only includes references to book-length, general introductions to television studies. Articles and books devoted to actual programmes, particular genres, histories, debates, methodologies etc. are not included (see individual chapters for details). In particular, this account should be seen as historically selective (it defines the contemporary as starting from the early 1970s) and nationally biased (most of the books are either British or American in origin). Nonetheless, it is hoped that this short bibliography will provide a brief overview of some of the major works that have helped define contemporary Television Studies as we know and understand it today. Needless to say that the bibliography at the end of this book is less descriptive but is obviously more comprehensive. Apologies in advance for any oversights that have been unintentionally made.

A SELECTION OF GENERAL INTRODUCTIONS TO TV STUDIES: 1974–2005

Williams, Raymond (1974), *Television: Technology and Cultural Form*, **London and New York: Routledge.**

Arguably this is where the contemporary academic study of television began, particularly in Britain. Perhaps more useful now as an historical document than an actual introduction to the subject, it nonetheless earns its right as a crucially important part of the Television Studies canon.

Newcomb, Horace (1974), *TV: The Most Popular Art*, **New York: Anchor Press.**

An early American account of television (chapters divided mainly into different genres) that helped lay down many of the subject's critical foundations. Inevitably dated, but still surprisingly insightful.

Newcomb, Horace (ed.) (1976), *Television: The Critical View*, **New York and Oxford: Oxford University Press.**

This early collection of articles has gone through various editions since 1976. Despite its age, it still offers a powerful overview of the subject from the programmes themselves to issues of production, television viewing, ideology, race and so on.

Fiske, John and Hartley, John (1978), *Reading Television*, **London and New York: Routledge.**

Classic text-based (rooted in semiotics) account of television that helped bring the subject firmly into the academy, particularly in Britain.

Bennett, Tony, Boyd-Bowman, Susan, Mercer, Colin and Woollacott, Janet (eds) (1981), *Popular Television and Film: A Reader*, **London: Open University and BFI.**

This is from the time when Television Studies still partly resided under the paternal wing of Film Studies. Nevertheless, it contains some interesting articles including the classic '*Days of Hope* Debate'.

Adler, Richard P. (ed.) (1981), *Understanding Television: Essays on Television as a Social and Cultural Force*, **New York: Praeger.**

A useful early American collection of articles that is divided into five parts: 'Overviews', 'Critical Approaches', 'Drama', 'News' and 'The Future'. Inevitably dated but includes interesting material on television aesthetics, genre, psychology and so on.

Ellis, John (1982), *Visible Fictions: Cinema, Television, Video*, **London and New York: Routledge.**

This is a classic account of television as a medium in its own right (particularly in comparison to the cinema). Essential for all students seriously committed to understanding the aesthetics of television and the origins of Television Studies.

Kaplan, E. Ann (ed.) (1983), *Regarding Television: Critical Approaches – An Anthology*, **Los Angeles, CA: American Film Institute.**

An interesting American collection of articles divided mainly into genres (soap opera, sport, news, daytime television and so on), but also chapters on video art, live television, history and television criticism.

Masterman, Len (ed.) (1984), *Television Mythologies: Stars, Shows and Signs,* **London: Comedia.**

As its title suggests, this is a mainly semiotic account of television and its programmes. Interesting and helpful but a little dated now in terms of texts, topics and methodology.

Fiske, John (1987), *Television Culture,* **London and New York: Methuen.**

A Television Studies classic, this was the most influential textbook for more than a decade. It includes accessible discussions of ideology, gender, audiences etc. Essential reading for any student new to the field or for those just wondering how the contemporary subject finally began to take shape.

Goodwin, Andrew and Whannel, Gary (eds) (1990), *Understanding Television,* **London and New York: Routledge.**

Inevitably some of the programmes will no longer be familiar, but this is a good general selection of essays divided mainly (although not completely) by genre and programmes.

Mellencamp, Patricia (ed.) (1990), *Logics of Television: Essays in Cultural Criticism,* **Bloomington: Indiana University Press.**

This challenging edited volume takes a loosely 'Cultural Studies' approach to television that tends to ignore genre-based critiques, focusing more on issues of audiences, reception, postmodernism, aesthetics, history and so on.

Allen, Robert C. (ed) (1992a), *Channels of Discourse, Reassembled: Television and Contemporary Criticism,* **London and New York: Routledge.**

This excellent collection of articles was originally published in 1987 but was later 'reassembled' into its final form in 1992. Despite its chapter breakdown being a little too reliant on literary theory, it is still an indispensable appraisal of television from various critical perspectives (semiotics, narrative, audiences, genre, ideology, psychoanalysis, feminism, Cultural Studies and postmodernism) written by some of the leading names in the field.

Butler, Jeremy G. (1994), *Television: Critical Methods and Applications,* **Belmont, CA: Wadsworth.**

With lots of discussion of camera angles, *mise en scène*, narrative structure etc., much of this American book examines the technical construction of television. It is a particularly useful reference for students hoping to produce detailed textual analysis.

Selby, Keith and Cowdery, Ron (1995), *How to Study Television,* **London: Macmillan.**

Perhaps a little dated by its heavy reliance on semiotics and its choice of programmes, this is nonetheless a useful introduction to anyone encountering the study of television for the very first time. Its description of camera angles etc. is particularly welcomed and accessible.

Caldwell, John Thorton, *Televisuality: Style, Crisis, and Authority in American Television* **(1995), New Brunswick, Rutgers University Press.**

Although not meant as an introduction to television, this is an interesting account of American TV that touches upon almost every aspect of Television Studies in the process.

Abercrombie, Nicholas (1996), *Television and Society,* **Cambridge: Polity Press.**

Although it does include chapters on 'text' and 'genre', this is a semi-sociological introduction to television studies. The chapter on 'Industry' is particularly welcomed.

Corner, John and Harvey, Sylvia (eds) (1996), *Television Times: A Reader,* **London: Arnold.**

Written by influential names in the field, this is an excellent selection of articles for the more advanced television student.

Holland, Patricia (1997), *The Television Handbook,* **London and New York: Routledge.**

With sections entitled 'The Practitioner's Perspective' and 'Making Programmes', this is a useful introduction to television mainly from the perspective of the people who actually make the programmes.

Newcomb, Horace (ed.) (1997), *Encyclopedia of Television,* **Chicago, IL and London: Fitzroy Dearborn.**

An extensive and comprehensive account of television programmes, biographies, histories and debates in three large volumes. Probably too expensive for the individual student to buy but should be ordered by your library if it does not already have a copy.

Geraghty, Christine and Lusted, David (eds) (1998), *The Television Studies Book*, **London and New York: Arnold.**

Similar in tone and style to Corner and Harvey (1996), although by no means comprehensive, this is still highly recommended for the more advanced student.

McQueen, David (1998), *Television: A Media Student's Guide*, **London and New York: Arnold.**

This was one of the first introductory textbooks to really try and bring together the whole of Television Studies under one accessible title. On the whole it offers a good balance of methods, histories and programmes, although sometimes lacking in detail. Nevertheless, a good place to start for the complete novice.

Burton, Graeme (2000), *Talking about Television: An Introduction to the Study of Television*, **London: Arnold.**

Similar in structure, style and content to McQueen (1998), this is nonetheless a well-balanced introduction to the major issues and debates for college and first-year undergraduates.

Ellis, John (2000), *Seeing Things: Television in the Age of Uncertainty*, **London: I. B. Tauris.**

Textual and contextual, this provides a useful and interesting guide to some of the most important issues and debates surrounding Television Studies today.

Corner, John (1999), *Critical Ideas in Television Studies*, **Oxford: Oxford University Press.**

A very useful introduction to many of the major issues and debates in television studies, this is an excellent introduction for the more advanced student.

Creeber, Glen (ed.) (2001), *The Television Genre Book*, **London: BFI.**

This is an accessible introduction to the study of genre through actual programmes and categories such as soap opera, drama, news, comedy etc.

Lealand, Geoff and Martin, Helen (2001), *It's All Done with Mirrors: About Television*, **Palmerston North, NZ: Dunmore Press.**

This is a general introduction from New Zealand. Most topics (ideology, genre, audiences etc.) are covered.

Miller, Toby (ed.) (2002), *Television Studies*, **London: BFI.**

This is an interesting introduction to issues and methodologies in Television Studies such as race, gender, audience studies and so on. It offers a good historical perspective on Television Studies as a whole.

Casey, Bernadette, Casey, Neil, Calvert, Ben, French, Liam and Lewis, Justin (2002), *Television Studies: The Key Concepts*, **London and New York: Routledge.**

This is a useful reference guide and general introduction to the subject as a whole.

Bignell, Jonathan (2004), *An Introduction to Television Studies*, **London and New York: Routledge.**

Similar to McQueen (1998) and Burton (2000), this attempts to bring the whole of 'Television Studies' together within one volume (including history, genre, postmodernism, production and so on) and is a good general point of reference.

Allen, Robert C. and Hill, Annette (eds) (2004), *The Television Studies Reader*, **London and New York: Routledge.**

Asked to do a third edition of *Channels of Discourse*, Allen (with Hill) preferred to assemble a collection of previously published articles that reflects the state of contemporary Television Studies. An interesting but challenging collection, this is perhaps more suited to the more advanced student.

Lury, Karen (2005), *Interpreting Television*, **London: Arnold.**

This is a useful and hugely accessible introduction to television analysis, with chapters divided into 'Image', 'Sound', 'Time' and 'Space', ideal for newcomers to the subject, particularly those who are interested in examining aspects of the television text.

1 Defining the Medium
TV Form and Aesthetics
John Ellis

When you watch television you don't dress up for it, you don't go out for it, you don't pay for it, the lights are on, and you do things and you talk, and all that is largely to the detriment of the experience – but if something is working it can be extraordinarily powerful because it sits right in the middle of all that mundaneness.

Dennis Potter, *Potter on Potter,* ed. Graham Fuller, 1993: 122.

There are many ways of talking about television, from trying to define what is specific about the **production** and **reception** of TV to discussing what is specific about the experience of TV. Questions of production (who made it, how and why?) and reception (who uses it, what for and to what effect?) have tended to dominate Television Studies. The question of the nature of television itself, which tends to receive less attention, is the subject of this first chapter.

Some people claim that TV has no **aesthetics**. By this, they mean one of two things. They may be treating the medium as a simple piece of glass that provides a transparent window or mirror on the world: the metaphor differs, but the idea is the same. This conception sees television as bringing nothing to that pre-existent world, a world which, moreover, does not include television. Or they may mean that the medium can make no claims to provide uplifting or inspiring experiences, or to transform the everyday into the sublime: that is, that it contains nothing of real **cultural value** (see Introduction).

Such ideas are increasingly difficult to sustain. Television has been for half a century or more an actor

in the word and an intimate part of the life of most of its populations. Events are routinely constructed for TV (in the search for 'publicity') and inflected by the involvement of TV within them. TV itself becomes an event, generating commentary and revising attitudes to the world. As Germaine Greer remarked of *Big Brother* (Channel 4, 1999–) 'Reality television is not the end of civilisation as we know it, it is civilisation as we know it' (cited by Shukor, 2005).

Society has become **mediatised**: to be significant and effective everything has to pass through the media, and everything involves the media. TV has a particular and prominent place in this ongoing process of mediatisation, and the form of TV that dominates is still that of **broadcast TV** (i.e. transmitted as [or as if] live). TV aesthetics tries to discover what is distinctive about the experience of broadcast TV and how it differs from other media and from other forms of human perception and experience.

TELEVISION AESTHETICS: A BRIEF THEORETICAL HISTORY

Since the beginning of TV, practitioners have tried to define what is new and special about their medium, clearly more than a crowded marriage of theatre, radio, cinema and journalism. **Medium theory** is also produced at an everyday level within television, growing from a severely practical need. People working in the medium have to understand the potential and limits of the form in which they work. Jason Jacobs' (2000) study of the pioneers of British TV drama brings this out clearly. Producers and directors tried to define TV as a medium that had something of theatre, something of cinema and something of radio, but was distinct in itself. The defining feature for them was '**intimacy**', a medium that worked best with close-up because it could provide a real-size image of the human face which would fill the screens of the time. Intimacy was therefore a concept that united production and reception in one aesthetic term: it described the scaled-down form of acting required, the felt connection engendered by live broadcasting and the domestic circumstances of the viewing: television's very private public.

Behind this working definition lies a fundamental desire to discover the importance of TV, how TV helps construct the world of which it is a part. But the problem is that speculations about the social role and effects of television, and the accompanying value judgments, can be made too quickly. The word 'aesthetics' itself has historically suffered from the same problem.

From the origins of the term there have been differing understandings of the word 'aesthetics' and the implicit value judgments that back them up. The German philosopher Baumgarten intended the term to be relatively value-free when he coined it in *Aesthetica* (1750). He envisaged aesthetics as a semi-scientific investigation into sensation and perception, the 'science of sensitive knowing'. However, his term was taken up by another German philosopher Immanuel Kant who, in *Critique of Judgement* (1790), tied it to one particular field of perception, that of *beauty* both in the natural world and in the creative arts. The particular force of Kant's definition lies in the moral value he gives to this experience, as one which refuses an instrumental attitude to the world. **Aesthetic pleasure**, in Kant's definition, is uplifting and transforms our relation to the world. It is one of the distinguishing features of our humanity. This definition gained wide currency in the nineteenth century, to the extent that the *Oxford English Dictionary* lists Baumgarten's notion, 'the science of the conditions of sensuous perception' as obsolete.

However, Kant's definition appeals to universal ideas of beauty gained through a process of transcendence of the everyday. This poses problems for an everyday medium like broadcast television, whose pleasures lie in the intimate involvements that it offers. Kant's definition also contains a central uncertainty: does the perception of beauty lie entirely in the eye or ear of the beholder (meaning, is it subjective?) or do the features of the object itself somehow set the conditions for such perceptions? Nowadays, as media proliferate and the very definition of a work of art is profoundly blurred, the uncertainty is often resolved by asserting that the object itself has a substantial role in provoking aesthetic responses. However, beyond the explicit value judgments and universalistic tendencies, Kant's definition does involve an important and often forgotten emphasis, the close connection between aesthetics and the attempt to define pleasure, or at least the conditions for pleasure.

A **television aesthetics** has emerged despite the tension with Kantian definitions of beauty and transcendence. It tries to define what is specific about television as a medium. It examines the technological set-up of TV, the feel of its images and sounds, the determining ways in which it is received and used, the distinctive nature of its texts, how it creates and organises meaning. It addresses the peculiarities of TV, how it is everyday and pervasive, much used and much despised. But given the problems inherent in Kant's definition, some thinkers have abandoned the use of the term 'aesthetics' for their attempt to define the specific objective conditions of sensuous perception proposed by TV to its viewers. Instead, they use the idea of 'medium theory', coined by Joshua Meyrowitz in his *A Sense of Place: Impact of Electronic Media on Social Relations* (1987), encompassing the work of Marshall McLuhan, Harold Innis and others who were as much inspired by anthropology as by any other discipline. Others, like Roger Silverstone, looked to the concept of '**poetics**' to outline the area of enquiry being discussed here (1999: 40–8). However, McLuhan's wonderfully sweeping definitions, nowadays unfashionable in the way that many 1960s' grand theories have become, nevertheless lie behind many current approaches, and his aphorisms like 'the medium is the message' and 'hot' and 'cold' media still have currency.

THE 'COOL' MEDIUM

Marshall McLuhan's work is a good place to start since his writings can be seen as an attempt to put aesthetics into the centre of the understanding of TV. It also demonstrates some of the pitfalls in doing so. He insisted that '**the medium is the message**' at a time when studies of TV concentrated on what was said or shown by the medium, treating it is a transparent window on the world. McLuhan looked at the *glass* rather than the *window*, asking how it framed things, how much light it admitted and in what spectrum, how much sound it allowed in and how it affected the other senses. McLuhan constructed a grand theory of media by examining the particular sensory set-up that they require in their users, and claimed that the dominant medium of an age would bring into being a particular balance between the senses and hence a particular kind of society.

McLuhan claimed that the arrival of print changed society, producing rationalistic and conformist regimes, and a particular form of opposition to them: 'If rigorous centralism is a main feature of literacy and print, no less so is the eager assertion of individual rights' (1962: 220). He breezily asserted that print changed world politics: 'of all the unforeseen consequences of typography, the emergence of nationalism is, perhaps, the most familiar' (1964: 192). He also classifies media into the '**hot**', which allow little participation and have an intensity of information (books and radio) and '**cool**' media which allow more participation and have a lower intensity of information. Television, for McLuhan, is therefore a 'cool medium', more like the telephone. A typical McLuhan claim is that TV 'rejects hot figures and hot issues and people from the hot press media. Had TV occurred on a large scale during Hitler's reign he would have vanished quickly' (ibid: 326).

Such a claim clearly demonstrates that McLuhan is deducing universal characteristics for a medium from a particular usage or stage of its development. He presents radio as a 'hot' medium because it allows individuals in public to create a personal space for themselves: 'the power of radio to involve people in depth is manifested in its use during homework by youngsters and by many other people who carry

transistor sets in order to provide a private world for themselves amidst crowds' (ibid: 325). In 1964, the transistor radio was a new phenomenon. Now such a role has been taken over by personal entertainment systems, and radio, having discovered the phone-in and texting, appears to be even more of a 'cool' medium in McLuhan's terms. Nevertheless, in TV aesthetics there re-occur attempts like McLuhan's to contrast television with cinema (where the physical circumstances of viewing encourage a 'hot' submission to the film's intense flow of experience and information). It can be seen in Ellis's (see later) contrast of the '**gaze**' at the cinema screen (itself derived from Metz [1982]) to the '**glance**' at the TV screen or Beverle Houston's (1984) psychoanalytic contrast of the textual experiences offered by the two media. Houston famously contrasted the pleasures involved: 'of cinema, the spectator says "I want the cinema experience again". . . of television we say "I want it as I have never had it"' (183–95). This intriguing formulation I will return to.

Another McLuhan term which has become common is '**the global village**'. By contrasting the linear nature of print with the instantaneity of TV he was able to claim that TV was constructing a form of society in which global citizens share a culture which is similar to that of oral societies (see also Fiske and Hartley's [1978] notion of 'bardic television'). Instant awareness of events reduces the relevance of both time and space, and hence individualism itself. Privacy and separation, the characteristics of the print world, are no longer tenable in this new global village. Writing in 1964, just twenty years after the start of regular TV services in the US, such a claim now seems to have been deliberately provocative and overstated. For today's global village may be instantaneous in its transmission of information, but that information very often brings home to viewers what separates and differentiates the world's cultures and beliefs, rather than bringing them into one whole community (see Chapter 9).

'FLOW'

McLuhan has fallen from favour because his effervescent style often leads him to see technology as the

'Glance Theory': television has to compete with domestic distractions

single cause of every social change. According to Raymond Williams (who wrote *Television: Technology and Cultural Form* [1974] partly as a response to McLuhan's technological determinism), McLuhan takes the current state of the medium as its essence, and then extends this view to become the single or main cause of changes in society. Where McLuhan was interested in the nature of the medium, Williams is, as a literary critic, more concerned about the nature of its **texts** (see Chapter 2). And this brings him to a puzzling phenomenon: whereas a book or a film are highly separate objects, TV is much more of a jumble of bits. What is more, it just keeps on coming. As he famously explains, this realisation first revealed itself to him on a visit to America where he experienced the highly commercial nature of US broadcast television for the first time (1974: 91–2):

One night in Miami, still dazed from a week on an Atlantic liner, I began watching a film and at first had some difficulty in adjusting to a much greater frequency of commercial 'breaks'. Yet this was a minor problem compared to what eventually happened. Two other films, which were to be shown on the same channel on other nights, began to be inserted as trailers. A crime in San Francisco (the subject of the original film) began to operate in an extraordinary counterpoint not only with the deodorant and cereal commercials but with a romance in Paris and the eruption of a prehistoric monster who laid waste New York.

Williams coined the term '**flow**' to define this type of phenomenon. He describes a typical evening's viewing as (95):

having read two plays, three newspapers, three or four magazines, on the same day as one has been to a variety show and a lecture and a football match. And yet in another way it has not been like that at all, for though the items may be various, the television experience has in some important ways unified them all.

Williams' notion of flow remains a key concept that has been built on by others. It emphasises the newness and the fragmented nature of the television experience, and its **serial nature**: one thing follows another in a seemingly endless stream, both on single channels and on the totality of channels available to a viewer at any one moment.

Williams remained concerned with the nature of an evening's viewing experience. But TV is a distinctive aesthetic form not only because of the fragmentary nature of its mixture of experiences, but also because of where those fragments come from and what they assume. Williams' guiding image is of a super-rich combination of live experiences. But the aesthetics of TV material involve a dense web of references to other TV material. Few programmes are totally singular entities; most are part of a series, referring to others through continuing plots, familiar characters, recognisable formats. TV is everywhere partial and nowhere whole. Beverle Houston (1984) summarised this in the formulation quoted above 'I want it as I have never had it'. She is describing not so much a feeling of dissatisfaction at this state of affairs as a distinct pleasure, one of experiencing many variants of an archetype which never fully appears. This powers the endless search of TV fans for the best or most typical episode of their favourite series (see Chapter 6). It is a feeling of belonging, of being within the TV series, a witness to it as an evolving world which continues to offer fresh surprises. The aesthetics of broadcast television in part tries to analyse the pleasures that come with this combination of inclusion (being 'inside' a series) and risk (not knowing what the next twist will be).

'SEGMENTATION'
Williams' metaphor of flow, as Gripsrud points out, 'carries what seem to be two diametrically opposed

images of the television experience: that of being swept away by an external force, and that of coolly and calmly regarding the river at a distance, possibly now and again distracted by what goes on in the immediate surroundings' (1998: 29). He contrasts Williams' approach to that of John Ellis's *Visible Fictions* (1982) which continued the project of contrasting cinema and television, using the developments in cinema aesthetics which had taken place during the 1970s.

John Ellis places a greater emphasis on the fragmentary, incomplete nature of the TV experience. He describes TV programmes as being constructed of **segments** lasting at most five minutes, with a relatively high degree of internal cohesion, but less linear connection with each other than is normally found in cinema. He claims that TV narratives multiply incident at the expense of forward narrative drive, and are much less self-contained than cinema films. For Ellis, the stripped-down quality of television (at least, compared to cinema) and the domestic environment in which it is watched (i.e. in natural light at home) results in a particular type of viewer concentration. In particular, he uses three essential characteristics to distinguish television from cinema. As this brief summary reveals (McQueen [1998]: 7):

- *The quality and size of the image:* The televisual image is of a lower quality than the cinematic image in terms of its resolution of detail as it is composed of electronically produced lines and is rarely more than thirty inches in diameter. The viewer is physically larger than the image: the opposite of cinema. Television is also usually looked down on, rather than up at, as in cinema.
- *The environment in which the medium is experienced:* Television is usually watched in domestic surroundings and is viewed in normal light conditions. Unlike cinema there is no surrounding darkness, no anonymity of the fellow viewer, no large image, no lack of movement amongst the spectators and far less 'rapt attention' to the screen.

'Gaze Theory': the big screen demands attention (*The Long Day Closes*, 1992)

- *The degree of concentration*: Television has a lower degree of sustained concentration from its viewers (who are often doing other things, such as talking, while it is on) but it has a more extended period of watching and more frequent use than the cinema.

Ellis crucially describes how these characteristics influence the viewer's relationship with the small screen. Following Christian Metz (1982), he defines cinema in terms of the spectator's fixated **gaze** directed to the cinema screen in conditions which favour a suspension of all physical activity (except that of eating and drinking). He contrasts this with the multiple distractions of the domestic space in which TV is viewed, claiming that the attention given to the TV screen is more that of a **glance**. This leads him to emphasise the '**immediacy**' of television (i.e. TV usually gives the appearance of going

out 'live') and the role of sound in television, calling the viewer's attention back to the screen, through vocal cues, music and effects.

'TELEVISUALITY'

This '**glance theory**', as it has become known, is strongly criticised by John T. Caldwell in his book *Televisuality* (1995). Caldwell emphasises an emerging phenomenon of television from the mid-1970s onwards: a greater emphasis on the 'look' of television, which Williams had foreshadowed in 1974 (70–1):

> One of the innovating forms of television is television itself. So many uses of the medium have been the transmission and elaboration of received forms, or have been dominated by the pressures of overt content, that it is often difficult to respond to some of its intrinsic visual experiences. . . . An experience

24 Hours News: characterised by its visual activity

of visual mobility, of contrast of angle, of variation of focus, which is often very beautiful. . . . Yet I see this as one of the primary processes of the technology itself, and one that may come to have increasing importance.

Caldwell similarly writes 'style, long seen as a mere signifier and vessel for content, issues and ideas, has now itself become one of television's most privileged and showcased signifiers' (ibid: 5). He points to two parallel developments. One is the increasing investment in creating a different and distinct look for each series, particularly but not exclusively in TV fiction series. The second is the universal use of graphics which emphasise the flat and electronic nature of the TV image (see Chapter 2).

Caldwell's contribution to the understanding of TV aesthetics is highly important. He makes us aware that the TV screen now provides, as it has for many years, a distinctive visual aesthetic of its own. It is an aesthetic where electronic images are seen not as images reflecting or presenting reality but as fragmentary flat images which sample and transform reality. TV feeds images into electronic formats which overlay writing on them, layer them in semi-transparent stacks, or place them in mosaic patterns. The visual activity of a twenty-four-hour news channel is typical of this new '**televisuality**' as Caldwell calls it. Be it Al-Jazeera or Sky or CNN, the typical format has a continuous ticker of written

information with its own logos running along the foot of a screen which also superimposes a banner headline or caption over footage of events (see Chapter 3). These are often displayed in a split-screen format with other events, images of the news anchor, or stock market information or trails of upcoming programmes. Despite the similarity of use of screen space, each channel is utterly distinct, having a graphic style, typefaces and palette of colours which is entirely its own.

This visual complexity provides Caldwell's grounds for criticising 'glance theory' since it seems to demand a more sustained and concentrated attention from the viewer. Ellis (2000) responds that such graphics are 'used to summarise, and to assemble within one frame or within a short sequence, providing layers of information . . . compressing material into a single but fractured space' (100). This is less than a disagreement: each writer is addressing a different aspect of TV aesthetics. Ellis is concerned to point out the forms of organisation of TV other than the obvious one of the programme, the single text.

THE SCHEDULE

One area of television notoriously ignored in the past is the way that the medium itself constructs its own particular catalogue of programming. Nick Browne's (1984) brief essay 'The Political Economy of the Television (Super) Text' was perhaps one of the first to reach out towards the higher level of organisation behind the fragmentary pieces of TV's flow. The rapid transitions between programme sequences, commercials, trailers, different genres within an hour's television on one channel are all immediately comprehensible to their audiences. This is because they have an underlying organisation. TV consists of an ordering of time, and a hierarchisation of material which is normally referred to as '**the schedule**'.

Scheduling is the perhaps the hidden determinant by which all television production and consumption is ultimately constructed (see Ellis, 2000: 130–47). This is the underlying organisation of television into blocks of clock time, providing the bulk of broadcast TV with a number of rhythms. Within the hour slot, it provides a sense of expectancy and ending and a habitual number of transitions from one kind of material to another (in the case of channels with spot commercials, sponsor messages and trailers). At the level of the day, the schedule provides a variety of material fitted into different 'day-parts', each with their own characteristics. For instance, the early-evening day-part in the UK is shared between news and magazine programmes or programming for a teen audience depending on the scheduling strategy of the channel concerned. At the level of the week, the schedule provides differing day characters, currently in the UK marking the distinction between weekday and weekend by the placing of soaps (weekday evenings), variety shows (Saturday), middlebrow drama (Sunday) and comedy (Friday). At the level of the year, the schedule changes according to seasons, and provides a range of predetermined and unanticipated events ranging from sport to TV-generated events like *Big Brother* to news-driven material.

Along with this comes a pattern of repetition of programme formats, generating the 'I want it as I have never had it' effect. This underlying structure closely imitates that of everyday life, and that is precisely where the strength of television lies. The aesthetics of broadcast television rely on a sense of **liveness**, not in the sense that the programmes are literally live, but in the deeper sense that the activity of television broadcasting itself proceeds in the present moment and addresses the present moment. Much of the feel of television and much of the pleasure of television emerges from this one fact. The sense of intimacy that was first defined by early practitioners springs from this, and it has enabled television to become the predominant taken-for-granted medium of our age (see the Introduction).

CONCLUSION

Critical work since McLuhan and Williams has identified and investigated an aesthetic of television, constructing a medium theory. The medium being defined is broadcast television, currently the predominant form that television takes. As I have described elsewhere (see Ellis, 2000: 39–74; 162–78), this has evolved through three distinct phases and the current phase, of 'plenty', seems to involve the reduc-

tion in dominance of the broadcast form of television (see Chapter 7). Other forms of television are emerging, or more accurately, the large screen in the living space is diversifying in potential uses. Living space screens have long been used to show material (both films and TV programmes) outside the flow of broadcasting, and are now being used to display information, to access the Internet, to show ambient images, to display our digital photos and so on (see Chapter 10). Some of these functions could be called 'television', others (like the Internet) consist of considerable amounts of material that could be called 'broadcast' (news sites, blogs etc.). Each will develop its own aesthetic. But there is no particular reason to assume that broadcast television, which still reaches deep into everyday life and consciousness, will cease to exist. Its dominance will end, it will no longer be used for inappropriate purposes or purposes for which it is inadequate. At that point, perhaps the nature of the aesthetics of television will become rather clearer than it has been in the past.

FURTHER READING

Brunsdon, Charlotte (1990), 'Television: Aesthetics and Audiences', in Patricia Mellencamp (ed.), *Logics of Television: Essays in Cultural Criticism*, Bloomington: Indiana University Press.

Caldwell, John Thornton (1995), *Televisuality: Style, Crisis, and Authority in American Television*, New Brunswick, NJ: Rutgers University Press.

Ellis, John (1982), *Visible Fictions: Cinema, Television, Video*, London and New York: Routledge.

Ellis, John (2000), *Seeing Things: Television in the Age of Uncertainty*, London and New York: I. B. Tauris.

Gripsrud, Jostein (1998), 'Television, Broadcasting, Flow: Key Metaphors in TV Theory', in Christine Geraghty and David Lusted (eds), *The Television Studies Book*, London and New York: Arnold.

Lury, Karen (2005), *Interpreting Televison*, London: Arnold.

McLuhan, Marshall (1964), *Understanding Media: The Extensions of Man*, London: Routledge and Kegan Paul.

Williams, Raymond (1974), *Television, Technology and Cultural Form*, London and New York: Routledge.

CASE STUDY
Issues in Television Authorship Catrin Prys

Notions of aesthetics and authorship are often closely connected. A work of 'art' has been so explicitly identified with an individual artist in the past that those cultural products without a clear author are sometimes dismissed as less 'worthy' of critical attention. Yet, to give media like film and television an 'author' is rarely a less than problematic exercise, sometimes resulting in the critic making a whole manner of unfounded and sometimes naive critical assumptions. In this case study the notion of television authorship will be explored, suggesting ways in which it can both aid and hinder our discussion and understanding of television texts, production and audiences.

REVIEWING THE CREDITS

When discussing a poem or a novel it is relatively easy to identify its author, his/her name can usually be found on the spine of the book or at the beginning of the text. However, authorship in television is rarely quite so straightforward. This is partly because television is primarily a **collaborative media** that frequently involves a large list of individuals in its construction. Directors, producers, writers, editors, actors, production designers, costume designers, musicians, choreographers, cameramen and composers and so on all play their part in creating what we finally see on the screen. As Edward Buscombe puts it (1980: 21):

> [t]aking all those before, during and after the work in the (television) studio the number of people working on a single drama series must run well into three figures if one includes those employed in the company infra-structure: accountants, telephonists, secretaries and so forth.

If this seems like an exaggeration simply take a look at the long list of credits that normally come at the end of a television programme. It would be impractical to list the full three figures that

Buscombe cites above, but some of the most important members of a television production team are listed below in alphabetical order (see also Holland, 1997: 27–44):

KEY TELEVISION PRODUCTION ROLES

- **Announcers**
  Announcers will narrate a sequence or a whole programme, usually working to carefully timed scripts.
- **Art director and production designer**
  The art director and production designer are concerned with the overall visual needs of a production, responsible for set design, *mise en scène* (see Chapter 2), graphics and so on.
- **Camera operator**
  Cameramen and women operate camera equipment both in the television studio and on location. An assistant camera operator can sometimes help with setting up cameras, camera movement, operating control and so on.
- **Casting director**
  A casting director helps to select and hire actors, often negotiating fees with agents.
- **Choreographers**
  Choreographers will create dance routines and train actors/dancers if necessary.
- **Composers**
  Composers will create or adapt a score, sometimes specifically written for a production. They will often work closely with the director to enhance the 'feel', atmosphere or mood of a particular sequence.
- **Continuity advisor**
  If an actor was to wear a blue tie in one shot, it would shatter the realism of a scene if it were suddenly red in the next. The continuity advisor is the individual concerned with ensuring that visual and aural detail is consistent between and within scenes.

- **Costume/wardrobe**
  The personnel who make up the wardrobe department take care of the dress and overall look of the actors while on screen.
- **Director**
  The director is, in many people's views, the most important individual in the television studio or on a set. Overall authority and responsibility for a production lies with him or her. Put crudely, the director is responsible for transforming a script into a piece of TV, making the artistic decisions regarding camera angles, type of shot, shot length, lighting, how the actors should interpret their roles, editing and so on.
- **Engineers**
  Engineers provide technical service to the production team as a whole.
- **Film editor**
  Shots are selected and arranged in order by the editor, giving a general shape, rhythm and structure to the programme as a whole.
- **Graphic designers**
  Graphic designers are responsible for producing computer-generated graphics that will create such effects as opening titles, credits and programme-information sequences.
- **IT specialists**
  IT specialists provide, operate and maintain the computer systems and software needed for a production.
- **Laboratory technicians**
  Laboratory technicians deal with film processing and back-room technical requirements.
- **Librarians/archivists**
  Librarians and archivists collect, collate, preserve and make available collections of recorded visual, sound, written and other materials for use by various productions.
- **Lighting specialists**
  Lighting specialists are responsible for correctly lighting the needs and requirements of a production.
- **Locations manager**
  The locations manager finds suitable locales for filming, sometimes also negotiating their use for the production.
- **Make-up and hairdressing**
  Make-up and hairdressing specialists work closely with wardrobe on the look of actors and individuals in front of the camera.
- **Management**
  Management teams work with the industry to ensure that areas such as the negotiation of national and international rights are looked after.
- **Marketing and sales**
  A marketing and sales team help to raise revenue for TV programmes as well as promoting and advertising the final product.
- **Musicians**
  Musicians will perform the music written by the composers.
- **Producer**
  Producers are important team leaders, sometimes involved in the original concept of a production and often responsible for helping to raise finance. Almost uniquely, the producer is involved in every stage of a programme's development from conception to broadcast. During production they perform a variety of roles that involve both management and creative tasks, helping to bring the various components of a programme together. As such, they play a hugely important role in overseeing the whole production.
- **Production assistants**
  Production assistants provide administrative and secretarial support to the producer and director.
- **Production management**
  Production management organises and arranges all the support staff and looks after such things as accommodation, transport and payment for the production team, actors and so on.
- **Production operatives**
  Production operatives perform the operational duties of a production such as vision mixing and autocues.
- **Researchers**
  Researchers acquire the background material needed for a production. This may include archival material (such as historical documents, film and information) or involve arranging contacts and interviews with relevant people or public bodies.

- **Runner/gofer**
  General assistants that take messages, make deliveries and so on.
- **(Screen)Writer**
  Writers produce a script from which a particular production will work.
- **Set technicians**
  Set technicians construct and maintain scenery, sets and props.
- **Sound editor**
  Much like the film editor, the sound editor (or 'dubbing mixer') assembles a single soundtrack from the multiple soundtracks recorded during production such as dialogue, music and sound effects.
- **Sound technicians**
  Sound technicians look after and create the type of sound needed for a production. An assistant sound technician will sometimes be involved with operating a boom microphone and other additional roles.
- **Stage/floor management**
  Stage/floor management co-ordinate and manage everything that happens in the television studio or set.
- **Story editor**
  Story editors refine and edit the script provided by the screenwriter.
- **Support staff**
  Support staff might include people involved in administration, catering, cleaning, driving and so on.

With such a long list of individuals involved in producing a piece of television (and this is by no means comprehensive), it would seem strange if critics and academics were to give the credit for a programme to only *one* individual. However, this is precisely what often happens in a large number of academic and non-academic accounts of the medium. Despite the collaborative nature of television, critics have frequently prioritised one individual as being the 'author' of a particular production. To make matters more difficult there is often confusion over which member of the production team should be priori-

Behind the scenes: many individuals go into making a single television programme

tised, a confusion that also exists between the different ways in which television is analysed in comparison to film.

THE AUTHORSHIP DEBATE

The authorship debate began most fiercely in Film Studies. For many decades, film critics argued over the logic and sense of prioritising the *director* as the true 'author' of a piece of cinema. Those in favour of this approach referred to it as the '**auteur theory**', a critical methodology that first gained significance within the pages of the French film journal, *Cahiers du cinéma* in the 1950s. Although the auteur theory has attracted much criticism in Film Studies it has remained a surprisingly resilient form of analysis. Both academic and non-academic cinema books are still often based on and around the director of a film rather than any other individuals in the production process.

For auteur theorists, a piece of cinema is defined by the creative eye of the director who oversees all aspects of the production and adds his or her own unique style of film-making in the process. As the American film critic Andrew Sarris has put it, the 'premise of the auteur theory is the distinguishable personality of the director as a criterion of value. Over a group of films a director must exhibit certain recurring characteristics of style which serve as his signature' (cited by Caughie, 1981: 13). Seen in this light, the director is responsible for the overall ***mise en scène*** (see Chapter 2) of a film i.e. its general look, visual style, prevailing tone, thematic preoccupations and so forth. Auteur enthusiasts argue that although there are clearly other influences (and individuals) at work on a production, ultimately the vision and the influence of the director remains paramount. Such critiques therefore spend a great deal of time identifying a list of distinguishing characteristics that help define a director's particular and personal '***signature***'. As John Caughie explains, it is 'in the disposition of the scene, in the camera movement, in the camera placement, in the movement from shot to shot – that the auteur writes his individuality into the film' (ibid: 27).

Although there has not been the same level of debate around authorship in Television Studies, there has been a tendency within the discussion of television to also locate a single 'author'. Yet, historically it has usually been the *writer* rather than the director that critical attention has focused upon. Certainly in

Dennis Potter: television dramatist as 'auteur'

Britain, television dramatists like Dennis Potter (*The Singing Detective* [BBC, 1986]), Lynda La Plante (*Prime Suspect* [Granada, 1991–]) and Jimmy McGovern (*Cracker* [Granada, 1993–6]) are certainly more well known than directors like Philip Saville (*Boys from the Blackstuff* [BBC, 1982]), Herbert Wise (*I, Claudius* [BBC, 1976]) and Simon Cellan Jones (*Our Friends in the North* [BBC, 1997]). An early academic account of television drama like George W. Brandt's *British Television Drama* (1981) certainly reflected this bias in critical thinking. Revealingly, this early account of TV drama divided its various chapters between prominent writers like Jeremy Sandford (*Cathy Come Home* [BBC, 1965]), David Mercer (*In Two Minds* [BBC, 1967]) and Jim Allen (*Days of Hope* [BBC, 1975]) while seemingly ignoring the input of hugely influential directors like Ken Loach and legendary producers like Tony Garnett who directed and produced all three of the above dramas (see Chapter 5).

This tendency to prioritise the television writer rather than director may date back to the days when television still had strong ties with the theatre in the 1950s and 1960s, a period when theatre productions were adapted for the small screen or when theatre writers were employed to produce original scripts for television (see Jacobs, 2000). Receiving prime billing in the theatre it would have seemed only natural to conceive these writers as the 'authors' of their television plays as well. The smaller dimensions of the TV screen also suggested a medium obsessed with dialogue rather than spectacle (see above), a tendency that tends to downgrade the input of the director and foreground the role of the writer (see Creeber, 1998: 20–2).

Unlike film, however, the notion of authorship in television has been even less consistent. While writers are often prioritised as the 'author' of television drama this is not always the case. For example, when the celebrated film director David Lynch became involved with the making of the television series *Twin Peaks* (ABC, 1990–1) his auteur status followed him directly to the small screen. This was despite the fact that this television drama was actually co-created by him and its writer Mark Frost (responsible for shows such as *The Six Million Dollar Man* [ABC, 1973–8]). In fact, there were twelve directors involved in the making of *Twin Peaks* as a whole and out of its thirty episodes Lynch directed only six (see Lavery, 1995: 196–7). Similarly, the TV war drama *Band of Brothers* (HBO, 2000) has often been referred to as being 'made' by the film director Steven Spielberg, yet the truth is that he was only executive producer of the series and never actually directed an episode.

To make matters more confusing, the director is also most commonly prioritised in discussion about television documentaries. This might be partly due to the fact that traditionally the scriptwriter in documentary is seen as playing a less important role, while directors like Molly Dineen (*The Ark* [BBC, 1993]) and Roger Graef (*Police* [BBC, 1982]) are generally regarded as overseeing the 'unscripted' action. This is further enhanced if a particular individual is also seen in front of the camera as in the case of Nick Broomfield (*The Leader, His Driver, The Driver's Wife* [Channel 4, 1990], *Tracking Down Maggie* [Channel 4, 1994]) and Louis Theroux (*Weird Weekends* [BBC, 2001]) (see Bruzzi, 2001: 130). Although less common, producers in both drama and documentary have also been singled out for attention. Indeed, individuals like Steven Bochco (*Hill Street Blues* [1981–7], *L.A. Law* [ABC, 1986–94]), Aaron Spelling (*Starsky and Hutch* [ABC, 1975–9], *Charlie's Angels* [ABC, 1976–81]) and Peter Watson (*The Family* [BBC, 1974]) have all risen to the level of auteur in their own right.

Nevertheless, this prioritisation of an auteur is not reflected across all television genres. Who, for example, is the 'author' of *Coronation Street* (ITV, 1960–), Britain's longest running soap opera? Although some critics have tried to prioritise its original creator Tony Warren as a possible auteur, it is, arguably, a limited means of examining the whole history of the programme (see Allen, 1992a: 109). And although many television dramas are still associated with auteur figures (Joss Whedon with *Buffy the Vampire Slayer* [WB, 1997–2001, UPN, 2001–3], Matt Groening with *The Simpsons* [Fox, 1989–] and David Chase with *The Sopranos* [HBO, 1999–]),

auteur credentials seem less easily applied to genres such as reality programmes, news programmes, quiz shows etc. This may partly be due to the low cultural status that such shows have with comparison to film or so-called 'quality' television drama. Indeed, authorship can sometimes be used as a means of granting **cultural worth** to a programme. By ascribing authorship to 'quality' television drama, the industry and critics are conceiving it as 'art' (i.e. the product of a single creative vision) rather than part of a collaborative (i.e. industrial) medium (see Creeber, 1998: 22).

Seen in this respect, television authorship is almost always implicitly tied up with economic considerations, frequently a way of simply selling a programme to an audience. On the strength of a 'brand name' like Russell T. Davies (writer of *Queer as Folk* [Channel 4, 1999–2000]) an audience may well be persuaded to watch a new drama also written by him. When an author is not ascribed to a particular programme, then it might also denote something else, i.e. a more formulaic or genre-based show. In this case the '**brand name**' may be the genre itself (i.e. a new detective drama or game show), a star name (such as Bill Cosby, David Jason or Sarah Michelle Gellar) or even a production company like MTM, HBO and Endemol. As the television industry has arguably little concern with artistic considerations, it is likely that they will use anything they can to promote a new piece of work.

It is important therefore that television critics do not just *accept* the form of authorship or '**branding**' provided to them by the industry but critically investigate the way that the programme is being conceived and marketed. As Matt Hills explains in his discussion of the authorial construction of Gene Roddenberry, the original 'creator' of *Star Trek* [NBC, 1966–9] (2004c: 197):

> Academic accounts which accept at face value the cultural status of *Star Trek* as authored . . . fail to see how bids for cultural value are staged through and around *Star Trek*. Such academic accounts . . . are in danger of simply affiliating themselves with one par-

ticular bid for *Star Trek*'s elevated cultural value. They fail to address different constructions and interpretations of the programme to different audiences. And as one of the longest running and most multifaceted programmes in television history, it would indeed be surprising if the *Star Trek* franchise could ever be convincingly reduced to one coherent and comprehensive 'reading'.

Such examples reveal the complex issues that surround authorship in television, a field that is rather inconsistent in the way that it constructs its critical approach to the medium. However, this does not mean that the notion of authorship is not a useful one or that it can never produce an insightful contribution to Television Studies as a whole. The answer is to always be aware of the approach that you *do* adopt and to be as critical and as self-reflective as possible when pursuing your own particular construction of a possible television 'author'.

   Below are a series of brief points that might assist you to avoid some of the major problems associated with applying authorship to television. If there is one golden rule, it is never to simply assume that you know who 'made' the programme under discussion. As we have seen, there are simply too many individuals involved in television production to be entirely sure how certain choices and decisions have been made. Of course, some individuals in the production team will always be more important and influential than others, but one can never assume that the prioritisation of a single creative vision is anything less than a particular methodological perspective – one that will always need some form of justification and discussion if it is to survive critical scrutiny.

APPLYING AUTHORSHIP TO TELEVISION: A GUIDE TO GOOD PRACTICE

- Never automatically assume that the authorship of a television programme is clear and unproblematic. Always question how and why a programme may have been perceived in such a way and your own reasons for choosing a particular notion of authorship.

- Be critical about individual claims to authorship no matter how convincing they might be. Always be aware of the way that other sources (both academic and non-academic) may unproblematically assume television authorship. Try to be as critical of these approaches as possible before embarking on your own.

- Whenever possible, try to be clear in your analysis what member of the production team may have been responsible for a particular effect. If it is not clear who made a particular production decision then be honest about it. Different members of the team will often argue for credit anyway so it is always advisable to remain as objective and as critical as possible when discussing creative input. (Note that DVD commentaries are very useful when trying to figure out particular creative input.)

- If looking at a long-running serial or series, always be aware of the different individuals responsible for separate episodes. Never assume that writers, directors, producers and so on remain consistent for a programme's entire run. Similarly, always be aware that many programmes are written by a team and that a single writer/director/producer is increasingly rare in television today, even when the programme itself may be marketed and discussed along those lines.

- Do not be afraid to make a case for authorship if you feel there really is one to be made. However, you will really need to substantiate your claims while also explaining why such an approach may be beneficial to your particular reading of a programme.

- Never assume that there can be only one auteur to a piece of television. If you want to prioritise two or more individuals in the production team then that is acceptable. Just be sure that you explain the reasons for your approach.

- Never set up a single individual as an 'author' of a programme simply because others have done so in the past. Your work will be all the more critical and convincing if you highlight and question the assumptions already made by others.

2 Analysing Television
Issues and Methods in Textual Analysis

Glen Creeber

> What our eyes behold may well be the text of life but one's meditations on the text and the disclosures of these meditations are no less a part of the structure of reality.
>
> Wallace Stevens, 'Three Academic Pieces, No. 1', in *The Necessary Angel: Essays on Reality and Imagination*, 1951 (orig. pub. 1942): 76.

Like all media, television can be analysed and interpreted using methods of **textual analysis**. At its most basic level, textual analysis is simply the means by which all texts (including books, films, plays, paintings, magazines, poems, fashion, photography and so on) are interpreted. This form of analysis is based almost wholly on critical interpretation and therefore clearly comes under the category of '**qualitative**' research i.e. speculative in nature and not scientifically verifiable (see the Introduction). Indeed, however rigorous it may be in its approach much of textual analysis is based on educated 'guess work', an analysis of the text (for our purposes a television programme) that simply attempts to uncover its potential meaning through detailed close readings (see McKee, 2003: 1–33).

It is primarily for this reason that textual analysis has come under increasing attack in recent years, critics arguing that it simply offers 'subjective' or 'arbitrary' readings of a text that are based on little empirical evidence. Although there are many forms of textual analysis (see below) this is an unavoidable issue and one that informs how you may go about using textual analysis or even whether you will employ it at all. In particular, there has been a great deal of debate about where the 'real' meaning of a text lies, whether it can be found somewhere in the text itself (sometimes located at the source of the 'author') or whether it can only be derived through a reader or viewer's interpretation. Added to this, some critics argue that textual approaches tend to focus on the text at the expense of wider contextual features such as institutional history and reception. This chapter will attempt to clarify these debates, hopefully offering suggestions that will enhance the reader's understanding and application of the approach and its relevance to Television Studies today.

TEXTUAL ANALYSIS: ORIGINS AND DEVELOPMENTS

In order to understand what textual analysis is and how it is employed, it is crucial that we first look back at its roots and historical development. This is because the reasons *why* and *how* such methods are undertaken can only really be understood as part of a larger intellectual tradition of methods and analytical procedures. In particular, the different forms and types of textual analysis employed today can be partly seen as a reaction against the type of methods and procedures used and employed in the past.

Textual analysis has probably been around, in one form or another, since human beings started painting on cave walls or telling each other stories. In terms of the modern world, many of its pedagogic and intellectual roots can be traced back to the work of the Greek philosopher and natural scientist Aristotle who was born in 384 BC. In particular, Aristotle set out some of the basic principles upon which notions of narrative structure and poetics are based. Both **genre** and **narrative** theory (see below) certainly owe a great debt to Aristotle and his conception and understanding of dramatic forms such as tragedy and comedy, notions that arguably still inform certain aspects of textual analysis today (see Lacey, 2000: 81–2). Indeed, it was not until the second half of the twentieth century that fundamental changes in our understanding and conception of the text began to produce a more contemporary form of analysis.

Before World War II most textual analysis could be found in the form of **Literary Studies**. Television, film and the media were only in their infancy and academics failed to really take such subjects seriously (see the Introduction). Literary criticism was particularly dominated in Britain during this period by the scholar F. R. Leavis. While Leavis is not the only example of this '**classical tradition**', he has since become synonymous with it because of his unusually high profile and strident views. However, much of the textual analysis offered by Leavis (most famously in his critical survey of the English novel in *The Great Tradition* [1948]) has since been discredited; critics argue that the texts he analysed simply provided him with a vehicle for projecting and reinforcing his own artistic, political and cultural prejudices. Lacking in any strict methodology, it is claimed that critics like Leavis were able to use textual analysis as a means of carefully reinforcing their own personal views and highly subjective opinions (see Storey, 1993: 27–33).

In particular, Leavis and his followers (**Leavisites**) were accused of using textual analysis to simply praise '**high culture**' (especially the 'great' English novel and their 'genius' authors) and downgrade or belittle the increasing rise of 'mass' or '**popular culture**' (such as magazines, newspapers, radio, cinema and television). Leavis clearly felt that such newer forms of culture were threatening the 'great' English 'classics' and he saw it as his role (and the role of his co-edited journal *Scrutiny* [1932–53]) to educate the masses out of their intellectual and cultural decline. As such, Leavis shared many similarities with the principles that founded the fledgling **BBC** (see Chapter 7). Although politically of the right, his attitude to popular culture was also ironically similar to the Marxist critiques of the **Frankfurt School**.

Mass appeal: early textual critics tended to dismiss popular culture like TV

While their political beliefs may have differed, they both distrusted the power and the rise of the mass media (see Chapter 3). Put crudely, Leavis saw his textual and cultural analysis as having two main functions. As Dominic Strinati explains, he wanted (1995: 20):

> first, to constitute an elite avant-garde which [would] substantiate and disseminate its interpretation of the rise of mass culture, and warn the population about, and try to reverse, the decline of serious culture; and, second, to regain its position of authority in education, and hence its position of authority as the ultimate arbiter of cultural and artistic taste and values.

The sort of textual analysis typified by literary critics like Leavis gradually became less credible after the war, particularly with the arrival of **structuralism** in the 1960s and 1970s. Structuralism implicitly questioned overtly subjective analysis by setting out a more rigorous and '**semi-scientific**' approach to the text. Put crudely, structuralism argued that all texts were composed of a complex system of '**codes**' and '**conventions**' that, if certain practices were followed closely, could be carefully '**decoded**' (see Chapter 3). **Semiotics** played a central role in this project, setting out a clear and coherent methodology by which the meaning of a text could be read as a complex system of '**signs**' (see below). This meant that textual analysis could (at least in theory) justify and account for its findings more thoroughly than in the past.

Just as importantly, this also meant that structuralism was less concerned with the cultural '*worth*' of a text. Now that all texts could be conceived as a '**system of signs**' it hardly mattered if they belonged to either the category of 'high' or 'low' culture. In contrast to critics like Leavis, structuralism implicitly suggested that a Shakespearean play could be 'decoded' in exactly the same way as a magazine advertisement, a photograph or even a child's drawing. The use of the relatively neutral term '**text**' was crucial in this project as it suggested that all cultural artefacts were essentially the same – at least on a very basic narrative or textual level (see Storey, 1993: 69–77).

Such reasoning was clearly at the heart of Roland Barthes' hugely influential book *Mythologies* (1957). *Mythologies* famously used structuralism and semiotics to analyse 'texts' such as wrestling matches, the Citroën car, Greta Garbo's face and soap powder (see Barthes, 1993). Other well-known examples of structuralist criticism include Umberto Eco's 'A Guide to the Narrative Structure in Fleming' (1979) and Lévi-Strauss's *Structural Anthropology* (1963), both classic attempts which offer 'semi-scientific' readings of culture. Such approaches to the text were particularly significant for the emerging discipline known as '**Cultural Studies**' (from which both Television and Film Studies were to partly evolve) that specialised in the analysis of 'popular' rather than 'high' culture (see Fiske, 1992). The influence of structuralism eventually helped to establish a clearer set of rules and procedures by which *all* forms of culture could now be analysed equally. This re-evaluation of popular culture certainly led structuralism to question a number of important critical assumptions. These included:

- **The notion of 'quality'**
  Whether a text is 'good' or 'bad' is not for structuralism to judge. Instead, it simply aims to find out how a text *works*, how it constructs meaning and how it transmits meaning to a reader. If notions of '**quality**' are employed at all, then they are usually strenuously debated or treated with great caution (with reference to Television Studies see Brunsdon, 1997 and Jacobs, 2001).

- **The notion of a canon**
  Originally deriving from the Greek word *kanon* (meaning to measure or rule), the term **canon** refers to the production of a list of 'important' or 'momentous' texts. While Leavis was happy to create a literary canon ('the *great* tradition'), structuralism tended to regard such canonised lists as invariably open to omissions, critical bias and cultural snobbery (with reference to Television Studies see Creeber, 2004a: xiii–xvii).

- **The notion of authorial intention**
  Structuralism challenged the notion of '**authorial intention**' i.e. that by uncovering the 'intention' of the author the critic could somehow discover the '*real*' meaning of a text. In contrast, **the 'intentional fallacy'** argued that the meaning intended by the author was not only difficult to locate (particularly so for a collaborative medium like film or television – see Chapter 1) but also not as relevant as other forms of interpretation (see Wimsatt and Beardsley, 1998).

However, structuralism itself came under increasing attack during the 1980s. Some critics found its 'semi-scientific' language (of the sort found in semiotics) particularly dense, while others criticised it for the way that it tended to over-emphasise the conclusive nature of the readings that it offered. In their desire to be seen as 'scientific', many structuralists were accused of producing 'pseudo-scientific' readings that were simply too rigid in their conclusions.

In contrast, **post-structuralism** attempted to foreground the *plurality* of meaning found in a text, suggesting that a text was always ultimately a product of *interpretation*. Barthes' the 'death of the author' may also be seen as relevant here because it argued that the 'death of the author' implicitly results in 'the birth of the reader' (Barthes, 1977b: 148). Put crudely, post-structuralism continued the structuralist development away from authorial intention but paid even greater attention to **textual indeterminacy** and **reader interpretation** (see below). Reader interpretation was also important in a strain of literary theory called '**reader–response criticism**'. Like Barthes, this approach to the text (particularly popular in America) argued that meaning was never *absolute* or *fixed* but mainly the product of the **act of the reader** (with reference to TV see R. Allen, 1992b).

The different forms of textual analysis used in Television Studies today can mainly be seen as deriving out of these structuralist and post-structuralist traditions, some dating back to Literary Studies (where the origins of structuralism and textual analysis lie) with others coming directly out of Film and Cultural Studies. This may partly explain why students new to the subject frequently find it such a difficult and confusing area of study, often not appreciating why certain methods and procedures have to be carried out and the reasons why they often take the form that they do. The varied origins of textual analysis also mean that there are now many different and contradictory schools of thought within this complex field of study, which can add to a profound sense of confusion and perplexity.

Such a rich intellectual history clearly means that there are now a variety of methods and approaches that can all be grouped together under the rather broad heading of '*textual analysis*'. These approaches include semiotics, narrative theory, genre study, ideological analysis, psychoanalysis, content analysis, linguistic analysis, discourse analysis and so on (see below). In turn, these approaches can be employed in an attempt to shed light on a varied array of critical readings such as feminism and gender politics, Marxism, Queer politics, post-colonial studies, Cultural Studies, modernism, postmodernism and so on. As a result, the field of contemporary textual analysis has become a complex combination of textual methodologies and critical perspectives. John Hartley has briefly summed up such a combination of approaches to the television text in this way (2002: 31–2):

- Close critical reading of audiovisual texts, derived from the traditions of literary critical reading.

- Semiotic analysis derived from Saussurian/ Barthesian linguistic structuralism and Russian formalism (Lotman, 1990; Volosinov, 1973).
- Analysis of visual images (still and moving) derived from art criticism and Film Studies (*Screen* [film journal]).
- Cultural analysis derived from 'Birmingham' Cultural Studies (Hall and Whannel, 1964; Hoggart, 1960) and Raymond Williams (1974, ideology/ hegemony analysis).
- Social-structured analysis, derived from Marxist sociology and political economy of the media (content analysis).
- Feminist criticism (Brunsdon, D'Acci and Spigel, 1997).
- Historical investigation of popular media forms (Sconce, 2000; Spigel, 2001).

Although a list such as this clearly reveals the dense complexity of the contemporary field as a whole, it is important not to be too overwhelmed by the number of textual approaches and critical perspectives you can now take to a television text. Contemporary textual analysis is a complex arena of critical methods, but with care and skill it can be broken down into a number of clear, coherent and complementary modes of television analysis that can help in any investigation of the television text.

TRADITIONAL METHODS OF TEXTUAL ANALYSIS

For the sake of clarity I will single out and briefly describe various forms of textual analysis that are used in Television Studies today. These separate approaches can be used in isolation, but any '**holistic**' approach to Television Studies will probably use a number of these critical perspectives (including non-textual methods if required), particularly if a more 'comprehensive' reading of a text is desired. There are no set rules about this, you can employ as many or as few critical approaches as you wish, but do be sure to make clear the approach (or combination of approaches) you aim to use. Like any other research method, textual analysis is less open to criticism if it employs a transparent and self-reflexive methodology.

Semiotics has been one of the most widely used methods of textual analysis employed in the study of popular culture. One of the first articles to apply this approach specifically to television was Umberto Eco's 'Towards a Semiotic Enquiry into the Television Message' first published in Italian in 1965 (see Eco, 1972). In its formative years semiotics certainly helped Television Studies to produce a form of analysis that was both versatile and analytically sophisticated. Pioneering work like John Fiske and John Hartley's *Reading Television* (1978) clearly based much of their analysis on this textual approach, while it has also informed later introductions to the field such as Len Masterman's *Television Mythologies: Stars, Shows and Signs* (1984) which was even dedicated to the French semiotician Roland Barthes. Introductory books to the subject like Keith Selby and Ron Cowdery's *How to Study Television* (1995) have continued this tradition in more recent years.

Originated by the Swiss linguist Ferdinand de Saussure and the American philosopher Charles Sanders Peirce, semiotics (sometimes referred to as the 'science of signs') was an attempt to bring 'scientific' theory to bear on the study of culture. Although a detailed introduction to semiotics is required for the uninitiated (for a general introduction see Chandler [2002] and for a more media-based introduction see Bignell [1998]), at its most basic level semiotics enables the critic to conceive and examine television with the rigour of linguistic analysis. By determining television in terms of 'signs' (exploring the cultural connotations that connect '**signifier**' with '**signified**'), semiotic textual analysis seemed to offer television academics the ability to organise their interpretations around systematic and exact procedures, also providing it with its own academic discourse (see Seiter, 1992: 32). Indeed, although semiotics is less explicitly used today than it was, it could be argued that much of the language and discourse of semiotics has remained in Television Studies as a whole, informing a great deal of the subject and its textual methodologies in the process.

Semiotics certainly informs aspects of **narrative theory** (or **narratology**). Originating in the work of the Russian formalists and Vladimir Propp (see

Propp, 1968), narrative theory attempts to unravel the means by which narratives are constructed, attempting to locate exactly what it is that turns a flow of words and images into a **story**. Originally employed for the study of literature (see Rimmon-Kenan, 1983), it quickly crossed over into Film Studies (see Bordwell and Thompson, 1990: 54–88) and later Television Studies with books such as Roger Silverstone's *The Message of Television: Myth and Narrative in Contemporary Culture* (1981). When applied to television, narrative theory reveals a medium that relies heavily on narrative structure and storytelling for a varied array of programming (see Kozloff, 1992: 69). So while Caren J. Deming (1985) reveals how a complex, multilayered television drama like *Hill Street Blues* (NBC, 1981–7) can still be reduced to a surprisingly straightforward narrative structure, other critics like John Hartley (1982) confirm its usefulness for analysing more factual programming like television news (also see Fiske, 1987: 293–308). As John Corner reminds us, '[a]lthough sometimes regarded as a self-evident indicator of trivialization or of distortion when found outside fiction, narrative organization is a necessary underlying principle of many broadcast forms' (Corner, 1999: 59).

Narrative theory is closely related to **genre theory**, a form of analysis that attempts to understand and categorise the fundamental characteristics of textual groups such as the sitcom, soap opera, documentary, cartoons and news and so on. Recognised by both viewers and the industry as a means of organising television into distinctive narrative categories, genre theory allows the critic to approach television in a systematic and methodical manner that may also take into account issues and methodologies such as ideology, discourse and semiotics (see Feuer, 1992: 145). Such ideas have since informed books such as Glen Creeber's *The Television Genre Book* (2001) that uses genre as a means of introduction to the study of television as a whole. Meanwhile, Jason Mittell's *Genre and Television: From Cop Shows to Cartoons in American Culture* (2004) shows how genre study can also be greatly enhanced through the application of other research methods

Hill Street Blues: narrative analysis can be used to examine even the most complex story lines

and contexts, particularly historiography, industrial practices and audiences.

However, all the above approaches to the text would amount to very little if they were not implicitly tied up with various forms of **ideological analysis**. Arguably, it is the ideological 'connotations' of the text that semiotics, narrative and genre theory attempt to '**decode**' through their structural analysis of television (see Gitlin, 1994). Indeed, without ideology at its theoretical roots semiotics would be little more than a semantic exercise, this is because its ideological underpinnings reveal not only how but also *why* texts are constructed the way they are. Originally informed by the ideas of the political philosopher Karl Marx, a traditional ideological conception of television focuses on the way that the text produces and perpetuates a *distorted* perception of the world; it prescribes and constructs reality in such a way that it maintains the structural inequalities of a capitalist society. Consequently, the portrayal of class, gender and race are frequently high on its list of critical priorities. More recently, traditional ideological analysis has been criticised for treating all audiences as '**passive dupes**' i.e. they are unable to resist the '**dominant ideology**' at work in a text. As a result, theories of **hegemony** (see Gramsci, 1971), **subjectivity** (see Althusser, 1971) and **discourse** (see below) have attempted to conceive notions of ideology in a less rigid and arguably more complex form (see Chapter 3).

Implicitly connected with forms of ideology, **psychoanalytic theory** has also proved an important tool in both Film and Cultural Studies, although to a lesser degree in Television Studies. Originating in the work of Sigmund Freud (and later theorists like Jacques Lacan [1979]), Film Studies has certainly applied psychoanalysis both in its examination of the text (i.e. looking for latent or '**unconscious**' meaning not immediately apparent to the viewer [see, for example, Metz, 1982]) and viewing practice, i.e. the very means by which we actually *watch* the media. Perhaps the most famous example of psychoanalytic theory and film spectatorship is Laura Mulvey's hugely influential feminist article, 'Visual Pleasure and Narrative Cinema' (1975). Although

Mulvey employs psychoanalysis to purely investigate and explore the voyeuristic environment of the *cinematic* experience, it is a good example of how useful psychoanalysis can be in unravelling the possible means by which desire and pleasure are unconsciously activated by audiences (see Chapter 3). Although it is tempting to adapt film theories of spectatorship to television, the profound differences in the two media (see Chapter 1) make such an enterprise notoriously problematic (see Flitterman-Lewis, 1992). However, newer developments in **cult TV** and **fandom** do appear to reveal a growing interest in psychoanalysis and television that may be developed in the future (see Chapter 6).

More commonly used in Television Studies is **content analysis**. Strictly speaking, more empirical, quantitative and 'scientific' than other forms of textual interpretation, content analysis attempts to simply record the amount of times that a certain piece of data is seen on TV. For example, a researcher might ask 'what percentages of people on British television today are black and Asian?' If it were possible, content analysis would then be used to count exactly how many black and Asian people have appeared on British television, perhaps in the last twelve months. As this is probably unrealistic (taking into account the number of channels and the amount of airtime involved), content analysts would probably choose a selected number of channels to examine during a chosen period (for the sake of argument, let's say a month). This data will then be transformed into statistical form from which a general pattern about contemporary British television would be formulated (see Barrat, 1986: 102–7).

One famous example of content analysis being used in Television Studies is the Glasgow Media Group's investigation of how industrial stoppages were covered by British TV news programmes. Published as *Bad News* (1976), their close content analysis (conducted over a six-month period) concluded that stoppages were usually attributed more to trade unionists than employers and that TV news was unfairly representing the interests of employers rather than workers.

However, critics of content analysis often dismiss

it as 'mere counting', revealing very little beyond obvious observations – unless, that is, other forms of analysis are employed (see Allen, 1985: 36–8). Other critics have also suggested that this form of analysis is not as objective as it tends to make out. In particular, critics draw attention to the practical problems of defining the topic of investigation, selecting the sample and units of analysis, choosing the categories and making judgments about how to implement them (see Fiske, 198**2**: 118–29). Yet, despite these criticisms, content analysis can still provide an important means by which a television text can be analysed, although it is clearly more '**sociological**' than the other forms of textual research discussed.

As this all too brief summary suggests, there are so many different forms of textual analysis available to the television critic that it is crucial to distinguish what kind of textual analysis you are employing from the start. It is also important to make clear why you are employing that method and perhaps foreground the benefits and the potential problems that it might bring with it. For example, a psychoanalytical reading of *The Sopranos* (HBO, 1999–) might help the critic to explain the complex portrayal of its characters, particularly the personal anxieties of its central protagonist. However, in doing so, such an approach might inevitably ignore the way that the programme operates within the narrative traditions of which it is clearly a part i.e. the gangster genre. Indeed, it might take a number of textual approaches and critical readings of *The Sopranos* (psychoanalysis, feminism, postmodernism, genre/narrative analysis, linguistic/semiotic analysis and so on) to ever do justice to its complex array of themes and narrative debates. David Lavery's edited book, *This Thing of Ours: Investigating* The Sopranos (2002a), suggests as much, its collection of articles using a number of textual methodologies and approaches to analyse this one television programme (see Chapter 5).

Whatever textual approach you may take to the television text (and this is by no means a comprehensive list) it is important to remember that all methods have their benefits and their deficits. To be aware of both is crucial if you are to produce an original and convincing reading of a television text.

RE-THINKING TEXTUAL ANALYSIS

In recent years such forms of critical interpretation have attracted a good deal of criticism. In particular, critics have increasingly argued that textual analysis (however loosely applied) can offer little more than wholly personalised and unfounded interpretations. If a text can be read in a number of (sometimes contradictory) ways then what makes one interpretation of a television programme more valid than another? Psychoanalytical approaches to the text have particularly borne the brunt of this sort of criticism. Many critics have argued that Freudian analysis can interpret a text almost any way it likes, finding exaggerated manifestations of the human unconscious in the smallest or seemingly irrelevant of details (and like semiotics the discourse of psychoanalysis can also be particularly complex for the uninitiated). As the film academic Martin Barker puts it in his book *From Antz to* Titanic: *Reinventing Film Analysis* (2000: 13):

> Without question, one of the main motives for writing this book is my dislike of psychoanalytic modes of film analysis. Partly, this is sympathy for students' frequent sense that to read the stuff is to take forced marches through jungles of jargon, behind whose every frond lurks a phallic snake, biting accusingly. Partly, it is because I share Bordwell's feeling that a great deal of such work is a rhetorical game, imposing arbitrary readings on films whose test of success is as much novelty as anything else. A sort of academic speaking in tongues. But mainly I reject psychoanalytic accounts because their findings resolutely refuse any kind of empirical verification.

Barker goes onto argue that psychoanalytic theories of film (and implicitly television) presuppose who the viewer might be. Following David Bordwell *et al.* (1985: 30), he suggests that such interpretations have in mind an '**ideal reader**' (sometimes known as an '**implied reader**' [see Iser, 1974]), a reader that may have strong similarities with the critic writing the analysis but not necessarily the rest of the audience. The consequences of these assumptions about viewers mean that varied interpretations are ignored and only one unsubstantiated reading is prioritised. A similar critique can be found in Justin Lewis's *The Ideological Octopus: An Exploration of Television and Its Audience*. For Lewis, 'the tyranny of the text' lies in its inability to accept the many and varied ways in which television can be read, semiotics being employed not to 'show what the text *could* mean, but to assert what it *does* mean' (emphasis in the original, 1991: 34).

These problems of textual analysis have led many television academics (including Barker and Lewis) to embrace audience analysis, opinion polls and **ethno-graphic research** as a whole. But perhaps the classic example of this wider shift can be found in David Morley's work on the British television programme *Nationwide* (BBC, 1969–83). Not satisfied with his (with Charlotte Brunsdon) semiotic analysis of the programme in *Everyday Television,* Nationwide (1978), he completely dispensed with semiotics and re-examined the programme from the perspective of its viewers, publishing *The* Nationwide *Audience* (1980) in the process (Chapter 6).

The attraction that audience studies seems to offer television critics like Morley is that it appears to avoid the issue of **'textual determinism'** i.e. tying meaning down to only one dominant reading. Instead, audience studies takes great pride in revealing the varied array of meanings by which readers and viewers make sense of a text. Rather than suggesting that meaning is somehow *embedded* in a text waiting for the discerning critic to uncover it, audience studies argue that individual viewers bring meaning *to* a text. Added to this, audience studies appear to be able to 'back up' their findings with **empirical evidence**. While textual analysis usually relies primarily on the qualitative interpretation of a lone critic, audience and reception research complement their findings with interviews, questionnaires, tables, graphs, statistics and so on (see Chapter 6). Compared to the frequently abstract and theoretical discourse that may accompany a textual reading of a piece of film or television, audience research may also appear refreshingly clear and exact in both their presentation and linguistic discourse.

However, such criticisms of textual analysis tend to ignore the fundamental changes that have taken place in this area of study in more recent years. While structuralism tended to heavily prescribe meaning to a text, **post-structuralism** usually emphasises the 'gaps' that occur between text and interpretation. In particular, post-structuralists tend to argue that only at the moment that a cultural product is 'read' by its audience does it even become a text, i.e. a complex site of struggle for meaning and understanding. As John Fiske puts it, 'Texts are the site of conflict between their forces of production and modes of reception', a '. . . program is produced by the industry, a text by its readers' (1987: 14). So, rather than prescribing a rigid or *fixed* meaning to a text, contemporary textual analysis tends to explore the playfulness and **open-ended** textures of textual meaning. As Ellen Seiter puts it (1992: 61):

> Post-structuralism emphasizes the slippage between signifier and signified – between one sign and the next, between one context and the next – while emphasizing that meaning is always situated, specific to a given context. . . . Theories of psychoanalysis and of ideology, under the influence of post-structuralism, focus on the gaps and fissures, the structuring absences and the incoherencies, in a text . . .

Added to this, critics have argued that '**post-modern**' texts are also increasingly '**open**', allowing great room for textual discussion and interpretation to take place. Rather than constructing a '**closed**', linear and straightforward narrative structure, the inter-determinacy of the postmodern text tends to deliberately indulge in ambiguity, pluralism and contradiction. Of course, many non-postmodern texts are also 'open' (or what Barthes refers to as '*writerly*' [Barthes, 1970: 4]), but postmodernism seems to celebrate textual indeterminacy with perhaps an even greater sense of irony, pastiche and **intertextuality** (i.e. when one text implicitly or explicitly refers to another). Such a view suggests that so-called 'postmodern' television (what Eco calls **neo-television** [1986]) arguably reflects the increasing slippage in meaning that occurs between text and reception by allowing greater room for audiences to experience the pleasures and anxieties of textual uncertainty (see

Chapter 5). As Jim Collins (1992) points out, this '**semiotic excess**' (i.e. the ever-proliferating bombardment of words and images from the media) is further enhanced by an increasing number of television channels and viewer **interactivity** that only adds to a television environment where the text is increasingly fragmented, distorted and forever resisting narrative closure (see Chapter 10).

The increasing use of **discourse analysis** may be viewed as reflecting part of these wider theoretical changes. Discourse analysis carries on much of the work once carried out by semiotic and ideological analysis but without being overly deterministic. Rather than heavily prescribing a single meaning to a text, discourse analysis is interested in the various means by which different socio-cultural discourses (gendered, sexual, national, racial, artistic, institutional and so on) compete for meaning. So, while discourse analysis still applies linguistic theory to the text and acknowledges the role that ideology can play in communication, it also attempts to reveal how various conflicting discourses (or '**linguistic genres**') are always battling to be heard. Subsequently, discourse analysis suggests that textual meaning is clearly much harder to pin down than traditional semiotic and ideological analysis would imply. As a result, this form of analysis is clearly more able to accept and actively reveal the textual inconsistencies, contradictions and ambiguities that may exist in a television programme (see Chapter 3).

Textual analysis is now also frequently employed alongside other forms of analysis, thereby offering various critical perspectives from which to view a text. For example, a study like Robert Hodge and David Tripp's *Children and Television: A Semiotic Approach* (1986) does not simply offer a fixed semiotic reading of a text. Instead, Hodge and Tripp attempt to explore the strength of their semiotic readings with detailed analysis of the child audiences who actually watch the programmes in question (see Seiter, 1992: 60–4). Similarly, it is increasingly accepted that textual analysis generally needs to be supported and developed around a wider **contextual** or **extratextual** framework. For example, a textual

approach to television from the 1960s would offer only a partial reading of the work if it were not set within its wider historical context (see Chapter 6). Television is not made or watched in a vacuum; the institutional, technological, social and political conditions in which a programme is produced, broadcast and consumed are inevitably an important area for discussion. Contemporary genre analysis, for example, would arguably offer very little if each genre were not placed firmly within its own '**generic genealogy**' (see Mittell, 2004: 123). This interest in extratextual information is perhaps even more pressing today because of the amount of material now available via fanzines, magazines, the Internet, merchandising and so on. Knowing where a 'text' starts and ends is not always as easy it might at first seem (see Chapter 7).

Consequently, some critics argue that some kind of 'textual analysis' will be involved in any form of cultural interpretation. Indeed, post-structuralists argue that everything we understand as 'real' is actually always mediated through language and interpretation. As a result, all knowledge is 'textual' because language articulates the way that we see and understand everything around us. As the post-structuralist Jacques Derrida famously put it, 'Il n'y a pas de hors-texte' ('there is nothing outside of the text' [1976: 163]). This does not deny the existence of reality, but it does suggest that human beings can only *access* reality through discourse. Consequently all that we perceive as real is always a matter of human interpretation (see Sarup, 1988: 35–41).

Such a view will certainly have implications on the so-called 'facts' produced by social scientists. Post-structuralists might argue that, after compiling all the interviews, graphs, tables, questionnaires and so on, audience researchers are simply left with yet another 'text' to be analysed i.e. the data they have produced. Despite their claim to be open to empirical verification their results inevitably rest finally on the interpretation of the critic or critics carrying out the research. Seen in this light, a methodological approach like audience studies does not get us any nearer to 'reality' but simply produces yet another 'text' for analysis. As Alan McKee puts it (2003: 84):

Audience research sometimes claims to find 'the reality' of the interpretations made by audiences. But this isn't the case – at least, not in the way it's often understood. Audience research actually produces more texts – tables, statistics, articles, books and newspaper stories. It doesn't produce 'reality' – it produces representations of reality. And just like other texts, these tables, statistics, articles, books and newspaper stories also have to be interpreted.

From this perspective, all forms of research in Television Studies are implicitly interpretative. Yet, whether the interpretative nature of the subject is a strength or a weakness is open to intense debate. Following Volosinov (1973), it was ironically Martin Barker (1989) who once suggested the potential offered by viewing ideology as a '**dialogic**' process. What Barker means by this, is rather than conceiving meaning as 'fixed' by ideology it is produced by a 'contract' or a 'dialogue' (i.e. a two-way exchange) between reader and text (see Chapter 3). Perhaps this 'dialogic' approach to ideology suggests how all forms of textual analysis may best be viewed in the light of recent post-structuralist theory. Different textual readings of a television programme may now be seen as simply forming a *dialogue* between different discourses or '**reading positions**'. As long as one single reading is never prioritised as the '*true*' one, then textual analysis can continue to provide an important role in producing a critical discourse around which textual interpretation, debate and discussion can be carried out.

To stick with an earlier example, a book like David Lavery's (2002a) edited collection on *The Sopranos* reflects a contemporary 'dialogue' of complementary and contradictory interpretations taking place around one television programme. Not only does it include various textual interpretations (genre studies, psychoanalysis, feminism, linguistic criticism and so on), there are also articles that employ both audience- and reception-based methodologies as well. Perhaps the great strength of such a book lies in the fact that no one reading is ever prioritised. Rather than endorsing a single particular perspective or methodology, all have their equal place in a *dialog-*

ic debate that reflects the wider spectrum of Television Studies as a whole (see Chapter 5). My personal view is that such a 'dialogue' should be encouraged rather than repressed, perhaps an inevitable reflection of a field in which all manner of methods and approaches can (and should) exist productively side by side. After all, this book is called 'Tele-Vision*s*', reflecting the plurality rather than the singularity of this highly inter-disciplinary and 'dialogic' field of study (see Corner 2004).

In summary, textual analysis refers to a number of critical perspectives and approaches in the analysis of the television text. Sometimes dismissed as subjective and deterministic, in more recent years the method has tended to be more open and self-reflexive about its subjective nature and less prescriptive in its findings. In particular, contemporary textual analysis (especially that informed by post-structuralist theory) does not generally attempt to offer a *fixed* reading of a text, but proposes various 'reading positions' (usually supported by a wider contextual framework) that may help form a 'dialogue' around which television programmes (and extratextual material) can be discussed. As this suggests, textual analysis is not always used in isolation and can often complement or add to the depth of other methodological approaches. Above all, textual analysis is a qualitative and unashamedly interpretative form of investigation, but one that (if used self-consciously and self-critically) can still provide an enormous contribution to the inter-disciplinary field we now call 'Television Studies'.

TEXTUAL ANALYSIS AND TELEVISION: A GUIDE TO GOOD PRACTICE

- Always be sure that the type of textual analysis you are applying is explained and clarified. 'I will carry out textual analysis' is rarely enough. Explain exactly what actual *form* of textual analysis it is you are employing and why you think this approach (or number of approaches) is best suited to explore the material in question.

- Always be aware that you are offering only *one* interpretation of a text. You may think that you are offering a relevant and convincing interpretation that few will disagree with. However, such is the nature of the subject that it is almost impossible to ever tie meaning down *absolutely*.

- Try not to make too many assumptions about the 'reader' of a text i.e. 'The audience will read this scene in this way'. We can never be entirely sure how a text will be 'read' (even extensive audience research is never completely trustworthy) so try not to assume you can guess an audience's reaction. Never be afraid to phrase your reading in the first person (i.e. 'I read this scene in this way . . .'), as it may be a good way of highlighting the subjective nature of the reading you are offering.

- Never be afraid to offer up a number of different readings of a text. This will not necessarily undermine your 'preferred reading' and may actually reveal the importance and significance of the reading you are offering. At the very least, your discussion of a number of other possible readings will reveal that you are aware of the textual complexity of your chosen material.

- Never be afraid to use textual analysis with other forms of research. For example, you may argue that your reading of a text is a prevailing one among many viewers and audience research could be employed to test and support your theory. Similarly, an historical context may give a much greater validity to your reading of a text from the past.

- Never be discouraged to carry out textual analysis because it is 'unverifiable'. Arguably all forms of media analysis are unverifiable (and inevitably 'textual' in nature), but that does not mean that they are not useful, relevant or important ways of approaching the subject.

- Always use textual analysis with confidence but do not make too many grand claims for it that may be difficult to defend. Regard your reading as part of a 'dialogue' with others rather than a piece of conclusive and indisputable evidence.

- Remember to always be critical and self-aware about your own particular methodology. Like every other research method, textual analysis has both its positive and negative features and you need to be self-reflexive about your approach.

- Feel free to use textual analysis if it is the form of research that you think best suits your material and the type of findings you are after. Television Studies is a highly inter-disciplinary subject and there is clearly room for *all* manner of techniques and different research methods. Tend to be suspicious of any approach that purports to be the *only* worthwhile way to study the subject.

TEXTUAL ANALYSIS: THREE IMPORTANT STAGES IN ITS DEVELOPMENT

1. The Classical Tradition:

Interested in cultural worth and what the *value* of a text is, consequently concerned with constructing canons and celebrating authorial 'genius' (see F. R. Leavis, *The Great Tradition* [1948]). This concern with value and judgment tended to prioritise high culture as the artistic creation of a single author and downgrade popular culture (such as film and television) as the product of industrial production (see Leavis *Mass Civilization and Minority Culture* [1930] and The Frankfurt School's notion of 'the culture industry'). This form of analysis was inevitably criticised for being far too subjective and arbitrary, relying heavily on personal opinion and offering few methodological procedures and little critical transparency.

2. Structuralism:

Less concerned with cultural value it focused on popular culture, applying a more rigorous ('semi-scientific') approach to the text (see Barthes, *Mythologies* [1957]). It was particularly identified with semiotics (following the linguistic tradition of Ferdinand de Saussure), narrative analysis (see, for example, the work of Umberto Eco) and uncovering the ideological codes and conventions of a text (see the Birmingham Centre for Cultural Studies). This focus on 'the text' crucially meant a movement away from the author as an unproblematic source of meaning and exposing the 'intentional fallacy' i.e. that you can ever be sure what the intention of the author was (see Barthes' 'The Death of the Author' [1977b]). It was eventually criticised for being too prescriptive i.e. 'this is the *only* (or true) meaning of a text' (sometimes known as 'the tyranny of the text').

3. Poststructuralism:
Best understood as a continuation of structuralism, but less prescriptive about meaning (see Barthes *S/Z* [1975]). This is partly because post-structuralism (akin to postmodernism) declares that all human knowledge (even the 'facts' produced by the natural sciences) is ultimately interpretative. See, for example, its critique of historical analysis which it sees as yet another form of 'textual analysis' (see Keith Jenkins *Re-Thinking History* [1991]). Consequently, it is at pains to acknowledge the active role of the reader in making meaning (see Stuart Hall, 'Encoding/Decoding in Television Discourse' [1980a]) and looking for multiple meanings within a 'polysemic text' (see Fiske, *Television Culture* [1987]). This can be witnessed by its movement away from traditional ideological analysis (particularly the notion of a 'dominant ideology') towards discourse analysis that is more concerned with identifying different 'discursive practices' that continually struggle to create power and meaning (see, for example, the work of Michel Foucault). However, this apparent 'relativism' leads to criticism i.e. if a text and its reader can produce so many meanings why bother carrying out textual analysis at all? However, post-structuralism would argue that if all meaning is interpretative then textual analysis is, at least, honest, transparent and realistic about what it does and what it can achieve.

FURTHER READING

Abercrombie, Nicholas (1996), 'Television as Text', in Nicholas Abercrombie, *Television and Society*, Cambridge: Polity Press.
Allen, Robert C. (ed.) (1992a), *Channels of Discourse, Reassembled: Television and Contemporary Criticism*, London and New York: Routledge.
Butler, Jeremy G. (1994), *Television: Critical Methods and Applications*, Belmont, CA: Wadsworth.
Creeber, Glen (ed.) (2001), *The Television Genre Book*, London: BFI.
Fiske, John (1987), *Television Culture*, London and New York: Routledge.
Lury, Karen (2005), *Interpreting Television*, London: Arnold.
McKee, Alan (2003), *Textual Analysis: A Beginner's Guide*, London, Thousand Oaks, New Delhi: Sage.
Miller, Toby (ed.) (2002), *Television Studies*, London: BFI.
Selby, Keith and Cowdery, Ron (1995), *How to Study Television*, London: Macmillan.

CASE STUDY
Shot-by-Shot Analysis Glen Creeber

All approaches to the textuality of television will rely on a basic understanding of sound and image and the language used to discuss them. This is normally referred to as a 'shot-by-shot' analysis that allows all textual approaches to examine television in a succinct and universal manner whatever the particular methodology employed. Unlike Film Studies (for example, David Bordwell and Kristin Thompson's *Film Art: An Introduction* [1990]), Television Studies has been surprisingly poor at providing students with a basic understanding of how to study and discuss the basic components of a television text. Indeed, it is surprising how few introductions to television (with the possible exceptions of Butler [1994], Selby and Cowdery [1995] and Bignell [2004]) even cover this sort of fundamental analysis. This is a great shame as, in my view, too many television students are leaving universities as skilled semioticians but without knowing the difference between a long shot and a close-up.

Karen Lury (2005) has recently examined the television text by breaking it down into four components i.e. 'Image', 'Sound', 'Time' and 'Space'. This is a useful way of looking at the different textual components of television and can provide a good source for further reading. However, for the purpose of this section I will loosely follow John Fiske's classic examination of television through ten major categories. According to Fiske, such an analysis should include examining these basic 'codes of television' (1987, 4–13):

- Camerawork
- Lighting
- Editing
- Sound and music
- Graphics
- *Mise en scène*
- Casting
- Setting and costume
- Make-up
- Action
- Dialogue
- Ideological codes

Fiske's inventory can act as a good checklist when writing an essay and it is certainly important to understand these categories in some detail before embarking on your own analysis.

CAMERAWORK

To be able to discuss the camerawork that distinguishes a piece of television is clearly an important first step in applying textual analysis to the small screen. For example, the size of a shot can clearly influence how a particular scene or piece of action is portrayed. While a **long shot** (or **extreme long shot**) may make the viewer feel distant from the action (this is why it is sometimes used as an **establishing shot** i.e. a shot that establishes where the action is to take place), a **medium shot** (sometimes known as a **head-and-shoulders shot**), **close-up** (or **extreme close-up**) can encourage the viewer's sense of intimacy with what is taking place on screen. Similarly a **point-of-view shot** (i.e. when the camera simulates the perspective of a particular character) may encourage the viewer's identification with an individual in the story, to see it 'through their eyes'.

The angle of a shot is also important in the way in which it constructs the action. For example, while a **high-angle shot** may encourage the viewer to feel a sense of power over the action, a **low-angle shot** may produce a sense of intimidation or inferiority for the viewer. Equally, an **eye-level shot** might construct a sense of empathy and equality between the viewer and the action. A **shot/reverse shot** may also be useful in these circumstances, a method by which two shots are edited together so as to follow the dialogue in a conversation.

Different types of lenses or focus can also be used in the construction of a shot. While a **standard-lens shot** tends to approximate the same depth of field and proportions as you get in real life, the **wide-angle shot** and the **telephoto lens** can dramatically alter the sense of depth or point of view (for example, the telephoto lens can create a greater sense of voyeurism).

Equally the use of focus in a scene can create a different style or mood. For example, **soft focus** may heighten the sense of romance in a scene while **deep focus** (where everything is equally in focus) is more likely to be used to create a sense of realism. **Shallow focus** (where parts of the scene are in focus and others are not) may be used to suggest a sense of documentary realism (where focus is traditionally harder to control) or used to direct a viewer's attention to a particular object or piece of action.

Finally, the type of camera used can influence the style and feel of a piece of television. For example, a **hand-held camera** or Steadicam (a camera that is strapped to the body of a cameraman) is often used in documentaries because it is lighter and generally easier to manoeuvre than other types of camera that might operate on a **crane**, **dolly** (a wheeled camera support) or tracks (known as **tracking**). However, when employed in drama a hand-held camera might produce a great sense of realism because its shaky, seemingly unrehearsed style gives a greater impression that the events on screen are taking place spontaneously. This effect may be extenuated with **whip pans** i.e. when a camera moves so fast that there is momentarily a loss of focus.

The choice between **film stock** (for example, **fine** or **grainy**) may also alter the general look and feel of a piece of television. While fine film stock

Cathy Come Home: Long shot (LS)

Medium shot (MS)

Close-up (CU) or head-and-shoulders shot

Extreme close-up (XCU)

may denote 'quality drama' a documentary feel is more likely to be achieved with a slightly more grainy stock.

LIGHTING

The way a certain scene is lit can often add to the mood or the style of a piece of television. To put it crudely, very **low lighting** can produce a sombre or depressing mood while very **high lighting** can add to a feeling of gaiety or optimism. In general practice a great deal of TV uses **three-point lighting** when a subject is lit from three sources, one light provides the main source, one light fills in the shadows and one light is placed behind the subject. Of course, in

modern TV this now usually involves more than three lights but the basic principles remain the same, producing an evenly lighted scene. As such, any deviation from this norm generally produces a striking or unusual effect. For example, if a subject is lit primarily from below (**underlighting**) it may create a more sinister effect while being lit primarily from behind (**backlighting**) can create a greater sense of mystery.

The choice between **soft lighting** and **hard lighting** can also make a difference to a scene. While soft lighting can enhance the warmth of a scene, hard lighting tends to produce the sort of harshness more commonly associated with documentary realism. A badly lit sequence with little contrast may also enhance the documentary feel of a scene, as documentary-makers usually have to rely on the light that is available to them. While in documentary a badly lit scene may be unavoidable, in drama it is probably done deliberately so as to produce a greater sense of actuality (see Chapters 4 and 5).

EDITING

As every ex-participator of *Big Brother* (Channel 4, 1999–) seems to agree, editing plays an enormous role in the way a viewer may interpret a piece of television. Editing can be done live (or 'as live') with multiple cameras or at the stage of post-production. Certainly in the *Big Brother* house a post-production editing process not only selects the action that its producers think is important, but it is pieced together in such a way that a story or narrative is constructed, often complete with heroes, villains, love stories and cliff-hangers. While **chronological editing** (sometimes referred as **continuity editing**) characterises the live coverage of the *Big Brother* house, **cross-cutting** between scenes in the edited highlights can not only speed up the action and add suspense but can also manipulate how certain participants are portrayed.

How two scenes are edited together may also have an effect on viewer perception. For example, a **dissolve** between shots may produce a seamless feel while a **jump cut** (an abrupt cut between scenes) is sometimes used to emphasise the juxtaposition of scenes. Although more usual in drama, *Big Brother* may also employ **flashbacks** (i.e. a scene from the past that comments in some way on the action taking place in the present) and even **montage** (a number of scenes quickly edited together) to create a sense of dramatic action (as in a housemate's 'best moments'). Montage, for example, is often used in TV advertising and music videos where a greater sense of intensity and information needs to be constructed within a strictly limited time.

SOUND AND MUSIC

Because television is a domestic medium and inevitably broadcasts while we are doing other things (eating, talking, ironing, and reading and so on) it relies heavily on sound. Theme tunes, continuity announcements, news readers, voice-over commentary, sound effects and so on all try to capture our attention in a space where there is much (unlike the darkened arena of a cinema or theatre) to distract us (see Chapter 1). As Rick Altman puts it, the soundtrack of a television programme continually shouts to us: 'Hey, you, come out of the kitchen and watch this!' (cited by Seiter, 1992: 45). This is not only true in the case of the most obvious musical sequences (think of the pounding drums that signify the beginning or end of *EastEnders* [BBC, 1985–]) but also in less obvious places (think of the loud thumping sound that accompanies the digital clock display as the seconds tick by in *24* [Fox, 2001–]).

While all sound clearly needs to be analysed, perhaps music is often the point where it is most obvious or powerful. Music can transform the moving image, making it more dramatic, moving or exciting. You don't have to be a musicologist to have opinions about the sort of music being used or the reasons why it has been chosen. However, you can be sure that music is rarely accidental as it can so clearly play a crucial role in the overall style and mood that a TV programme is trying to create (see Lury, 2005: 57–94).

In terms of terminology, **diegetic** sound or music means that it is clearly meant to be coming from a source within the story or scene. For example, in *EastEnders* you may hear a pop song on the jukebox in the pub or from the radio in the café. However, when the music or sound arrives apparently from 'nowhere' then it is **non-diegetic** i.e. the music or sound has no recognisable source within the narrative world (see Butler, 1994: 204). Of course, sometimes it is the lack of music or sound that is notable, perhaps apparent in a drama that is hoping to capture a greater sense of documentary realism. This may be the reason why a soap opera like *EastEnders* rarely uses non-diegetic music, as to do so would risk breaking the form of realism that it strives so hard to achieve. However, this does not mean that diegetic music is not frequently used for effect because it clearly is.

Mise en scène = everything seen on the screen

Technique	Effect
Establishing shot (ES)	Usually sets the scene (e.g. a shot of the house where the action takes place)
Long shot (LS)	Distancing, removed, neutral (often used in an establishing shot to set the scene)
Extreme long shot (XLS)	Distant, removed
Close-up (CU) (head-and-shoulders shot)	Intimacy, empathy
Extreme-close up (XCU)	Emotion, drama, a vital moment
Shot/reverse shot (SRS)	Creating a dialogue between two people
High-angle shot (HAS)	Domination, power, authority
Low-angle shot (LAS)	Weakness, powerlessness
Eye-level shot (ELS)	Equality, empathy
Point-of-view shot (POV) (usually simulating a character's view of a scene)	Individual perspective
Wide-angle lens	Dramatic
Standard lens	Everydayness, normality
Telephoto lens	Voyeurism
Soft focus	Romance
Deep-focus (everything is in focus)	Everydayness, normality
Shallow focus (a scene only partially in focus)	Draws attention – 'look at this'
Three-point lighting (a subject is lit three ways)	Normality
Low-key lighting (or *chiaroscuro*)	Sombre, depressing, gritty
Underlighting (light source from below)	Sinister
Backlighting (light source from behind)	Mysterious, enigmatic
Soft lighting	Complimentary, warmth
Hard lighting	Realistic, gritty
Fine film stock	Natural, everydayness
Grainy film stock	Documentary realism
Hand-held camera (Steadicam)	Shaky, documentary realism
Whip pan (momentary lack of focus)	Documentary realism
Cross-cutting (two scenes edited together)	Allowing one scene to comment on the action of another
Dissolve	Continuity
Jump cut	Juxtaposition
Flashback (a scene from the past)	Narrative and temporal depth
Montage	Action, intensity, drama
Diegetic music/sound (from an identifiable source in the narrative)	Realistic
Non-diegetic music/sound (not from an identifiable source in the narrative)	Dramatic and emotional

Figure 2. A Summary of Television Techniques and Their Potential Effects.
Adapted from Selby and Cowdery (1995: 57).

GRAPHICS

One aspect of television not mentioned by Fiske (1987) in a great deal of detail is its use of graphics. Graphics have always been important to television, look at any old newsreel and you will see maps, diagrams and tables constantly being employed as a form of illustration. However, in more recent years (particularly since the introduction of **computer-generated images [CGI]**), graphics have become increasingly foregrounded in the television image. Indeed, printed words and graphic images increasingly determine the look, style and meaning of a television image. Whether graphic images are responsible for a whole set (as is often the case in modern news programmes) or are superimposed over the image (sometimes running, for example, along the bottom of the screen), television increasingly uses graphic images and written text to add meaning and style to all of its programmes. Like sound and music we may not always be aware of graphics being used (how often, for example, do you even notice a channel's logo in the corner of the screen?), but to ignore them in analysis is to leave out a hugely influential element by which meaning is clearly produced.

MISE EN SCÈNE

All these elements (and more) of composition are generally referred to as the **mise en scène**. Originally a theatre term meaning 'staging', it simply refers to everything that can be seen on the screen (see Corner, 1999: 31). According to Jeremy G. Butler, '*mise en scène* thus includes all the objects in front of the camera and their arrangements by the director and his or her minions. In short, *mise en scène* is the organisation of *setting, costuming, lighting* and *actor movement*' (1994: 101). It is, therefore, a useful term when trying to describe or locate the overall **style** or **composition** of a programme or a particular sequence. For example, the general *mise en scène* was dark and gloomy, bright and optimistic and so on.

CONCLUSION

It can take time and practice to get used to these terms, but Figure 5 may provide a crude but useful summary of some of the major points. This table is inevitably reductive and simplistic. The codes and conventions of television vary greatly under different cultural, historical and economic systems. To say A + B = C in terms of television sound and image is to ignore the inevitable differences that exist between different societies and the sometimes subtle differences by which individuals and different audiences determine their own meanings (see Chapter 6). This is one of the greatest problems with textual analysis, its apparent willingness to predetermine and categorise *all* meaning for *all* viewers. Nevertheless, it is hoped that such a table simply helps the student to isolate and understand some of the ways in which a particular technique *may* effect and influence a viewer's reading of the text.

Figure 5 can certainly tell us a great deal about the television sound and image. While not trying to determine universal meanings between 'technique' and 'effect', it does reveal how there is inevitably a strong relationship between the two. For example, it explicitly reveals how **realism** is always as constructed a televisual form as fantasy, and that all forms of programming construct the viewer's point of view in such a way that meaning (if not predetermined) is clearly being manipulated. It is the job of textual analysis to reveal that process of manipulation, and while it may not always be 'accurate' in its assessment (or empirically verifiable in its results), it can clearly remind us of the potential ways in which that manipulation can operate. While it needs to be used with great care, textual analysis provides us with a form and language through which the possible results of that manipulation can be analysed, discussed and debated.

3 Decoding Television
Issues of Ideology and Discourse
Glen Creeber

One nation/under god/has turned into/one nation under the influence of one drug – television, the drug of the nation . . .

'Television, the Drug of the Nation', The Disposable Heroes of Hiphoprisy.

This chapter could have centred on many forms of television analysis ranging from semiotics, psychoanalysis, narrative theory, genre study and so on (see Chapter 2). However, the reason why **ideology** was chosen over all other forms of analysis is because it plays such an important role in almost every other approach. Critiques such as semiotics and narrative theory clearly rely on fundamental notions of ideology to offer conclusions about textual signification, while matters of institutional and political theory would be of little use without its conceptual underpinnings. Despite ideology becoming rather unfashionable in recent years for its sometimes deterministic approach to the television text and context (hence the rise of **discourse theory** – see below), ideology remains an important concept around which television has been formed and discussed.

WHAT IS IDEOLOGY?

A simple definition of ideology is difficult because it is a complex and highly contested term. But at its most basic level ideology refers to the ideas and beliefs by which human beings come to understand the world and their place in it. There are, of course, different ideologies that attempt to explain the world to us (religious, political, philosophical and so on),

but whatever form it takes, ideology is a particular way of seeing the world that is articulated through language, imagery, gesture, metaphor and so on. The term ideology first appeared in post-revolutionary France at the end of the eighteenth century to simply mean 'a science of ideas' (see Cormack, 1992: 9), but the notion of ideology that we understand today owes most to the definition of the concept originally outlined by classical **Marxism**. In particular, Karl Marx (who established the fundamental principles of Communism in work such as *The Communist Manifesto* [1848] written with Friedrich Engels) used the term to describe the way in which those in power *distort* meaning.

According to classical Marxism, capitalist society is profoundly unjust, constructed in such a way that only the ruling class (or **bourgeoisie**) benefits economically from its form and structure. In particular, it argues that the bourgeoisie (owners of the 'means of production' i.e. factories and other industries) exploits the working class (or **proletariat** i.e. the workers who sell their labour power) for economic gain, a social imbalance that is reflected in all aspects of capitalist society. The bourgeoisie manages to retain this supremacy over the proletariat by making the economic inequalities in society look perfectly normal and unchangeable. It is ideology that does this, distorting the profound inequalities of capitalist society until they appear completely *natural*.

For Marx, the **base** (i.e. the economic structures upon which a society is based) directly determines the **superstructure** (i.e. the legal, political, religious, aesthetic, cultural, moral and philosophical ideologies) around which a society operates. As Marx and

Engels famously put it in *The German Ideology* (1998 [orig. pub. 1845]: 67):

> The ideas of the ruling class are in every epoch the ruling ideas: i.e., the class which is the ruling *material* force of society is at the same time its ruling *intellectual* force. The class which has the means of material production at its disposal, consequently also controls the means of mental production, so that the ideas of those who lack the means of mental production are on the whole subject to it.

As this suggests, ideology *normalises* the dominant ideas of the ruling class until they become accepted by all sections of society as perfectly natural. An example of the way the dominant ideology might '**naturalise**' societal norms is the notion behind 'the divine right of kings'. Such a concept decrees that God has chosen certain families to rule and so their power and wealth is beyond question or dispute. Similarly, when the Christian hymn, *All Things Bright and Beautiful*, originally included the lines: 'The rich man in his castle/The poor man at his gate/He made them high or lowly/And ordered their estate', it gave the impression that different levels of social class are actually ordained by a higher power. Seen in this light, the hymn proposed an ideology that attempted to explain and naturalise the huge differences in wealth that exist in society as literally *God given*. Indeed, Marx famously proclaimed that religion is 'the opium of the people' (Marx, 1982: 131), meaning that religion dulls the pain caused by oppression. While the Christian notion of eternal damnation makes the proletariat fearful of breaking social norms, the promise of a heavenly reward keeps them satisfied with the hardships they experience in their present life.

For Marxists, all social institutions (not only religion, but also the government, the law, the media and so on) construct a similarly distorted view of the world. From a classical Marxist perspective, the proletariat live in a state of '**alienation**' or '**false consciousness**', constantly denied real insight into the true nature of their own exploitation. Mike Cormack has recently summed up these major points (2000: 94):

1. Ideology is a false (or at least distorted) way of seeing the world of social relations (i.e. the ways in which people, or groups of people, interrelate with each other).
2. It is based on the economic and social structure of society, to the extent that it is seen as arising naturally from that structure. Thus the economic structure of society gives rise to a particular social structure and out of this ideology emerges.
3. It is linked only to the dominant [ruling] class in society, which attempts to impose its ways of seeing the world on to the subordinate classes.
4. Its essential character is to present as natural, and almost God given, a form of society which systematically works in favour of a few (those who profit from the organisation of society by being in the dominant class), against the interests of the majority (those whose work supports the dominant class but who do not themselves greatly profit by this work).
5. It is thus not a conspiracy invented by the dominant class, but rather a way of seeing the world which even the members of the dominant class see only as natural.

Changes have clearly taken place in the contemporary notion of ideology (see below), but this original conception of ideology undoubtedly influenced a great deal of Television Studies, particularly its early development.

APPLYING IDEOLOGY TO TELEVISION

For the purpose of Television Studies it is important to understand the role that TV (and the media in general) plays in maintaining the ideological power of the bourgeoisie. Although Marx himself said very little about the media (of course, television was not even invented during his lifetime), Marxists today would argue that it is crucial that television critics examine the means by which the medium reflects the views and concerns of the ruling class. They might argue, for example, that TV quiz and game shows validate and perpetuate the materialist aspects of capitalist society with their expensive prizes and huge cash wins. They might also argue that they help to create the misleading illusion that great wealth is available to all members of the public regardless of their social class, reinforcing the misconception that knowledge (and skill) always produces high rewards (see Fiske, 1987: 266).

This classically Marxist notion of ideology was clearly reflected in the critique of television offered in the 1930s and 1940s by the **Frankfurt School**. The Frankfurt School was one of the first groups of intellectuals to take television seriously and used a Marxist understanding of society to explain the medium's role in forming important aspects of capitalist ideology. In particular, they coined the term '**cultural industries**' to suggest the way that modern capitalist societies produce some forms of culture like mass-produced *commodities*. Whereas high culture like classical literature and classical music possessed artistic integrity, mass (-produced) culture like newspapers, magazines, popular music, pulp fiction, radio, television etc. churned out standardised and formulaic cultural products, simply designed to keep the masses happy and deluded in their exploitation (see the Introduction). For Theodor Adorno, 'the concepts of the order which it [the culture industry] hammers into human beings are always those of the status quo'. Its effects are profound and far reaching, 'the power of the culture industry's ideology is such that conformity has replaced consciousness' (1991: 90).

Classical Marxist notions of ideology were also at the very heart of **structuralism** and **semiotics** (see Chapter 2). Roland Barthes' famous semiotic account of culture in *Mythologies* (1973 [orig. pub: 1957]) clearly could not have been conceived without incorporating this type of social critique into its analysis. Put crudely, Barthes argues that 'myth' is simply the illusion by which ideology is presented to the world as natural. According to Barthes, a 'conjuring trick has taken place; it [myth] has turned reality inside out, it has emptied it of history and has filled it with nature . . .' (1973: 142). So when Barthes analyses a *Paris-Match* cover photograph of a young black soldier saluting the French flag, his description of the mythological 'connotations' of its message (that 'France is a great empire, that all her sons, with-

out colour discrimination, faithfully serve under her flag' [ibid: 116]) essentially offers an ideological critique.

This belief in the ideological structure of culture and storytelling was also reflected in aspects of structuralist **narrative theory** (see Chapter 2). According to Tzvetan Todorov (1977), narrative structure is not, in itself, either radical or conservative. However, more than likely the narrative structures common in any given society are usually used to perpetuate the status quo. For example, narrative theory has argued that we do not come to understand the world innocently but learn to see it through a system of opposites. In the history of Western thought these '**binary oppositions**' might include 'good versus evil', 'mind versus matter', 'speech versus writing', 'man versus woman', 'white versus black', 'West versus East' and so on. However, these binary oppositions are not defined equally but hierarchically i.e. the second term is usually seen as a *corruption* of the first. This means that the very structures by which we understand the world are inherently ideological i.e. white is superior to black, man is superior to woman, the West is superior to the East and so on.

These binary oppositions have important implications for ideological analysis. For example, television news may be seen as constructing images of the political world that works on the binary opposition of 'us' and 'them'. For American and European television this could mean presenting the West as 'good', 'fair' and 'just' and the East as 'chaotic', 'untrustworthy' and even 'evil', as this small list of binary oppositions reveals with reference to the media coverage of the Iraq war (cited by Lacey, 2000: 69):

We	*They*
Our missiles cause . . .	*Their missiles cause . . .*
We . . .	They . . .
Precision bomb	Fire widely at anything in the skies
George Bush is . . .	*Saddam Hussein is . . .*
At peace with himself	Demented
Resolute	Defiant
Statesmanlike	An evil tyrant
Assured	A crackpot monster

Similarly, the general structure of storytelling (order/disorder/order restored) implicitly suggests that things should (and will always) remain as they are. In a world of immense poverty, famine, war and hardship, the fictional happy endings consistently produced by the big and small screen suggest that everything will eventually turn out well, that society is essentially just and fair. In this narrative universe cowboys with white hats will always succeed over the ones in black hats, and good (as it is defined by the dominant ideology) will always triumph over evil. However, the notion of 'good' and 'evil' projected by such narratives is inevitably biased. Just ask the Native Americans who were so often caricatured in Hollywood Westerns as blood-thirsty, cunning savages (see Wright, 1975).

This kind of **stereotyping** is another example of how ideology *naturalises* culture, creating distorted myths about different social/national/racial groups. The word stereotype was originally a printing term, derived from the process where rows of type were literally fixed on a plate (called the 'stereotype') which then makes an impression on paper. So the term implies monotonous regularity – each page printed from a stereotype is *exactly* the same. As this suggests, stereotypes enforce a form of rigid uniformity on whole groups, simplifying individual characteristics into social and ideological clichés – examples might include the savage Red Indian, the black mugger, the Islamic terrorist, the Asian shopkeeper, the nagging wife and so on.

Television is particularly susceptible to the use of stereotypes because the medium often needs to

Are You Being Served?: stereotypes are commonplace on TV

establish character almost instantly before an audience loses interest and switches over or off (think, for example, of the kind of stereotyping often used in television advertising). While sometimes harmless, stereotypes can also be damaging and socially divisive (see Perkins, 1979). In particular, Richard Dyer (1977: 30) argues that stereotypes often work by 'splitting' i.e. dividing people so that we inevitably have those that have done the stereotyping and those that have been stereotyped. This, of course, leads to a classic binary opposition between 'us' and 'them'; our 'normality' is reinforced by placing anyone seen outside our norm as 'strange' or 'suspicious'. For example, critics have argued that this was often the case in early TV portrayals of homosexuals that tended to either portray gay and lesbian characters as evil or objects of ridicule (see, for example, Capsuto, 2000). The ideology hidden in stereotypes is therefore often used as a means of keeping so-called 'minority' cultures subordinate, simultaneously re-establishing a dominant culture or ideology in the process.

Whatever approach to ideology you take it will usually involve similar issues of **representation**. Ideological criticism consistently reminds us that rather than *innocently* reflecting the world, television **re-presents** reality i.e. it constructs and articulates it from a particular perspective or point of view. This does not just take place in the explicit political bias endemic in factual TV programmes such as news and current affairs, although clearly this is an important source of ideological distortion (see below). It also clearly takes place in apparently less politically motivated genres such as soap opera (see, for example, Mumford, 1995), the TV action series (see, for example, Buxton, 1990), the police show (see, for example, Clarke, 1986) and the sitcom (see, for example, Wagg, 1998). From this perspective, television consistently 'naturalises' the world around us, forever turning ideological bias into a seemingly '*natural*' representation.

RE-THINKING IDEOLOGY

Classical Marxist notions of ideology have not been without criticism. In particular Marx's original conception of ideology allowed little or no room for resistance against the dominant ideology.

Consequently, such a critique of the media tends to conceive audiences as passive '**cultural dupes**' that are unable to see beyond their ideological manipulation. This kind of approach to Media Studies has often been referred to as '**the hypodermic needle**' (or '**magic bullet theory**') approach because the media are seen as having a *direct* influence on the individual, as if a hypodermic needle (or 'bullet') had been put directly into their veins to administer a mind-altering drug (see Williams, 2003: 171–2). Such an approach tends to treat the public as *passive* consumers, who are never able to read against the grain or form their own opinions.

Critics have also questioned the **economic determinism** of the dominant ideology theory, arguing that other ideologies may also exist that are not strictly reliant on Marx's economic model. In particular, it has been argued that the Marxist obsession with social class ignores other forms of ideology such as gender or racial ideology that can sometimes cut across class lines. Finally, critics have argued that if there is a 'false consciousness' then there is also clearly a 'true consciousness'. It is a concept that is not only dangerously totalitarian but also risks appearing philosophically limited and naive (see Eagleton, 1991).

Over the years, various Marxist critics have attempted to answer or explain these apparent problems with the classical notion of ideology. Roland Barthes, for example, accepted that resistance can take place against the dominant ideology. However, he argued that resistance is only allowed to take place as a form of '**inoculation**' against greater threats. Just as a disease like polio is prevented by injecting a tiny amount of it into the body (thereby immunising the patient), so society allows a small amount of resistance to take place only in order to counteract complete dissent. As Barthes puts it, 'One immunizes the context of the collective imagination by means of a small inoculation of acknowledged evil; one thus protects it against the risk of generalized subversion' (1973: 150). In this way, Barthes managed to continue the drug metaphor that Marxists had applied to religion, but added a convenient and plausible twist that explained how and why capitalist society allows resistance to take place (see Fiske, 1987: 39).

The Algerian critic Louis Althusser also added more complexity to Marx's original conception of ideology, particularly in his most famous essay, 'Ideology and Ideological State Apparatuses' (1971). Most crucially, Althusser investigated the notion of *subjectivity* a great deal more than Marx, drawing on the work of the structural anthropologist Lévi-Strauss and the post-Freudian developments in psychoanalysis. He argued that ideology cannot simply be explained through economic determinants alone, nor is it something simply imposed forcefully on the passive individual by the ruling class. Instead, **ideological state apparatuses** (ISAs such as religion, education, politics, the law, the family, media and culture) function in favour of the dominant ideology by '**interpellating**' (or '**hailing**') us as individuals (see Althusser, 1971).

As John Fiske (1992a) points out, the implication of Althusser's work is that ideology is not a 'static set of ideas through which we view the world, but a dynamic social practice, constantly in process, constantly reproducing itself in the ordinary workings of these apparatuses. It also works at the micro-level of the individual' (287–8). Consequently, Althusser concluded that we should see ideology as part of the very fabric by which we understand ourselves as **subjects**, the very means by which we articulate and construct our personal identities. We can consequently never step outside ideology as classical Marxism may have suggested because the subject is a *social construction*, not a natural one. Like Barthes, then, Althusser does not criticise Marx explicitly but attempts to explain, in detail, the means by which ideology continues to retain control over individuals within modern capitalist societies.

Althusser's understanding of ideology partly grew out of the work of the Italian Marxist Antonio Gramsci, who also developed Marx's original conception of ideology in books such as *The Prison Notebooks* (written between the years 1929 and 1935). In particular, Gramsci employed the term '**hegemony**' to explain the complex and sophisticated system of power that modern capitalist society

operates. Although dominant interests will prevail for most of the time, Gramsci argued that there are places within society where real dissent is felt and heard (see Tony Bennett *et al.* 1992). Contesting the original Marxist notion that ideology is simply a reflection of the economic base of society, Gramsci argued that ideology exists in a form of both *force* and *consent*. In other words, ideology may control society but how it does so is frequently a matter of **negotiation** (see Gramsci, 1971). Consequently, ideology is always a complex system of domination, resistance and compromise. As Michael O'Shaughnessy puts it in 'Box Pop: Popular Television and Hegemony' (1990: 89–90):

'Hegemony' recognises the role of the subordinate groups in producing ways of 'making sense' of the world. It suggests that the 'hegemony' or power of the dominant groups can only be maintained through a struggle and tension between dominant and subordinate groups. Out of this struggle, ways of 'making sense' of the world are produced which both groups contribute to and can agree with. What this means is that although the interests of the two groups are fundamentally opposed they have found a way of living in harmony or consent because the subordinate groups have won enough concessions to make them accept their domination while the dominant groups' overall structural power base is maintained. As long as *this* is not challenged the subordinate groups can continue to win more and more concessions and have an effect on the constitution of the resulting state of hegemony.

The influence of Gramsci and Althusser on British Cultural Studies during the late 1970s saw a resurgence in the use of ideology in the humanities generally. This was particularly spear-headed by the work done at the University of Birmingham's Centre for Cultural Studies (CCCS) under the leadership of Stuart Hall (see, for example, Hall, 1982). Gramscian notions of ideology certainly influenced Hall's ground-breaking article 'Encoding and Decoding in Television Discourse' (1980a) that attempted to reveal how all television texts are '**polysemic**' i.e. they can be read by audiences in a number of ways. Such an approach to television clearly revealed how audiences do sometimes accept the '**dominant**' reading of a programme. However, Hall went on to argue that they can also *resist* that 'encoded' interpretation, offering '**negotiated**' or '**oppositional**' 'decodings' in their place (see Hall, 1980a).

It was Hall's article that arguably inspired the rise of **audience studies**, which became increasingly popular in Television, Film and Media Studies in the 1980s and 1990s (see Chapter 6). When it was recognised just how **active** audiences could be at decoding programmes the notion of a dominant ideology indoctrinating *all* viewers in the exact same way seemed overly simplistic (see Chapter 2). However, Hall's notion of a 'preferred' reading was eventually criticised for suggesting that the critic could ever be sure which reading was preferred or that there was even one preferred reading at all. Despite granting audiences with the power to offer various readings of a text, his notion of a 'preferred' reading still suggested that there was a 'dominant ideology' at work, even if resistance to it could take place (see Morley, 1980).

Ideological analysis was certainly losing favour during the 1980s and 1990s with critics like Nicholas Abercrombie arguing that once academics abandoned the very notion of a dominant ideology that ideological analysis itself was redundant (see Abercrombie *et al.*, 1980). Meanwhile, Martin Barker's *Comics: Ideology, Power and the Critics* (1989) continued to develop the classical notion of ideology by introducing Volosinov's notion of *dialogism* into the debate. Instead of conceiving ideology as a one-way process, Barker argued that ideology forms a 'dialogue' between text and reader (see Chapter 2).

The problems associated with ideology and the shift in the political climate generally towards the right (Thatcherism in Britain, Reaganism in the US and the general decline in Communism, particularly the collapse of the Berlin Wall in 1989) may partly explain the unpopularity of ideological analysis after the mid-1980s. In particular, the heavy attention of Marxist theory on social class was now regarded as a little too narrow in its focus. As the clear-cut binary oppositions of the Cold War began to break down, so the race, class and gender wars also seemed to be acquiring more complicated cultural patterns. This appeared to be reflected in a growing interest in '**identity politics**' that, while still interested in social class, also focused more on issues of gender, sexuality, ethnicity, national identity and so on. As the feminist mantra 'the personal is political' appeared to suggest, critics argued that we were now living in a world where more than just brutal economics could determine human consciousness.

Originating in socio-linguistics, **discourse theory** proved particularly attractive to this new development in Cultural Studies. Discourse theory argues that there are a number of different 'discourses' at work within society at any one time, actively constructing the world around us and making sense of and reproducing reality by fixing meanings. These discourses might include institutional discourses such as legal, medical, educational, journalistic or even popular discourses such as pop music, slang, regional dialects and so on. So, although these discourses are not ideologically neutral and do fix meaning, they are not seen as dominant or eternal, neither are they always economically determined (see Chapter 2).

Michel Foucault is particularly associated with the origins of discourse analysis in Cultural Studies, his work investigating the means by which different discourses influence the social production of meaning. Through his **post-structuralist** (see Chapter 2) critiques of society he showed how legal, medical and even sexual discourses fix the way in which the treatment of crime, illness and deviancy have been dealt with over time, influencing the way definitions such as 'sane' and 'insane' and even 'good' and 'evil' have been historically constructed (see Foucault, 1984). As Danaher *et al.* put it (2000: 6):

Foucault was far more interested in, and receptive to, work, which, instead of trying to understand the 'one and only' truth of things, tried to 'historicise' the different kinds of truth, knowledge, rationality and reason that had developed in cultures.

For many critics, then, the problems associated with earlier notions of ideology are eased by the flexibility of discourse theory that does not treat ideology as completely dominant, ever present and timeless. Not every text is driven as ideologically as every other and sometimes ideology may not even be the best way to approach a particular programme or genre at all. However, it would be misleading to suggest that discourse theory entirely replaces ideological analysis, for many critics ideology is still an important aspect of discourse analysis, just not the only one. As Norman Fairclough puts it in *Media Discourse* (1995: 47):

> My view is that media discourse should be regarded as the site of complex and contradictory processes, including ideological processes. Ideology should not be seen as a constant and predictable presence in all media discourse by definition. Rather, it should be a working principle that the question of what ideological work is being done is one of a number of questions which analysts should always be ready to ask of any media discourse, though they should expect the answers to be variable. Ideology may, for example, be a more salient issue for some instances and types of media discourse than for others.

As Fairclough's comments imply, it would certainly be premature to announce the death of ideology in Television Studies completely. Most general introductions to the subject (see Abercrombie [1996], McQueen [1998] and Lealand and Martin [2001]) still spend time defining and explaining the approach while also making clear what the problems may be with it. It clearly remains a useful way of uncovering the implicitly 'political' nature of television and particularly the means by which social identities are reflected and articulated by the small screen. It is no longer the only or even primary method of textual analysis but it does frequently add insight and depth to other forms of methodological interpretation. Some critics have even argued that ideology provides the theoretical 'teeth' of the field, an area of study that risks simply becoming toothless,

banal and apolitical without its insightful critical perspective (see Morris, 1990).

FEMINIST TELEVISION CRITICISM AND IDEOLOGY – A BRIEF OVERVIEW

Notions of ideology and discourse have clearly influenced a great deal of Television Studies. The investigation of class, race and gender have particularly benefited from the systematic analysis of social stereotypes and constructed forms of identity that such approaches have to offer. However, simply for the purpose of this section I will concentrate on feminist critiques of television, to provide a small case study by which I can illustrate how these issues have specifically influenced at least one area of textual and cultural debate within Television Studies as a whole.

Feminist interpretations of the media began in earnest during a period now known as '**second-wave feminism**'. While 'first-wave feminism' is generally identified with the early origins of feminism (particularly Emmeline Pankhurst and the Suffragette movement), second-wave (or 'radical') feminism grew up alongside the political movements of the 1960s such as the Black Civil Rights movement, the New Left student activism and the Anti-Vietnam War protests. Like these movements, feminism (or 'the women's movement') was politically motivated, identified with women's groups, 'consciousness-raising', campaigns for women's health and childcare, demonstrations against pornography and so on. In terms of the media's representation of women there was clearly much debate, some of which frequently turned into direct action. In 1970, for example, 100 representatives from the National Organisation of Women (NOW) in the US occupied the premises of one of America's leading magazines, demanding the appointment of a female editor, childcare for employees and the publication of a 'liberated issue'.

Rather than perceiving a person's sex as biologically determined (i.e. 'God given'), second-wave feminism was interested in uncovering the means by which gender was culturally and ideologically constructed. Indeed, using the word '**gender**' rather than 'sex' can be seen as an attempt to foreground the cultural rather than biological construction of female and male behaviour. Translated into English in 1953, the French feminist, Simone de Beauvoir's *The Second Sex* (1949) was particularly influential in this project. According to de Beauvoir, men and women have been culturally differentiated in terms of 'first' and 'second' gender, a notion that clearly sets up gender in terms of a '**binary opposition**'. In patriarchy, men are clearly 'The First Sex' because masculinity embodies everything defined as culturally *positive* and *normal*. In contrast, women are stereotyped as 'The Second Sex' because femininity tends to be associated with the *negative* and the *abnormal*. Seen in this light, a woman 'is not regarded as an autonomous being . . . She is defined as differentiated with reference to man . . . He is the Subject, he is the Absolute – she is the Other' (1988: 16).

This concept of the '**Other**' is one that is important to Cultural/Media Studies as a whole, revealing how certain groups in society are culturally constructed around notions of 'normality' and 'abnormality'. In terms of gender, the list of binary oppositions below reveal how feminists traditionally argued that 'masculinity' is frequently connected with the *primary* or *superior* value while 'femininity' is more commonly associated with a *secondary* or *inferior* opposition (C. Nelson, cited by Fiske [1987]: 203):

MASCULINE	:	FEMININE
active	:	passive
presence	:	absence
validated	:	excluded
success	:	failure
superior	:	inferior
primary	:	secondary
independent	:	dependent
unity	:	multiplicity
organized	:	scattered
intellect	:	imagination
logical	:	illogical
defined	:	undefined
dependable	:	capricious
head	:	heart
mind	:	body

subject	:	object
penis	:	vagina
firm	:	soft
sky	:	earth
day	:	night
air	:	water
form	:	matter
transcendence	:	inurement
culture	:	nature
logos	:	pathos

Second-wave feminism clearly saw the media as playing a large role in the gendered construction of these binary oppositions. Books such as Betty Friedan's *The Feminine Mystique* (1963) accused the media of simply emphasising the ideological role of woman as 'the happy housewife', defined only in relation to men, the home and family. Gaye Tuchman's edited book *Hearth and Home: Images of Women in the Mass Media* (1978) came to similar conclusions, her own article entitled 'The Symbolic Annihilation of Women by the Mass Media'. Like Friedan, Tuchman relied heavily on content analysis (see Chapter 2), arguing that women on television were markedly under-represented, men tended to dominate programmes, men were represented pursuing careers, women did not appear in the same professions as men, and women were shown as ineffectual (not as competent as their male counterparts). As Helen H. Franzwa put it (1978: 273–4):

. . . televised images of women in large measure are false, portraying them less as they really are, more as some might want them to be. . . . Television women are predominantly in their twenties . . . portrayed primarily as housewives . . . restricted primarily to stereotyped positions such as nurses and secretaries . . . portrayed as weak, vulnerable, dependent, submissive and frequently, as sex objects.

Such notions of ideology were also reflected in film and cultural theory of the 1970s, particularly of the kind most closely associated with the British cinema journal *Screen*. First published in *Screen* in 1975, Laura Mulvey's 'Visual Pleasure and Narrative

Star Trek: women on TV have traditionally been portrayed as passive

Cinema' was certainly influential in feminist and media theory during this period and beyond. Although Mulvey did not explicitly refer to notions of ideology (she relies more heavily on psychoanalytic notions of subjectivity) her conclusions do still rely on the notion of a dominant '**male gaze**' – a form of 'ideology' that all members of the audience seemingly buy into when entering the cinema. In particular, Mulvey argued that in patriarchal society masculine desire had constructed the cinematic gaze in such a way that it simply reflects the structure of the dominant male unconscious. 'In a world ordered by sexual imbalance', she argues, 'pleasure in looking has been split between active/male and passive/female. The determining male gaze projects its phantasy on to the female figure which is styled accordingly' (1975: 19). Seen in this light, all members of the audience (regardless of their gender) are powerless to resist the 'dominant ideology' of the male gaze.

However, such traditional notions of ideology were increasingly challenged by books such as Lorraine Gamman and Margaret Marshment's *The Female Gaze: Women as Viewers of Popular Culture* (1988) in which you can clearly detect the influence of Gramsci. Explicitly drawing on Mulvey's conception of the 'male gaze', they argued that women are not always dominated by patriarchal structures and that there are means by which the female gaze can actually infiltrate and *resist* dominant forms of representations. For example, discussing the female cop show *Cagney and Lacey* (CBS, 1981–8), Gamman argued that it offered great scope for '**female spec-tatorship**', far beyond the limited restrictions of the male gaze (1988).

Such critiques also brought a greater interest in women's genres (particularly soap opera [see Brunsdon, 2000]) and in the possibility that they could actually offer up avenues of **resistance** to more dominant modes of ideology. Books such as Ien Ang's *Watching Dallas: Soap Opera and the Melodramatic Imagination* (1985), Mary Ellen Brown's *Television and Woman's Culture* (1990), Christine Geraghty's *Women and Soap Opera* (1991), Andrea Press's *Women Watching Television* (1991), Lynn Spigel's *Make Room for TV* (1992), Ann Gray's *Video Playtime* (1992) and Julie D'Acci's *Defining Women: Television and the Case for* Cagney and Lacey (1993) all attempt-ed to re-investigate the complex (and frequently active) relationship between women and the small screen (see Brunsdon *et al.*, 1997). As Mary Ellen Brown put it in *Soap Opera and Women's Talk: The Pleasure of Resistance* (1994: 2):

> It can be said that soap operas in some way give women their voice. The constant, active, playful dis-cussions about soap opera open up possibilities for us to understand how social groups can take a some-what ambiguous television text and incorporate it into existing gossip networks that provide outlets for a kind of politics in which subordinated groups can be validated and heard.

Perhaps one of the most often quoted examples of this sort of criticism in Television Studies can be found in John Fiske's *Television Culture* (1987). Here Fiske argued against traditional readings of Madonna's music videos that regarded them simply as pandering to patriarchal tastes by continuing the sexual objecti-fication of women. For Fiske, Madonna was actually *taking on* patriarchy by parodying traditional notions of femininity, using her body and sexuality as a signi-fier of resistance. Fiske concludes that Madonna videos are a 'site of semiotic struggle between the forces of patriarchy and feminine resistance, of capi-talism and the subordinate, the young and the old' (1987: 39; see also Kaplan, 1987 and Kaplan, 1992).

This approach in Television Studies can now clearly be seen as heralding the arrival of what some critics have contentiously called '**third-wave femi-nism**' (sometimes confusingly known as '**post-feminism**'). Rather than viewing television simply as an instrument of the dominant ideology, third-wave feminist critiques of the media attempt to recognise the complex means by which female rep-resentation is both constructed and *actively* consumed by its audience. Refusing to regard ideology as uni-vocal or total, this approach tends to conceive gen-der as part of an ongoing process by which subjects are constituted, and conceiving identity as increas-ingly fragmented and dynamic. Influenced by post-structuralist notions of subjectivity (see Chapter 2), it defines gender as a discourse that, by definition, can break away from rigid binary oppositions (active/male, passive/female) to become a site of per-formance, resistance, style and desire. As Liesbet van Zoonen puts it (1994: 34):

> A poststructuralist notion of discourse as a site of contestation implies that the disciplinary power of discourse, prescribing and restricting identities and experiences, can always be resisted and subverted. Dominant male discourse can therefore never be completely overpowering, since by definition there will be resistance and struggle.

You can certainly detect this kind of critique in more contemporary readings of television pro-grammes such as *Absolutely Fabulous* (BBC, 1989– [see Kirkham and Skeggs, 1998]), *Buffy the Vampire Slayer* (WB, 1997–2001, UPN, 2001–3 [see Wilcox and Lavery, 2002]) and *Sex and the City* (HBO, 1998–2004 [see Akass and McCabe, 2004]). Here there is much discussion of the means with which certain television texts (and their audiences) play around with, subvert, ridicule, investigate, resist and even transcend traditional male (heterosexual) ide-ologies. As this suggests, contemporary approaches to television hope to add complexity to the whole notion by which gendered ideology is produced and consumed rather than simply erase its power and sig-nificance altogether. It is not a complete break from

Sex and the City: an example of third-wave feminism?

the past (and the term 'post-feminism' certainly does *not* mean that feminism is over) but a re-articulation of the theoretical terms upon which traditional notions of gender and ideology were once based. As Elspeth Probyn puts it (1997: 137):

> far from initiating a break from feminism, I think that the current discursive landscape is a condition of possibility for generations of feminist analysis. And in the midst of the reborn family and the refurbished home, it is more important than ever that we make the personal political and theoretical.

Such a view suggests that it would be a grave error if the notion of ideology (however it is theoretically conceptualised) were allowed to disappear from Television Studies completely. The changing notions of ideology and discourse have certainly been a pivotal tool through which Television Studies has grown and developed since the writings of the Frankfurt School. To clearly appreciate and understand this is to understand a great deal about the subject as a whole.

FURTHER READING

Cormack, Mike (1992), *Ideology*, London: Batsford.

Gitlin, Todd (1994), 'Prime Time Ideology: The Hegemonic Process in Television Entertainment', in Horace Newcomb (ed.), *Television: The Critical View*, New York and Oxford: Oxford University Press.

Miller, Toby (ed.) (2002), *Television Studies*, London: BFI.

Mumford, Laura Stempel (1995), *Love and Ideology in the Afternoon: Soap Opera, Women and Television Genre*, Bloomington and Indianapolis: Indiana University Press.

O'Shaughnessy, Michael (1990) 'Box Pop: Popular Television and Hegemony', in Andrew Goodwin and Garry Whannel (eds), *Understanding Television*, London and New York: Routledge.

Wayne, Mike (2003), *Marxism and Media Studies: Key Concepts and Contemporary Trends*, London: Pluto Press.

White, Mimi (1992), 'Ideological Analysis and Television' in Robert C. Allen (ed.), *Channels of Discourse, Reassembled*, London and New York: Routledge.

Zoonen, Liesbet van (1994), *Feminist Media Studies*, London and New Delhi: Sage.

CASE STUDY
An Ideological Analysis of Sky News Mike Wayne

There can be no more important issue or event for the media to critically scrutinise than when a country declares war. In March 2003 the United States and Britain invaded Iraq on the grounds that its dictator, Saddam Hussein, posed a threat both to the region and the world because he was in possession of 'weapons of mass destruction' and that he intended to either use them himself or pass them to Al Qaeda-linked terrorist groups.

My **qualitative** analysis of Sky News focuses on its 10pm edition on 28 June 2004. This was the day of the surprise 'handover' of power in Iraq. It was a surprise because it had been officially scheduled for 30 June but had been brought forward unexpectedly, for reasons that were not entirely explored by the news programmes themselves. The 'handover' marked the *formal* end of the occupation by the American-dominated ('-led' in news programmes) coalition forces (essentially America and its 'junior lieutenant', Britain). The key question then to be asked on 28 June was to what extent this marked the *substantive* and not just *formal* transfer of power to Iraqis? Was the 'sovereignty' (that is independence and autonomy) real or highly partial, selective and contradicted by other less visible power relations?

After the title sequence of Sky News, one of the two news anchors, Emma Crosby, speaks the first words of the programme: 'Tonight on Sky News at 10, the first steps of withdrawal from Iraq'. This is then followed by a cut to President Bush, speaking at a press conference in Istanbul, Turkey, where he and other politicians were attending a NATO (North Atlantic Treaty Organisation) summit. Bush says: 'We pledged to end a dangerous regime, to free the oppressed and to restore sovereignty [to Iraq]. We have kept our word.' What is extraordinary about this opening is that even though (according to opinion polls) Bush was held in very low regard by the British public and even though by the time of this broadcast a clear majority of people in the UK did

not support the war, Sky News, by placing him visually and aurally at the top of the programme, makes Bush the ***primary definer*** of the meaning of the formal 'handover' of power.

Sky News was not alone in the media in interpreting the handover as part of an Anglo-American 'withdrawal' from Iraq. The length of time of any such withdrawal (two years? five years? ten years?) was not explored by Sky, nor was 'withdrawal' itself defined. For example, senior US military figures have been talking about the need to secure 'basing rights' for US forces in Iraq. The Project for the New American Century (PNAC), a pressure group made up of right-wing figures many of whom hold leading positions in the Bush administration (such as Dick Cheney, the Vice President at the time), openly writes of the need to have US armed forces in the Middle East, as part of its 'power projection' (see Rampton and Stauber, 2003: 121).

The Sky News extract from Bush's speech is a clear example of the ideological strategy of **universalisation**, here given uncritical amplification (and priority) by television. Universalisation works to make the dominant social classes and *their* interests appear to be aligned with the general, universal interest (see Cormack, 2000: 102). We are asked to believe that the son of a wealthy family with extensive oil interests, whose presidential campaign was backed by millions of corporate dollars from the energy sector (including from the corrupt and now collapsed Enron), undertakes actions with the aim and the effect of representing the best interests of the Iraqi people. Rupert Murdoch, head of News Corporation which owns BSkyB, was perhaps closer to the mark concerning the motivations behind the war when he said that: 'The greatest thing to come out of this [the war] for the world economy, if you could put it that way, would be $20 a barrel for oil. That's bigger than any tax cut in any country' (Greenslade, 2003). As I write, the price is $43 for a barrel of American oil so things did not quite pan out as expected. Corporate members of the ruling class are, however, often remarkably frank about the real nature of the economic system they preside over. Unlike politicians they do not have to 'dress up' their motivations for public consumption in high-minded rhetoric. Such comments, however, do not often make it to the front page of the newspapers or the top (or bottom) of a television news programme, but remain tucked away in the business pages (or in this case in the media section of *The Guardian*).

The separation of social spheres into *apparently* discrete compartments means that such comments do not qualify for entry into the world of political reportage. The Marxist concept of **appearance forms** is useful here (see Wayne, 2003). It refers to the way social reality presents itself 'officially' and most visibly through our major institutions (such as politics and the market) and how it appeals to simple observation (without sufficient analysis). At the level of appearance forms, politics and economics are separate and television news faithfully duplicates this reality of the appearance. But appearance forms are ideological because they are unable to 'embody the full social relation on which the system ultimately rests' (Hall, 1977: 323). In this case, the 'full social relation' that news cannot represent is that politics and economics are inextricably intertwined.

There are two key components by which television news freights a host of connotations that seek to affirm the veracity of their reporting, **naturalising** the procedures of news gathering as much as the actual 'content' of any actual report. They are ***proximity*** and ***liveness***. After the Sky News title sequence, which typically invokes the global reach of news technology and the rapid circulation of information, we are taken into the studio setting. Here the anchor(s) sits at the centre of the authoritative hub from which we are introduced to news stories from around the world. These are followed by news reports from journalists who are located in geographical proximity to the events taking place. The movement of the viewer from the studio to the location report implies that we are getting *closer* to the events and that the proximity of the reporter to those events enhances the veracity of the report. In fact it would be entirely possible for journalists to produce much more searching analysis of events from a studio location, but then the reports would lose those connotations of directness and immediacy.

Proximity is also coupled with liveness. It is now standard procedure to follow major news reports with a return to the studio where the anchor conducts a live exchange with the reporter in the field. This further buttresses our sense that the report we have just watched is close physically and in terms of explanatory power, to the events unfolding. It also affords the opportunity to get an 'update' on events and a summary from the journalist on the implications of the events which often involves some **pseudo-mediation** of the conflicts involved. Pseudo-mediation refers to attempts to 'mediate' between conflicting interests or positions in a way that offers a premature and thus largely imaginary solution. In fictional narratives it is key characters that work to mediate, that is bring to some (premature) reconciliation conflicting positions. Colin McArthur (1985) gives a nice example of this process at work (without using the concept of pseudo-mediation) in his discussion of an episode of the classic 1970s' series *Upstairs, Downstairs* (ITV, 1971–5) that focuses on Britain's 1926 General Strike.

The 28 June Sky News programme placed a lot of emphasis on liveness. When we return to the anchors after they have introduced trails to the other news of the evening, Alan King tells us that they have live reports from the Iraqi capital. We are told that there have been three or four reported explosions in the city and are shown a night shot of Baghdad. Then back in the studio King studies the monitor in front of him: 'I'll just try and bring you the very latest on that because information is coming in as we speak . . .'. At the bottom of the screen, graphics underpin the sense of urgency and immediacy: 'SKY NEWS FLASH. BREAKING NEWS'. A little later in the programme a 'whoosh' sound effect is dropped in over the graphics. Sky News appears to be frighteningly close to the classic and prophetic satire of television news, *The Day Today* (BBC, 1994), starring, among others, Chris Morris, Steve Coogan and

Armando Iannucci. *The Day Today* satirised the pompous authority of television news, its use of special effects and dramatic and metaphorical language to conceal its utter banality and vacuousness. The report on Sky News by Tim Marshall that follows the studio introduction ends with the words: 'Iraq is a test tube. If it overheats it will shatter', which is barely a notch below the sort of tabloid discourse that the fictional journalists would speak on *The Day Today*.

Before introducing Tim Marshall's report, Emma Crosby informs the audience that the 'handover' of power came two days early in order to prevent 'terrorists' wrecking the proceedings. This is an interesting choice of words. The lack of popular support for the war and the widespread recognition that Iraqis did not welcome the US and British forces with open arms (as political leaders and the news media had desperately suggested they would before and during the war) required many broadcasters to refrain from repeating US and British military definitions of those who have opposed their violence with their own. Thus other terms are often found such as 'insurgents', 'rebels', 'militants', 'radicals' and so forth. However, Sky News abandons even this elementary distance between itself and the US and British military and political elites.

There was, however, another reason why the handover came two days early. It was part of the political choreography by which President Bush and Prime Minister Blair could overcome the embarrassing reality that it was simply not safe enough for them to travel in triumph to Iraq to attend a pre-appointed ceremonial occasion. However, requiring some sort of political occasion as a platform, they chose the beginning of the NATO summit in Turkey. The fact that the images from this **political theatre** were used by the television news broadcasters without question demonstrates how easily the news agenda can be manipulated by the political elites without fear that their **news management strategies** will be scrutinised by the news broadcasters.

As on ITV and BBC news, Sky News used the same **standardised** images of the events. The ideological effect of standardisation is that cultural forms only repeat a narrow repertoire of expressive means

and therefore are unable to meet the challenges of new situations or events or develop new thinking in relation to old or established or recurrent events. All three broadcasters:

- Opened with the images of the US proconsul Paul Bremer signing over 'power' to the Iraqi Prime Minister Iyad Allawi;
- Showed images of Paul Bremer about to board his plane (implying that American political control really has ended);
- Showed images from the NATO summit where Bush receives a note informing him that the handover has taken place;
- Showed Bush whispering the good news to Tony Blair sitting next to him;
- Showed the pair shaking hands ('the special relationship on display' gushes Tim Marshall for Sky News); later of course, in another news management strategy, the note was released to the media for 'posterity' and we could see Bush's scribbled response: 'let freedom reign' (only the BBC used this);
- Showed clips from the subsequent press conference where Bush and Blair try to justify their war by pointing to Iraq's new found 'freedoms'. Sky News and ITV news even have the *same* Iraqi in a vox pop apparently showing support for the day's events as he talks about the hopes Iraqis have for a prosperous future (presumably they could only find one so they had to share).

Unlike Sky News, at least ITV news followed their vox pop with another man who expressed doubt about the ability of the new government to bring security and stability.

The decision to select a quote about 'security and stability' was significant because that was a familiar theme in the coverage of the 'handover' of power. While security and stability are clearly important, they are not unconnected to the issue of democracy and the legitimacy of the Iraqi government in the eyes of the Iraqi people. It is remarkable, given the emphasis the television news places on proximity, that the broadcasters make so little use of the possibilities of accessing a range of Iraqi voices and letting

Sky News: ideological bias presented as 'hard facts'?

us hear them speak (instead of having what they say summarised by the reporters). No broadcaster bothered to interview Ayatollah Ali al-Sistani, for example, the most senior Shiite cleric in Iraq who had argued for an elected constituent assembly.

Indeed, over the entire Sky News coverage that night, there was only one passing mention that the Iraqi government was 'appointed' and not elected. Sky News and the other broadcasters that evening passed over in silence the fact that the new Prime Minister, Iyad Allawi, is a former CIA spy who before that was a low-level spy informing on dissidents for Saddam Hussein's regime. Tim Marshall tells the Sky audience that: 'Sovereignty means Iraqi police backed by multinational forces patrolling the streets. That Iraqi politicians head all twenty-six ministries.' There are a number of important **omissions** here. The 'multinational force' includes 160,000 US troops over whom the 'sovereign' Iraqi government has no control whatsoever. On the alternative news Internet site ZNET, David Edwards noted that 'during discussion at the Security Council over the interim administration's rights, the French insisted on an Iraqi veto over any large-scale 'coalition' military offensives. Prime Minister Allawi refused to support the French demand' (Edwards, 2004). Indeed all US soldiers, coalition employees and private contractors (including thousands of mercenaries) are immune from Iraqi law. Meanwhile, the politicians who 'head' the ministries will be advised by some of the 2,000

staff at the US 'embassy', the largest embassy in the world. Those politicians will also work within a number of US edicts signed into law for a period of five years by Paul Bremer before he left, which cover tax law, crime and foreign policy.

The ideological strategy of **de-historicisation** means that the news refuses to look at earlier examples of a colonial strategy bearing remarkable similarities to the so-called 'handover' of power. Historical contextualisation provides crucial resources by which to assess what is going on in the present. A recent study called *Bad News from Israel*, for example, found that a large majority of people from a variety of social groups, were unaware that Israel was created in 1948 by driving Palestinians off their own land (Philo and Berry, 2004: 212–17). Indeed many viewers thought it was the Palestinians who were occupying Israeli land. The conflation of 'news' with what is apparently 'new' or happening 'now', today, is profoundly ideological because it cuts the 'new' off from the past. As Tariq Ali noted on ZNET, 'all Iraqis remember, this is a farcical repeat of what the British did after World War I when they received a League of Nations mandate to run Iraq' (Ali, 2004). Recalcitrant Iraqi villagers were bombed from the air by the newly formed RAF, while the British embassy ran the country through a constitutional monarchy until 1932. A similar strategy was tried by the Americans in Vietnam: they sought to 'Vietnamese' the conflict by shoring up an unpopular puppet regime in the south of the country.

The ITV late evening news on the 28 June did, at least, raise some questions about the nature of the power being handed back to Iraqis. In his report, Julian Manyon described Allawi as 'publicly, at least, the most powerful figure in Iraq'. Later in a live two-way exchange with anchorman Trevor McDonald, Manyon stressed that the new government needed to be 'allowed, and I stress allowed, to gain credibility in the eyes of Iraqis'. He made it clear that meant acquiring some independence from the Americans. This is a classic case of pseudo-mediation. It seeks to reconcile the irreconcilable and pose the possibility of a regime utterly dependent on the Americans acquiring some independence from them.

4 Analysing Factual TV
How to Study Television Documentary

John Corner

We can see two types of truth here. One is the raw material, which is the footage, the kind of truth that you get in literature in the diary form – it's immediate, no one has tampered with it. Then there's the other kind of truth that comes in extracting and juxtaposing the raw material into a more meaningful and coherent storytelling form, which finally can be said to be more than just raw data.
Albert Maysles, cited by G. Roy Levin, *Documentary Explorations: 15 Interviews with Filmmakers*, 1971: 227.

Maysles' 'two types of truth' and his ideas about 'raw material' may be open to question, as sections of this chapter will suggest, but his remarks usefully illustrate the way in which any serious attention to documentary quickly faces the complexities of its manufacture and the problems of integrity that follow. As an object of study, documentary television is uniquely fascinating and offers students a rewarding challenge, both **sociological** (about our understanding and evaluation of the historical world) and **aesthetic** (about our ways of representing this world, including through the pleasurable, satisfying practices we call 'artistic'). Studying documentary can not only tell us a great deal about the character and conventions of television more broadly, it can open out to cover a range of fundamental issues concerning the use of images in communication and the use of recorded speech. We can characterise the analytic allure of documentary as something to do with the way in which it lies between the areas of 'news' and 'drama' in television's **generic system** (see Chapter 2), as well as often having more than a little of the talk show and the travel programme in its make-up. It appeals to our inquisitiveness about the ways by which the media produce knowledge but it also generates a strong creative and narrative appeal for our critical appraisal.

I shall primarily be concerned with what we can call '**formal analysis**', an approach to looking at how documentary television is constructed involving the critical investigation of its uses of image and language. Such an approach can benefit from an attempt to classify some of the different kinds of image and speech to be found in documentary work. After this, examples from different kinds of programme will be selected to explore the principal communicative methods at work and to point the way towards the future analysis that readers may want to undertake on their own. Other kinds of study can be followed which give emphasis, for instance, to the production practices of documentary or to the ways in which different documentaries engage with the same theme or topic. Study of the economic and **institutional contexts** for documentary work is also important (see Chapter 8). However, some attention to the communicative design of documentary work is a useful preliminary to any other kind of enquiry.

DOCUMENTARY AND COMMUNICATIVE DESIGN
The use of photography, cinema and television as ways of presenting information and knowledge goes back to the origins of these technologies as methods of '**recording**', collecting images taken directly from the world itself and therefore representing that world in a way utterly different from painting and drawing.

Radio was a way of collecting speech and sounds in this direct manner. Whatever suspicion we have about the use of the idea of 'recording' or of the 'direct' (aren't photographs to a large degree constructed? don't they show what photographers want to show? isn't television's capacity to depict the real world often in serious doubt?) we should not underestimate the special, if often complex, relationship that exists between a recorded image and the reality it portrays. It is certainly possible to talk about documentary writing and documentary painting and, indeed, these are interesting topics to explore, but it is only with the recorded image and recorded sound that the special kind of challenge and force of documentary work becomes apparent. A number of early film-makers understood this, although in Britain it was John Grierson in the 1920s and 1930s who expressed it most powerfully in a series of writings which accompanied his own work as a pioneer film director and producer (Hardy, 1979).

Television documentary has come to differ from cinema work in a number of ways, not always marked. The much smaller screen size has implications for the way in which images can be used and the length of time shots can be held (see Chapter 1). The **domestic** rather than 'public' context of viewing encourages a more intimate range of spoken address. And the location of television documentary

John Grierson: a pioneering documentary film-maker

within the wide range of television factual and fictional output gives it an '**inter-generic**' character, a responsiveness to change in other areas, which has been quite significant in the last decade.

Documentary has always been regarded, and was so even by Grierson, as a loose and rather leaky category, only roughly defining an area of practice and representation. However, it is only with the arrival of the academic study of film and television that sustained pressure has been placed on issues of definition, with some commentators insisting that the category is almost meaningless and, at worst, an attempt to install a claim to the 'real' and the 'truth' which is essentially fraudulent. Documentary, this view claims, is a category word designed to elicit our **trust**. But the more we look at what goes on within the category, the less trustful we should be. There are some good reasons for adopting a suspicious approach, but the *dismissal* of documentary as an empty and possibly deceitful category goes too far. It misses recognition of the commitment, creativity and honesty of many documentary projects, and the continuing values, political and social, of work in the documentary vein. An approach which is able to be critical but also to be appreciative seems to me to be a better way of engaging with the topic and that is the approach I shall adopt here.

Of course, it is not hard to see why documentary should be a controversial area of media practice. By attempting to produce extended accounts of the world, using images and speech organised to provide coherent and persuasive bodies of knowledge and often to make judgments, it is immediately open to the charges of **manipulation** and **distortion**, conscious or otherwise, which have become a key reference point for public debate about television and a principal theme in its academic study. All media students know very early in their studies that media representation is not 'transparent' or 'direct' but is the product of a whole range of interventions and constructive acts (see the Introduction). The contrast between what might appear to be the status of the image and the real conditions of its production is perhaps most strong in '**observational**' work, work which has attracted the use of the revealing (or concealing) term '**fly-on-the-wall**'. It is interesting how the recent discussion of '**reality television**' has heightened general awareness of fakery here, although it is not clear just what impact this has had on public perception of other, more 'serious', kinds of documentary work.

I take the idea that documentary is the result of **constructive practice**, a series of interventions in the production and assembly of materials, as the *starting part* of analysis not, as some have appeared to do, the finishing point. It is only by acknowledging an essential level of '**artificiality**' in the documentary project that we can begin to get anywhere with serious study, and with an appreciation of its considerable achievements in engaging with reality and truth. Elsewhere (Corner, 1995) I have outlined three transformative stages in the production of documentary. Briefly, these are:

1. **Planning**: when it is decided precisely what to film and whose speech to record in respect of the chosen topic.
2. **Shooting**: when critical decisions about the organisation of any action, objects and people within the shots and the use of the camera (e.g. lighting, positioning and movement) and microphone are made.
3. **Editing**: at which point a whole range of judgments about sound/image combinations, about narrative continuity and expositional development occur, together with the possible addition of music at various points and the use of visual effects both to enhance individual shots and to ease the transitions between shots.

This process necessarily takes us a long way from the raw 'realities' of, say, the working life of an air-traffic control officer or the recent history of the arms trade in Britain. It also leaves out the further transformation that occurs when a television documentary is watched by a viewer using their own experience and values as a basis for interpretation, a topic which could receive more attention from research than it has hitherto (Hill, 2005).

Before looking at some examples of how particular documentaries employ these creative transfor-

mations in their accounts, it might be useful to look at some of the principal ways in which image and speech, separate and combined, are put to work in the business of representing the real.

First, we need to look at the **modes of documentary depiction**. By 'modes' I mean the particular ways in which image and language perform their communicative tasks as part of the 'documenting' activity of a programme. The separation of modes I suggest seems to me to be a useful way of reaching a preliminary analytic understanding of the key components out of which most documentaries are built. Other writers might choose different categories, refining mine or perhaps placing together what I have chosen to categorise separately. I have attempted an outline of modes before (Corner, 1996) but here I do it with the express intention of helping a student reader and so what follows varies from my previous accounts even though it draws on them.

The relationship between image and speech varies significantly throughout most documentaries. Which can be considered primary, the looking activity or the listening, can shift even within the same sequence and the precise form of their combination alters too.

THREE MODES OF DOCUMENTARY IMAGE

It is the pictures of documentary that are most instrumental in providing directly access to the real world, even though it is often the speech that provides the most direct information and argument. We both 'look through' documentary images, treating them as virtually transparent means of engagement with what is shown, sometimes providing '**visible evidence**', and yet also 'look at' them, picking up with varying degrees of self-awareness on their particular pictorial organisation and the pleasing formal properties at work within their assembly and design. In order to strengthen this element of documentary viewing, some directors work with a concern to offer rich and beautiful images.

A three-mode outline hardly does justice to the variety of possibilities, but it does allow some important basic distinctions to be made.

1. ILLUSTRATIVE

In a number of ways, documentary images serve to '**illustrate**' the theme under expositional development or to carry the narrative forward. The visual material might be archive (library) footage or it might be newly shot. It might involve considerable planning and/or intervention to obtain (e.g. a lifeboat being launched off a rocky coast) or it might be easily got (e.g. congested traffic in a city centre). In an **expositional structure**, perhaps led by continuous commentary (e.g. on the future of the British fishing industry), the images may not only have different sources but may illustrate different places and times. Some of the illustrative work will be of the most general kind (an image of a trawler simply to illustrate a reference to 'deep-sea fishing') while at other times the illustration will be tightly specific (an image of a trawler to illustrate a specific vessel that was involved in a disaster due to faulty design). Illustration may play a strong role as presented evidence (e.g. police footage of the car in which the death occurred, showing bullet holes in the door despite official talk of an accident).

The direct, evidential use of images is one of the most powerful tools of the documentary, enabling it to recruit viewers to become '**second-hand witnesses**' in ways that can impact significantly on social knowledge and attitudes. Programmes compiled from many different image sources that nevertheless want to achieve a good level of narrative continuity (e.g. a programme about the Allied invasion of Normandy in 1944) may sometimes struggle to achieve this, requiring a strong commentary to carry across the sharp transitions in archive visuals. Looking closely at how documentaries organise our experience of seeing as one of illustrated explanation or argument is therefore an important task.

2. OBSERVATIONAL

Observational material differs from illustrative insofar as it purports to follow continuous activity or behaviour with the intention of allowing us to engage with this (e.g. candidates being interviewed for the job of an airline pilot) and derive knowledge from it. The conditions under which observational

Nick Broomfield: using 'fly-on-the-wall' techniques

material is produced have perhaps come under more scrutiny and suspicion than any other aspect of documentary production. It was only with the arrival of lightweight cameras in the 1960s that documentary directors really had the mobility to follow action as it happened (to produce the 'fly-on-the-wall' effect) but this seductive possibility also ushered in a whole new set of options for documentary artfulness. A paradox at the core of most observational footage is that the people we observe in it seem unaware of the presence of the camera even though we know they cannot easily ignore it. This has led to endless debate about the '**truthfulness**' of what we see in such material, quite apart from anxieties about outright '**fakery**'. It is interesting that in some of the more recent observational material, including that within the broad 'reality television' category, awareness of the camera's presence by participants has been more marked, giving participants a sometimes awkward status as both observees and performers. This combination is not without its pleasures for the viewer, and in some respects it merely brings out a tension that was always latent in the very conventions of the observational approach.

It is worth mentioning here the increasing use on television of an observational form in which some of the problems discussed above are unlikely to occur. This is material shot clandestinely by hidden cameras, a situation in which the participants are simply unaware of their being recorded. Understandably, there are severe limitations on the scope and mobility of the visual presentation that can be obtained from this kind of practice (quality of sound often suffers too, given restricted microphone placement) but the strength of such material is grounded in its immediate and perhaps shocking **evidential impact** rather than in the more sustained, steady and often 'quiet' yield of knowledge typical of most observational work.

3. SYMBOLIC/ASSOCIATIVE

It is risky to make a separate category of this kind since all documentary visuals, whatever their primary status, can carry **symbolic/associative** meanings. So, for instance, a sustained shot of surf pound-

ing a beach may well illustrate a point about the problem of erosion or serve to make the viewer think of holidays or connect with some deeper, less conscious, associations of waves and the sea. However, in many documentaries there are sequences which clearly give symbolic and associative work a primary function. Composition, framing, editing and the use of music are sometimes indicators of this. **Symbolic resonance** can be achieved in a variety of ways. For instance, simply holding a shot for a longer period than one would normally expect can cue the viewer to read something deeper and less specific from it (e.g. a shot of an old man looking out to sea from a promenade bench becoming more generally resonant about retirement and old age as the camera very slowly pulls back – see Chapter 2).

SIX MODES OF DOCUMENTARY SPEECH

A brief account of the variety of documentary speech can usefully identify six principal modes, all of them active in combination with images. Dramatic dialogue is included here, since the speech in **docudrama** productions often has quite distinctive communicative duties to perform.

1. COMMENTARY

The offering of a spoken account, continuous or intermittent, across a sequence of images is the 'classic' mode of speech in documentary. It has been dubbed the '**voice of god**' (see Nichols, 1991), a phrase which attempts to characterise both its disembodied sourcing and its authority. Early documentaries relied extensively on this method for two reasons. First of all, many of them had a didactic, if not propagandistic, intent and a commentary account fitted this purpose well. Second, location interviews were technically difficult if not impossible because of the limitations of contemporary sound-recording equipment. However, it would be unfair to see all uses of commentary speech as following the examples of early didacticism. Depending on the particular project of the documentary, sustained description and explanation is only possible through speech of this kind, whatever the legacy of authoritarianism. The use of more colloquial and relaxed voicings of commentary quickly followed the arrival of television documentary. This reflected the move to more personalised, informal registers of speech across the medium as a whole, following from the domestic settings for reception and a need to establish a more intimate communicative bonding with the audience (as radio had already succeeded in doing).

Commentary regulates the viewer's interpretation of the image flow, a point that has received extensive analytic attention with regard to the 'truth' of documentary portrayal. Typically, it is the commentary which identifies what we are seeing, its relationship to other things or factors, and its general significance for the theme being pursued. Here, it is important to note the way in which documentary exposition varies in its degree of generality or particularity. A documentary about loneliness in the city works with a general topic, whatever particular examples it chooses to illustrate its theme. A documentary about the changing look of London's Piccadilly Circus works with a quite specific focus on the physical world. There are many examples in between, but whatever the level at which the engagement is made the filmed images can only be of particular things, while the commentary can refer both to particular detail and general circumstances. The terms of this play-off are often complex, particularly where specific images are used to underpin broad, general claims to the 'truth' or the 'real' and where (as is often the case) there are shifts in the level of generality throughout a documentary, changing the kind of language used in the commentary.

2. PRESENTER ADDRESS

Presenter speech involves the speaker not only in shot but also facing the camera and appearing to address the viewer directly. The implications of such '**direct address**' have been given extensive debate in media research (see, for example Fiske and Hartley, 1978). The gaze and demeanour of the presenter now become involved in the interpretation of the speech, the relationship is more strongly personalised than in commentary speech, with consequences for the kind of trust relationship established and the

grounding of truth in the account. Speaking directly to the audience, the presenter's address is set within the broader communicative context of the shot and its development. The background will often be significant itself (what places can be seen, what action is occurring, perhaps partly off camera). During a presentation, the speaker (and the camera) may move to bring other sights into view and to meet people, possibly for the purpose of an interview. Set within a specific event-world like this, the address clearly has a spatial and temporal relationship to the visual depiction that cannot occur in commentaries. Words like 'that', 'there', 'this', pointing to features of the scene, are common, making the most of this relationship and partially aligning the gaze of the presenter with that of the viewer in a manner often designed to encourage assent.

3. INTERVIEW SPEECH IN SHOT

Interview speech in shot is a central component of much documentary construction. As analysts point out, it is speech designed to be overheard, even though it purports to be dialogue. This play-off between its character as a form of public speaking and its adaptive use of the format of the private conversation is central to understanding its communicative power and the continuing controversy around it. The degree of interactivity involved in its production and its level of continuity is variously revealed or hidden in the final, edited sequence, i.e. as it appears on screen. Many documentarists prefer to remove the questions from the soundtrack and not to show the questioner at all, thus keeping the visual and aural focus firmly on participants. In these circumstances, speech often has the character of voluntary testimony, with the face usually shot in a three-quarter profile that directs speech to the corner of the frame (just off-camera) but is sufficiently close to direct address to create something of that mode's effect. However, other directors use a full interactive presentation, with both questioner and interviewee in shot (either in a '**two-shot**' or by intercutting), and the questions can be heard, so that the interviewee's speech is then clearly read as response rather than testimony.

Whatever the method used, interviews are invariably edited down from their original length, both to give them optimum significance within the final design of the film and to manage overall duration within the limits. Given the constraints of time and the need to sustain a good level of thematic focus and development, shifts in the order of answers may be introduced as well as cuts to answers. These alterations to the original speech have often been the cause of dispute following the release of a final version, particularly in cases where the interviewee was speaking in an official capacity and therefore 'accountable' for what they said. Interviews are inevitably prepared for and will vary considerably in their degree of apparent spontaneity and in their articulation. Fluency is not always sought, however, since hesitation can be a **marker of authenticity**, especially in relation to sensitive, personal themes.

4. INTERVIEW SPEECH AS VOICE-OVER

Where interview speech is used as **voice-over** it often links the interpretation of the image to a dimension of experience as well as of knowledge. The speech of a participant frequently frames what is shown within the terms of the personal and perhaps of memory. It may lack the direct informational authority invested in a commentary or a presenter but it adds a distinctive dimension to portrayal, in part providing a '**first-hand**' verification for the professional assembly of images over which the voice is heard. For instance, we might hear the voice of a prisoner telling of his experiences over shots of prison conditions.

5. OVERHEARD INTERCHANGE

Overheard interchange is a key component of observational film-making (discussed above), in which the fiction that participants are unaffected by the camera and the microphone, and indeed act as if they were unaware of their presence, is frequently maintained. With no direct connection to producer discourse (unlike interview answers), observed speech in documentary varies in its plausibility as '**natural**'. In general, it is more convincing when it occurs as part of an official task being performed (e.g. an airline check-in counter, police cautioning a

motorist) than when it occurs simply as 'casual' (in domestic settings, for instance, or in workplace chat). However, in all cases the modifying effect of the documentary team upon what is said and how it is said remains an issue. In the forms of 'reality television', observed speech has often had a self-conscious and performative character, aligning it more with the display of the talk show than with the attempted naturalism of classic observational work. Game shows like *Big Brother* (Channel 4, 1999–) have clearly brought further complexities into the relationship of the natural to the artificial in what is 'overheard'.

6. DRAMATIC DIALOGUE

Dramatic dialogue is the scripted (or possibly improvised) dialogue occurring between actors in sequences of dramatised documentary. Although it shares features with 'overheard interchange' as part of its desire to be naturalistic, it is usually carefully constructed to develop character, sustain narrative and reveal context and circumstances. Compared with

Big Brother: reality TV, social experiment or game show?

most naturally recorded speech, its constructions will be more considered and coherent and the delivery more fluent, even allowing for a naturalism of hesitation and repetition. The conversational plausibility of the speech is sometimes in tension with its descriptive, explanatory functions (it might seem to be saying more than is 'realistic' or being too explicit, almost like a commentary). The further issue, of how far it might approximate to what was really said in the situation being reconstructed, is a longstanding point of contention in the discussion of films and programmes using this approach.

Listing the basic modes of documentary speech leaves out the way in which documentaries make use of '**actuality sound**' itself, either directly to support the image (e.g. crowd noise, birdsong, train whistles, gunfire) or as an ambient context for location speech. More importantly, it also leaves out the important role of **music** in strengthening the formal organisation of a programme, helping to bridge shifts of time and place and, most obviously of all, cueing moods appropriate to what we are shown. Music allows documentary-makers to work with images much more creatively and confidently than they could do if the sound overlay consisted solely of speech. I have briefly reviewed the role of music in documentary in a recent article (Corner, 2002).

These, then, are the major means by which most documentaries are assembled and understood. Of course, how these factors influence an audience's understanding of 'the real' is a complex and difficult area of debate and one that can only really be satisfactorily explored with reference to specific examples (see below).

FURTHER READING

Bruzzi, Stella (2000), *New Documentary: A Critical Introduction*, London: BFI.

Corner, John (1996), *The Art of Record: A Critical Introduction to Documentary*, Manchester: Manchester University Press.

Dovey, Jon (2000), *Freakshow: First Person Media and Factual Television*, London: Pluto Press.

Holmes, Sue and Jermyn, Deborah (2004), *Understanding Reality Television*, London and New York: Routledge.

Izod, John and Kilborn, Richard, with Hibberd, Matthew (eds) (2000), *From Grierson to Docu-Soap: Breaking the Boundaries*, Luton: University of Luton Press.

Kilborn, Richard and Izod, John (1997), *An Introduction to Television Documentary*, Manchester: Manchester University Press.

Paget, Derek (1998), *No Other Way to Tell It: Dramadoc/Docudrama on Television*, Manchester: Manchester University Press.

Winston, Brian (2000), *Lies, Damn Lies and Documentaries*, London: BFI.

CASE STUDY

Different Documentary Modes: *World in Action*, *Hotel* and *Wife Swap* John Corner

Having discussed some of the principal communicative modes out of which documentaries are constructed, I want now to look at three examples. This will allow us to explore a little further just how these modes work to produce the documentary effect. In each case, I will focus on the opening few minutes of the programmes, although I will also indicate their overall design. This is to allow proper attention to detail in the space available.

1. *WORLD IN ACTION*: 'PROFIT BEFORE PRINCIPLE' (GRANADA, 1997)

'Profit before Principle' was made for Granada's *World in Action* series, which ran for four decades (1963–98) and produced some of the most influential documentary journalism on British television. The programme looks at the continuation, despite the election of a Labour government in 1997, of a British export trade in military hardware to countries in violation of human rights. It focuses on the figure of Jose Ramos-Horta, winner of the 1996 Nobel Peace Prize and a campaigner for the people of East Timor against the Indonesian dictatorship. In using Ramos-Horta to further its own enquiries into the British arms trade, it employs a wide variety of documentary modes as outlined above, including material filmed by **hidden camera**. Indeed, its whole approach to its topic makes it very much a 1990s' programme, even though *World in Action* had been pursuing similar themes since the 1960s (see Goddard, 2004).

Its structure as a piece of enquiry but also of exposition involves the use of **commentary, filmed report**, **interview**, **observation**, **archive film** and **photographs**. Although primarily framed as **exposition,** it has set within it a strong narrative grounded in undercover investigation.

Let us look at how the programme opens. It uses a short pre-title sequence in the manner that became conventional in the increased competition of the 1990s as a means of 'hooking' audience members who might be contemplating a switch of channels. First of all, there is **library footage** of Ramos-Horta receiving his Nobel Prize, with the initial visual focus on the Nobel certificate he is holding. Then we see him inside an office and in a jeep (1). We see someone pointing to military vehicles in a garage, shots which, by the nature of the image and lighting, look like hidden camera footage (2). A man in shirt-sleeves stands outside an office block (3). The same man (hidden camera again) speaks from behind a desk (4). How are these various images to be read? A commentary voice carries us through them in the sequence as follows:

1. 'Tonight, the current holder of the Nobel Peace Prize goes undercover with *World in Action* to investigate British businessmen who supply arms and equipment to the Indonesian dictatorship'.
2. 'The defence salesman, whose company sells guns to the Indonesian Army'.
3. 'And the British Territorial Army captain who claims influence in Downing Street'.
4. (Speech within hidden camera footage 'We are

very, very heavily involved in Indonesia'.)
So as samplers of the programme, we are given a strong taster of what will follow if we continue to watch. We know it will involve a story of undercover enquiry. We know it will involve revelations, including those that implicate the Government.

This sequence is followed by the *World in Action* titles and music, after which the programme re-opens in a more relaxed mode. A male hairdresser is busily at work styling and colouring the hair of Ramos-Horta. We are given close-ups of his actions and of Ramos-Horta's face in a mode that inclines towards the **observational** as we watch this 'everyday' business. The commentary tells us that this stylist works for Vidal Sassoon and that his previous clients have included 'supermodels and the Spice Girls'. However:

> Today's client is Jose Ramos-Horta, the current holder of the Nobel Peace Prize. He's being disguised because he's agreed to join *World in Action* in an undercover investigation into Britain's support for Indonesia's brutal military occupation of his homeland, East Timor.

So the business is far from 'everyday'. It is the preparation of disguise. We are watching someone being prepared for espionage. We are being taken from the celebrity world of 'supermodels' to the realm of international politics. This is the start of a potentially exciting story as well as of a report.

Ramos-Horta speaks in interview about his objectives, to reduce the flow of arms to Indonesia. Over archive pictures of Tony Blair and his wife entering Downing Street amid cheering crowds on the day of his election victory, the commentary pushes further with the political implications of the programme: 'Tonight, *World in Action* asks if under the new Labour government Britain will continue to put profit before principle.'

This ends the programme's establishment of its topic, its declaration of intent. The next sequence is of eight photographs of bodies under torture or corpses that show physical damage. Ramos-Horta is shown with the photographs at a press conference explaining what they confirm about the Indonesian regime's reputation for torture and murder, even though the Indonesian government has declared the photographs to be fakes.

The programme then broadens out to offer political background on the situation in Indonesia, interviewing two student activists and a human rights observer who has further photographic evidence of the use of military violence at peaceful demonstrations. It brings together shots of weapons and weapons training, including the use of anti-riot vehicles equipped with water cannon exported from Britain. Having shown hidden camera footage from a reconnaissance visit to the company that has been chosen as the 'target' for the undercover mission, the main enquiry of the programme gets under way. Disguised and wearing dark glasses, accompanied by *World in Action* reporters, Ramos-Horta gets into a limousine: 'We set up a second meeting with the Procurement Services International. Ramos-Horta was to pose as the head of a *World in Action* front company. We phoned before we arrived.'

With shots of the travelling car, the show is truly on the road and the 'sting' plot – to send a distinguished opponent of the Indonesia regime on a quest ostensibly to buy arms for it – has the context needed to give viewing impact and significance. The programme has established the stature of Ramos-Horta, it has provided images and testimony of torture and civil rights abuse and it has provided early visual evidence that arms exports to Indonesia are still going ahead despite Labour promises of an 'ethical' foreign policy. In a few minutes, we have been given access to the preparation of Ramos-Horta's disguise, to photographs of torture, to hidden camera footage of arms trading in Britain, to the streets of Jakarta and the testimony of those caught up in Indonesian repression. We have been told something of the background to the Indonesian situation and the Downing Street celebrations have reminded us of the hopes, aspirations and claims that went along with Labour's election victory. Now, we are following the principal figure undercover, to collect more evidence from a hidden camera and microphone. An intriguing story, involving an international celebrity,

has been set in train and it is within the spaces opened up in its narrative flow that a broader journalistic exposition is developing.

2. *HOTEL* (BBC, 1997)

Hotel was a successful **docusoap** series for the BBC, drawing on many elements of the more familiar **fly-on-the-wall** programming that had been successful with audiences for over twenty years (see Izod and Kilborn, with Hibberd, 2000). Its docusoap identity was achieved by an approach that brought out the entertainment potential of the topic as much as, if not more than, any serious social knowledge. The programmes explore aspects of working life in a celebrated, Liverpool hotel, the Adelphi, built in the early twentieth-century grand style. A feature of the **observational** mode employed here is a much higher degree of participant self-consciousness than traditional programmes tend to encourage. Not only do many of the scenes in *Hotel* show people aware that they are on camera but they often show them 'playing up' to it, with remarks aside and little performances and gestures that would not fit easily with earlier 'fly-on-the-wall' approaches. This increases the *sociability* of the programmes even if it potentially reduces the level of viewer trust in the **authenticity** of the circumstances and actions depicted. Given the lightness of tone, however, such a reduced sense of specific trustworthiness (would this really happen like this were the cameras not there?) may not be a big problem.

The title sequence starts with a shot of the hotel at night, with its windows lit. There follows a sequence of sixteen shots showing aspects of working life in the hotel. Some of these are framed by the lit windows of the hotel, with zooms, reverse zooms and pans across the front of the hotel to focus on action in other windows (an effect of overlay editing). The sense of 'peering into' its routine working life is thus given **graphic reinforcement**. Of the sixteen shots, seven show people in confrontation with each other, either pointing or finger wagging. One shows the manageress and the head porter in dispute, literally bent towards each other with heads touching (itself a clear indication of the performative level that overlays much of the 'realist' portrayal). The final shot shows the manageress wiping her brow. We are then returned to the hotel front at night, with a sign 'Hotel' in blue neon in the top left corner and a gold neon 'Adelphi' flickering across the whole image.

Across all of this sequence a bright tune with a strong beat has played. Several of the last shots in the sequence show people apparently moving their arms or hands in time to the music (a shot of three receptionists facing the camera shows them 'hand-jiving' to it).

What does this tell us about the programme and (since this is the first episode) the series? It presents us with a **documentary promise**, certainly, but it also encourages us towards the expectation of entertainment. There will be confrontations, but there will be good fun. There is conflict, but there are smiles. We might expect to get to know more about some of the people who work there. The connection is implicitly made with the television grammar of situation comedy (*Fawlty Towers* [BBC, 1975–9] and its drama of 'coping' in bizarre adversity seems always to be there in the background, despite the very different kind of hotel).

The 'busy'ness of the credit sequence gives way to the more expansive **observationalism** that will be the principal mode for the series. We overlook and overhear. The manageress is seen on her rounds of the main public rooms, giving out orders and admonition to those involved in routine cleaning and preparation

> Put that there. And I want that lifting down . . . I don't want her lifting. You know she's having a baby? It's called consideration, son. . . . Do we have a stray stool? Can we give it a home? . . . We've got dirty ashtrays in the Crosby room.

Over this progress, and subsequent scenes at the reception desk, where queries and complaints are being handled, the commentary runs:

> Grand National weekend, the busiest three days of the year for Liverpool's Adelphi Hotel. General

Manager Eileen Downie copes with a full hotel. Senior Receptionist Christine must keep track of 391 rooms sold. Whoever wins today's big race, the Adelphi is favourite to make big profits. This weekend's cheapest single room is £95. Christine is building up to her own big event, the birth of her first baby. And today she has to check in over 700 guests.

This is a very different use of commentary from the one in the *World in Action* example. It is more relaxed and, like the address of the title sequence, more sociable. As well as setting us up for a narrative of **occupational pressure** (a key ingredient of 'docusoap' formats) it also moves in to offer some selective, personal information. Christine is part of the 'cast' of hotel workers we are going to get to know (only a small minority of the full hotel staff) and information that might seem extraneous in a conventional documentary is here entirely within the framework of depiction.

The provisional design of the programme can be seen to be a day's events compressed into thirty minutes, the chronology itself providing a coherent framework for observation. The **'day-in-the-life'** model is a classic documentary design, still much used for the organisation it brings to material and its continuing imaginative appeal. In this case, however, the programme departs from what one assumes was the initial plan when the Grand National has to be cancelled due to a bomb threat. This turns the narrative into a crisis story, how the Adelphi copes with the extra pressure on facilities, and the chaos, following the emergency evacuation of the racecourse and the postponement of the race until the Monday. The programme quickly moves to the afternoon cancellation in order to give itself space for the aftermath and the extension of the account into the following two days. A revised, and strengthened, **narrative sequence** is dictated by the turn of events. Whatever had been shot prior to the bomb scare, selection and editing could easily organise it within the new design, with its new chronology and new emphases. As a matter of course, the commentary would only be added in the final stages.

Wife Swap: a mixture of social experiment and entertaining observation

3. *WIFE SWAP* (CHANNEL 4, 2004)

My third example is taken from one of the most successful reality programmes on British television at
the time of writing. *Wife Swap*, with the sexual innu-
endos of its title, was greeted by some critics as indi-
cating a further slide in the integrity of factual output. However, since then, it has received cautious
critical appreciation. The basic idea of *Wife Swap* is
to take two very different families and have the wives
swap homes, setting up temporary new relationships
within the household. For the first week they follow
the rules of the home they've moved to, for the second week they can make the rules. In most episodes
of the series, it is the relationship with the children
rather than the (non-sexual) one with the man that

is most important, although the insertion into a new
domestic routine obviously involves both.

Wife Swap has learnt from docusoap about how
to do **entertaining observation** but it moves further than docusoap in openly setting up the circumstances in which observation will be carried out. In
this respect, it follows the '**social experiment**'
model of *Big Brother*. The localised action you are
watching may (or may not) be true to what really
happened, but it only happened in the first place
because television arranged the circumstances. The
play-offs between truth and falsity at the level of the
general situation and at the level of the *specific behaviour*
have often been confused in discussion of the 'reality' conveyed by this kind of programme design.

Each episode of the programme opens boldly. We are introduced to the two families, depicted snapshot style and described by a chirpily voiced commentary. The contrasting aspects of their lives are sharply brought out.

Shot 1: Meet the Maxi-Juckes. Emily and Larch have been together for eight years and live in a forest near Swansea with their three year-old son, Sage and their five-year-old daughter, Rowan.

Shot 2: Meet the Kingstons. Bernard and Joanne have been married for twelve years and live in a four-bedroom house in suburban Liverpool with their nine-year-old daughter, Talia.

The two wives have agreed to swap homes, husbands and children for two weeks to see what they can learn about their own lives.

So, despite the marked promise of entertainment (again, as in *Hotel*, partly a matter of personal confrontations sometimes generically close to situation-comedy routines), the programme wants to claim a more serious character as an exercise in learning.

This episode then thickens out the specific entertainment on offer a little, showing 'trailer' footage of material from later in the programme. Over shots of scenes in the contrasting households, now with their swapped wives in place and clearly unhappy, the commentary offers playful 'What happens when . . .?' questions to give us a preview of some of the embarrassments, tensions and outbursts that will follow from the deliberate mismatching at the core of the programme design.

The basic pattern of switching regularly between the two households to show the roughly co-extensive developments (a pattern central to many reality shows) is started in earnest with a brief exploration of each family's values and way of life. We learn that one family has 'no interest in material wealth' and has no fridge, phone, bath, mains electricity or car while to the other 'appearances are everything' and they have a half-a-million-pound house and a luxury car. Brief visuals in the '**illustrative**' mode are offered here but

the depictive work is done using a variety of documentary modes, including commentary over visuals, interview (both set-piece and while carrying out tasks) and interview voice used as commentary over visuals. This gives a mix of 'external' views of the two families (the tone of the commentary places the viewer as an amused outsider waiting for things to go wrong) and 'internal' views. The use of interview voice over visuals (e.g. one partner comments on another's qualities over shots of him playing with the children) is the strongest mode for giving the internal view since, unlike interview to camera, it gives the participants themselves the temporary authority of commentary, anchoring the images around their perceptions. This mode has been used extensively both in 'access television' work (such as the BBC's *Video Diaries* [1990–4] series) and in reality programming, which has variously exploited the strong contemporary appeal of what Jon Dovey has called '**first-person' formats** (Dovey, 2000).

More than most of the visual sequences in *Hotel*, and much more than anything in 'Profit before Principle', the status of the visual depictions in *Wife Swap* have the character of display rather than observation, although this is unlikely to stop viewers judging at least some of what they see as behaviour 'true' to the participant's personalities and attitudes. As I noted earlier, the situation they are in is entirely the result of their acceptance of television's invitation to participate. In a way, we might see them as game show competitors, notwithstanding the real-life settings of their 'challenge'. This implies a self-consciousness of their televisual status exceeding that of the subject of conventional observational filming or even of docusoap observation. Whereas in most docusoap formats, the expression of personal attitudes and the display of personality are an important incidental dimension of a narrative grounded in occupational events, in *Wife Swap* they are core ingredients – the basis for the programme design.

In its central sections, *Wife Swap* shifts to a more extended observational mode, looking on and overhearing becoming for periods, as in *Hotel*, the primary viewing relationship. However, the programme's need to keep alternating between the two households and to maintain a commentary-led development of how things develop across the two-week period, with regular participant interviews, necessarily breaks any observational continuity.

By deliberately intervening in the world in order to encourage an entertaining drama of personal contrasts, *Wife Swap* departs from conventional documentary practice and aligns itself with the game show and with sitcom. However, by using real domestic settings and routines it exposes some of the rhythms, tensions and contradictions of everyday living and indeed the structures of wealth, class and culture, in ways not open to more conventional treatments.

I started this chapter by saying how the analysis of documentary was both fascinating and an important entry point into our understanding of visual media and of the power of pictures in contemporary culture. My categorisation of some of the ways in which images and words can be constructed and organised in documentary will, I hope, give students something they can work with, 'building blocks'. My brief examples indicate only some of the production options available and are subject to continuous adaptation and innovation. So get in front of your VCRs (or DVD players) with notebooks in hand and start taking documentaries apart. And try to maintain a due regard for the craft that went into their making as well as the critical alertness necessary in discussing all forms of representation.

5 Analysing TV Fiction
How to Study Television Drama
Robin Nelson

A first-class radio program is like no theatrical or motion picture presentation that ever was. It is a new thing in the world. Similarly, it is quite likely that television drama will be a new development, using the best of the theatre and motion pictures, and building a new art-form based on these.

David Sarnoff (1942), cited by Horace Newcomb, *TV: The Most Popular Art*, 1974: 3.

This chapter is concerned with television drama and matters that relate specifically to fictions on the small screen, as distinct from issues relating, for example, to news coverage or documentary. There is inevitably some overlap, however, between aspects of studying television as a medium and studying drama distributed *through* that medium. Just as there is concern about the influence of the news and the extent of its 'bias', for example, so the impact of TV drama on aspects of behaviour have concerned some people. Pervasive sex and violence depicted in dramas has traditionally been regarded as unacceptable in a medium that is transmitted directly into people's homes. In the UK, the 'nine o'clock watershed' marks a limit before which certain material cannot be shown for fear of corrupting minors. What is acceptable at different times and under different conditions remains a matter of debate and, broadly speaking, TV drama has become increasingly permissive (see the discussion of Home Box Office [HBO] below). Such an example certainly reveals why it is important to be actively aware of both the **text** and **contexts** of television drama, and this chapter will attempt to keep both firmly within the scope of its analytical approach to small-screen fiction.

WHAT IS TELEVISION DRAMA?: TEXTS AND CONTEXTS

The term 'small-screen fictions' is intended to cover narrative fictions shown on television, made-for-TV movies and (more recently) television movies alongside dramas made specifically for the small screen. While recognising that the borderlines between categories may not be firmly drawn, TV drama is a sub-category of 'small-screen fictions' defined for the purposes of this chapter as narrative fictions in dramatic form (that is, stories enacted as distinct from being merely told orally) made to be distributed through the medium of television in the first instance. TV drama forms thus include soap operas, series, miniseries, serials and single plays/films that are made primarily for television.

Differences as well as similarities in studying TV drama and studying television more broadly become apparent. Where for all modes of television study the text can insightfully be located in its production and reception contexts, the textual forms themselves are distinctive in ways which have consequences for the mode of engagement with audiences (see Chapter 6). A news programme or documentary typically purports to be revealing something about the living world and events in it, to be making a truth claim about the actual world which can be tested against evidence (see Chapter 4). Fictional forms make no such claim, though in different ways some, such as **social realist** dramas, do offer insights into the way life is lived. Since the stories are fictions and – as the traditional disclaimer has it – 'any resemblance to actual persons (living or dead) is purely accidental' – it would not make sense to challenge a drama's veracity in the way in which viewers might want to challenge a news item.

However, it should perhaps be acknowledged, up front, that any sharp distinction between fact and fiction has been questioned in much contemporary theory. In particular **discourse theory**, theory about the way language works and meanings are shaped and exchanged, admits no neutral uses of language (see Chapter 3). In this view, 'objective' accounts of the world are impossible since the language medium (e.g. words and images) encodes the message in ways which colour the account with the perspective (ultimately the ideas and beliefs) of the teller. Hence there is much interest in Television Studies in identifying 'the spin' consciously or otherwise put on any given account. For the purposes of this chapter, however, a distinction between fact and fiction, between a story which is knowingly and avowedly fabricated and one which involves an overt truth claim about the world, is taken as core to the television medium's own categories. News bulletins or documentaries are presented as distinct from the fictional forms of narrative film and dramas.

Whatever your conception and understanding of television drama, actual programmes almost certainly benefit from being placed within their wider, social, technological, economic, historical and institutional context. In the early days of television in the UK there was only one channel (BBC1) with the introduction of ITV in 1955 affording a choice of just two channels until 1968 (see Chapter 7). In today's **multichannel environment**, of course, there is a huge range of choice. At the turn of 2004, the majority (just over 50 per cent) of British homes had gone digital and, subject to the purchase of a digital box, were eligible to receive some forty channels free of charge (beyond the UK licence fee) (see Chapter 10). By subscribing in addition to commercial suppliers, viewers may receive up to 500 channels with more choice promised. This development of the television environment makes the questions above even more necessary if we want to understand what is on offer and how it came to be there.

With the advent of **satellite technology** (the capacity that is to transmit a beam to a satellite orbit-ing the earth and vastly extend the range of reception of the transmission by bouncing the beam back at a wide angle to broad swathes of the terrestrial globe) **transnational** distribution, bypassing national markets and regulatory frameworks, became possible (see Chapter 9). This technological revolution facilitated production that may not have been viable on a national scale alone. The **telenovela**, a south American form of soap opera emanating from Brazil and made in Spanish, can now be transmitted directly to the whole of the Spanish-speaking world. Additionally, countering the anglophone dominance of material made in the US, it is now economically viable to make television movies with budgets approaching those of theatre movies and transmit them around the world dubbed into a range of languages.

Although some national public service broadcasters remain, such as the BBC in the UK funded by the licence fee paid for using a television receiver, television globally is also an increasingly commercial medium. The power over worldwide programming of multimedia conglomerates (such as AOL Time Warner or Rupert Murdoch's News Corporation) also inevitably raises concerns about cultural influence. Some people perceive the influence of American-based transnational media conglomerates to be one-way traffic overwhelming any local product (see Dowmunt, 1993). Such allegations of US industrial domination might equally be debated in relation to the sitcom *Friends* (NBC, 1994–2004) as to the shopping channels. Dissemination of – and resistance to – the **dominant ideology** (see Chapter 3) of global consumer capitalism is a matter of analysis in the domain of drama just as it is with regard to CNN (see Chapter 9).

Technological changes have also brought a transformation to the way television drama looks. The quality of the digital image, not to mention its relative size on large widescreen monitors, allows television now to approximate to cinema in its use of the visual image. In the very early days of television, the image was so small, so poor and, of course in black and white only, that the medium was more like radio

Marty: an early example of American TV drama

with illustrative accompaniment and consequently words were privileged over visual images reinforcing the more literary approach to drama, and commentary upon it. Today, the opposite is the case with visual effects in some instances dominating pared-down dialogue with high-quality soundtracks greatly extending the use of music in TV drama.

Historically, TV drama has been constrained in comparison with cinema by the domesticity of the predominant viewing environment and hence the relative conservatism of most of its audience. Drama has also been constrained by its high production costs, in the context of television, which typically have prevented creative people from being able to experiment. Compared, for example, with game shows, quizzes and 'reality TV', drama is more expensive to make and less certain of success. The costs of failure are thus relatively high, particularly if TV drama aspires to be like cinema. With the exception of some British and Australian soaps deriving from a largely outmoded multi-camera studio production tradition, today's TV drama is shot on film with post-production editing in a process mirroring cinematic output. Recent 'American Quality Television' arises out of production circumstances which have allowed 'the creatives' to be more experimental as we shall see in a discussion of *The Sopranos*

(Opposite) *24*: a TV drama where budgets are approaching those of film

(HBO, 1999–) to follow and in exceptional cases such as *24* (Fox, 2001–) whose budgets approach those of film.

There is an irony here in that soaps, which draw some of the numerically biggest television audiences, are very cheaply made (in Britain and Australia, for example) in comparison with what the Americans call 'theatre films', that is films destined to be distributed at least in the first instance through big-screen cinema networks. That many of those films are ultimately shown on small screens, through mainstream terrestrial channels, specialist satellite film channels or videotape complicates the issue. So a key task of the study of TV drama is to define its domain. We must first attempt to clarify the means by which television drama has been studied in the past, thereby clearly setting out the way in which this form of television is currently analysed, understood and contextualised.

THE STUDY OF TELEVISION DRAMA: A BRIEF HISTORY

Early criticism focused on the quality of '**the play**' since, both in the UK and the US, the very first TV dramas were televised versions of stage plays. In the UK, 'Armchair Theatre' (ITV, 1956–74) and 'The Wednesday Play' (BBC, 1964–70) are well-documented strands (see Brandt, 1981 and Cooke, 2003) while, in America, strands such as 'The Pulitzer Prize Playhouse' (ABC, 1950–2) and 'The Goodyear TV Playhouse' (NBC, 1951–60) presented live versions of some of the works of Shakespeare alongside more modern playwrights such as Ibsen as well as original plays written for television by contemporary writers such as Paddy Chayefsky (see Thompson, 1996). Plays were judged mostly in terms of their literary merit and the quality of the actors' performances in the tradition of theatre criticism. One of the first academic books on TV drama, George Brandt's (1981) *British Television Drama*, formulates quality in these terms and has chapters on the works of playwrights such as Peter Nicholls, Jeremy Sandford and Dennis Potter.

With the emergence of **Cultural Studies**, notably at Birmingham's Centre for Cultural Studies

in the UK in the early 1970s, attention was paid by a group of critics associated with Marxist perspectives to the messages more covertly conveyed by television texts (see Chapter 3). Stuart Hall (1980a), for example, formulated an influential 'encoding/decoding model' which suggested how the dominant ideology was inscribed (encoded) in the text and was in the main uncritically accepted (decoded) by an audience whose values were constructed by the powerful influence of mass culture (see Chapter 7). Debate surrounded the political impact of seminal TV dramas such as *Days of Hope* (BBC1, 1975) (see Bennett *et al.*, 1981). Hall's model acknowledges, however, the possibility of '**resistant**' or '**oppositional**' readings by those viewers placed at the social margins who would not readily concur with mainstream values. He thus sets up the possibilities of the next phase of television criticism in the 1980s which, through ethnographic study (see Ang, 1985 and 1991; Morley, 1986 and 1992), placed emphasis on what people *do* with television.

Such became the emphasis on audience research into variant resistance through readings, as opposed to reception of textually inscribed meanings, in this later approach that Schroder came to assert that '[t]he text itself has no existence, no life, and therefore no quality until it is deciphered by an individual and triggers the meaning potential carried by this individual' (1992: 207). 'Meaning in potential' has shifted, it should be noted, from the text to the reader, a shift to what Fiske (1987), in a standard primer, calls '**producerly texts**'. This shift took place in an intellectual climate (post-structuralism) in which any firm and stable relationship between the '**signifier**' and the '**signified**' was being called into question. Derrida (1978), among others, pointed to an ultimate deferral of closure of meaning in an endless chain of signifiers (see Chapter 2).

Amid the changes of approach, a broader range of TV drama texts was established as worthy of study. Tulloch (1990 and 2000; Tulloch and Jenkins [1995]) welcomed the recognition of the potential for meanings and pleasures of those popular, 'machine-made' series and serials which Brandt considered to be undermining the theatrical play tradition. But he also noted the limits on meaning production through reading. The '**agency**' of readers, their freedom to make meanings or determine their own lives, is constrained by the structures of texts, of television institutions and of societies (see Tulloch, 1990 and Nelson in Creeber, 2001: 10–11). Thus, understanding of viewers' readings through ethnographic study might best be balanced by study of the institutional contexts of both production and reception. Millington and Nelson's study (1986) of *Boys from the Blackstuff* (BBC2, 1982), for example, took a broader view of a force-field of influences on the production, the text and its reception and still serves as a useful model for study.

Though scepticism among some academics about the value of studying drama on television remains to this day, popular series as well as the more 'arty' end of the spectrum are indeed worth studying to understand their cultural as well as textual significance. TV drama now has sufficient history, moreover, to afford retrospective studies such as Bignell *et al.*'s *Television Drama: Past, Present and Future* (2000). Most recently, emphasis is again being placed particularly on the principles of composition and even the aesthetics of the TV drama text in an increasingly visual, as opposed to the earlier literary, culture.

HOW TO STUDY TELEVISION DRAMA: FROM PRODUCTION TO RECEPTION

To unpack the range of issues above and to address some deceptively simple questions such as 'What kind of drama do we get on television?', 'Why do we get it?' and 'What do we do with it?', this chapter takes the American television series, *The Sopranos* (HBO, shown in the UK on Channel 4) as a worked example. In focusing on *The Sopranos* and drawing comparisons with other well-known TV dramas, three key stages are outlined ('**The Production/Distribution Context**', '**The Text**' and '**The Reception Context**'), explaining how a specific example, and TV drama in general, might be studied.

1. THE PRODUCTION/DISTRIBUTION CONTEXT
Who Made It and for Whom?

If you pass through a room in which the television is switched on to an HBO programme you recognise it immediately by the dialogue alone. Your attention once drawn by the scatter-gun deployment of four-letter expletives, the impression is likely to be confirmed by explicit visual imagery in 'scenes of an adult nature'. Typical in *The Sopranos* are the glimpses of the scantily clad lapdancers who work the floor of the Bada Bing. Seldom dwelt upon in the intrusive, prurient manner of the camera on an overt porn channel such as Red Hot Dutch, an explicit openness to sexual acts is simply taken to be part of adult television life. HBO is not a porn channel (though it does show full sex in its Real Sex strand), indeed its products such as *The Sopranos*, *Sex and the City* (HBO, 1998–2004) and *Six Feet Under* (HBO, 2001–) are typically quite sophisticated. But, since it is a subscription channel HBO bypasses the cultural and regulatory constraints which historically have moderated free-to-air material.

In the network era, television's disposition not so much to please the audience but to sustain numbers by offending the smallest number of people, led to an inherent conservatism. HBO sets itself up in explicit contrast to this approach with its slogan, 'It's not television, it's HBO!' Implicitly condemning the blandness of the LOP (i.e. 'least offensive programming') approach to television, HBO announces its aim to please not everybody but primarily its target market. Since viewers in America pay directly through subscription for HBO, they are deemed in regulatory terms to elect to watch its products in full knowledge of their content. If they do not want to watch it – or have their children inadvertently exposed to it – viewers need not subscribe, where, with free-to-air television, viewers do not have the choice or control. For UK airings on Channel 4, some of the more challenging material is edited.

The general point to draw from this account is the need to be aware of the production and distribution context of the programme of study. Questions to ask include: 'Where was it made and by whom?'; 'What channel is it aired on and at what time?';

'Where is it re-transmitted?'; 'What is the target market?'; 'How do viewers access it?'; 'How many people typically watch it?'; and 'What is the **demographic** composition of the audience?'.

WHO PAYS FOR IT?

Television drama is ultimately paid for by viewers: directly, by obligation, in licence fees (the BBC in the UK); directly, by choice, through subscription (e.g. to HBO in the US); and indirectly through advertising or sponsorship on commercial channels (e.g. the American networks), funding which is ultimately costed in all the consumer goods viewers buy.

   Though the costs of setting up a satellite-delivered programming network are extremely high, they are affordable by today's highly capitalised media conglomerates (see McMurria in Jancovich and Lyons, 2003). Hallmark, the greetings card company, for example, has horizontally integrated its business with other media and progressed from sponsoring TV movies for the 'Hallmark Hall of Fame' on CBS to become a satellite distribution network with global reach. As McMurria reports (2003: 80–1):

> The channel broadcasts sixteen different feeds in twenty-three languages as of 2001. Each channel typically premiered thirteen to twenty TV movies per month. . . . Each feed consists of a single programming stream, with space for up to six different language subtitling tracks. Regional offices in London (Europe, Middle East, Africa), Miami (Latin America) and Hong Kong and Singapore (Asia) execute sales and marketing campaigns, and co-ordinate subtitling/dubbing.

As a result of the advent of such media empires as Hallmark and, on a more modest scale, subscription channels such as HBO, TV drama products are more varied than ever and increasingly shaped to please specific segments of the global market, either separately or aggregated. Thus, if in studying drama on television, we aim fully to understand why products are formed as they are, we need to ask the above

(Opposite) *The Sopranos*: 'It's not television, it's HBO!'

questions about the **production** and **distribution** context.

2. THE TEXT
What Type of Drama Is It?

Though it has high production values and is shot on film, *The Sopranos* is neither a theatre movie nor a TV movie (see Lavery, 2002a). Movies typically have a single (though sometimes complex) continuous narrative arc aimed to take us on a journey from point A to point B over a continuous timespan of 100–140 minutes. Though as noted, many movies are now shown on television, the shape of TV drama differs from the cinematic form because the industrial imperative is to fill more time. Some television channels now provide a twenty-four-hour service. Even in its earlier days, television aspired to offer entertainment in a domestic context which, besides a peak evening viewing span of perhaps six hours per day (17.00–23.00 hours), also offered 'daytime television'. Many hours need to be filled to complete a schedule. For drama to make the substantial contribution for which it had viewing potential, new forms needed to be developed specifically for the medium. The one-hour-long single play, derived in the early days of television from its antecedent in the theatre, would not suffice.

   Traditionally the scheduling year (fifty-two weeks) of a mainstream terrestrial channel such as BBC1 in the UK was divided into quarters, that is, four quarters of thirteen weeks each. From a scheduler's point of view, it was convenient if a serial or a series might run for thirteen weeks to fill a slot for a quarter year, or in practice twelve weeks to allow a spare week when an international soccer match or other 'national', one-off event might demand the precedence of airtime. Given, as noted, that TV drama is expensive to make and risky in terms of its success, the thirteen-week quarter, might be broken down into two six-part miniseries, with a spare week. The key point is that the **industrial medium** of television demanded long-order, enacted narrative forms of its drama. In America, an industry structure based on profits made ultimately from syndication to the various networks, longer runs of, say, twenty-two weeks were required. Today, a series like *The Sopranos* runs in several series, each comprising around thirteen episodes.

Narrative Structure

John Ellis (1982) long ago observed that the soap form, ongoing serial narrative, is television's distinctive contribution to narrative form. A popular product with a seemingly limitless output made by an industrial process capable of three (or more) prime-time episodes per week is a scheduler's dream. The form ideally suits the medium of television in being inexpensive to make, in drawing a large audience (15 to 18 million in the UK) and in keeping them watching in a social ritual year on year. Following Ellis, Nelson has identified what he calls the '**flexinarrative**' form (see Nelson, 1997), a hybrid mix of serial and series forms derived from prose fiction, distinctive of the majority of TV drama output today. 'Flexi-narratives' are mixtures of the series and the serial form, involving the closure of one **story arc** within an episode (like a series) but with other, ongoing story arcs involving the regular characters (like a serial). This hybrid form maximises the pleasures of both regular viewers who watch from week to week and get hooked by the serial narratives and the occasional viewers who happen to tune into one episode seeking the satisfaction of narrative closure within that episode. *The Sopranos* serves as an example of the form.

The Sopranos has extended over four 'series', each comprised of thirteen episodes. The main characters and setting are common but, in each episode, a story complete in itself is told to satisfy the occasional viewer seeking the pleasure of one-off narrative closure. In an episode entitled 'Commendatori', for example, several of the key characters make a trip to their family homeland, Italy, specifically Naples, with the aim of importing to the New Jersey mob a young 'soldier' with 'old-school' values. The episode ends with their return to America, mission completed. At the same time, ongoing serial narratives are built in to sustain continuing interest.

Most episodes interweave several story arcs in parallel. For example, 'The Happy Wanderer' runs the

story of Tony's taking over his father's and Uncle Junior's 'executive game' of high-stake poker featuring Frank Sinatra Jr in parallel with the story of Meadow's appearance in the school show (part of her bid to achieve a place at a good college). Other arcs are ongoing, for example Tony's feud with Richie Aprile, day-to-day tensions in both Tony's families, and his consultations with Dr Melfi, resumed towards the end of the second series. Thus, in comparison with a more traditional, goal-oriented police or detective drama where the law enforcement agencies get their man and the mystery is resolved, the drive for narrative closure in *The Sopranos* is not strong, despite most episodes introducing and bringing at least one story arc to at least a weak closure.

Viewer interest in *The Sopranos* would not appear to lie primarily in the satisfactions of narrative closure traditionally associated with goal-oriented male desire (see Fiske, 1987). Instead, interest lies more perhaps with a circular economy of family issues which fluctuate between an everyday friction of rubbing along together in less than perfect harmony and occasional crisis points which are never fully resolved. This **narrative economy** has traditionally been located in soaps and with women's viewing pleasures (see Fiske, 1987). As we shall see when considering audience reception in 'The Reception Context', however, the target audience for *The Sopranos* is primarily AB1 males rather than women, though its distinctive mix has broad appeal.

Genre

Another key aspect in characterising a TV drama is '**genre**', the type of thing it is. However, as *The Television Genre Book* (Creeber, 2001) explains, 'genre' is a contested and changing concept. Located in New Jersey, *The Sopranos* deals with the life and times of a contemporary Italian-American family linked to its historical roots through the involvement of its main characters in the mob, the Italian Mafia operating in New Jersey/New York. In this respect, it is tempting to place *The Sopranos* in the genre of 'gangster', or more precisely 'Mafia', movies such as *The Godfather* (Coppola, I, II, and III) which are overtly referenced in the series. Besides debate about which 'generic' cinematic influence is greatest on *The Sopranos* (see, for example, Pattie and Creeber in Lavery, 2002a), there is a strong case for saying that the series defies genre classification because it is a **hybrid** of several forms.

Extending its 'flexi-narrative' mix of the series and serial narrative forms, *The Sopranos* also taps into the soap genre. If the narrative economy of soap, as Jane Feuer has remarked, involves a tendency towards 'integration into a happy family . . . a balance between harmony and disharmony but no one couple can remain in a state of integration' (1984: 113), *The Sopranos* fits the bill. Indeed, Tony Soprano is the head of two families, his kinship and Mafia families, each just about sustaining family identity but each threatening continually to implode. Besides his Uncle Junior (Tony's father's brother), Tony's kinship family includes his wife, Carmela, his children, Meadow and 'young' Anthony, his sister Janice (aka Parvati) and his fearsome mother, Livia. The regular mob characters are members or acquaintances of Tony Soprano's crew such as Pauley Walnuts, Christopher Moltisanto, Richie Aprile and Salvatore (Big Pussy) Bonpensiero along with neighbourhood associates such as Artie Bucco, proprietor of the Vesuvio restaurant.

Further extending the genre mix, the psychological well-being of central character, Tony Soprano, is explored in relation to his social role in a manner untypical of the gangster movies to which this TV drama is intertextually, and to some extent generically, related. The main device, set up in the pilot episode to explore Tony's inner being, consists of his visits to an attractive female therapist, Dr Jennifer Melfi, who appears to be thoroughly intrigued by Tony, opening up the additional narrative and generic possibilities of a romantic or sexual liaison. The notion of '**intertextuality**' is important in contemporary TV drama and operates on several levels. If genres are 'marked by a particular set of conventions, features and norms' (Neale in Creeber, 2001: 01), viewer knowledge of the kinds of texts they like attracts them to particular programmes. In the process of building audience by aggregating a mix of interest groups, mixed genre, or hybrid, forms such as *The Sopranos* have the potential to appeal to a range of audiences. In making overt or covert, 'intertextual' references to other texts known to a media-literate audience, the text can function on several levels: to reassure viewers that the text they are watching is the kind of thing they like; to make viewers feel superior because they are knowledgeable about this textual genre; to add an element of playfulness ranging from spotting the allusions made through to a full **post-structuralist** awareness that textuality is all (see Chapter 2).

Visual Style

The concept of 'flexi-narrative', besides noting the dominance of a conflated series–serial cultural form in contemporary television, recognises a relation between the mode of televisual storytelling and the cultural moment. In particular, it indicates the fast pace and high temperature of today's television drama achieved largely through the **rapid intercutting** of several storylines in any given episode. Assuming an advanced level of television literacy in today's viewers, editors can cut from high point to high point of the storyline in each narrative arc keeping up the overall temperature of the drama. The cutting rhythm will, of course, vary to afford light and shade but the overall impact will be dynamic. *The Sopranos* achieves such dynamism with style. Though it does not quite use the squish-pan camera search of *NYPD Blue* (NBC, 1993–), the camera is frequently on the move. In editing, very sharp cuts are made from the core of one scene, perhaps a more reflective scene of Tony Soprano opening up to Dr Melfi, slap into high, often violent, action in which somebody inevitably gets 'whacked'.

Besides violent scenes, another feature of *The Sopranos*' visual style is the casually incorporated sex scenes, such as the shots inside Bada Bing, the strip joint which is the front for Tony's office. In most episodes, glimpses of the bare-breasted girls are cut in almost in passing as mob characters move across the Bada Bing space. Likewise overt sexual acts are shown frequently but not dwelt upon, being swiftly intercut as part of the camera's restless roving through the New Jersey neighbourhood. Sequences such as these and those involving travel in cars across the 'hood are used to inject a dynamic of motion in counterpoint to the more static scenes of dialogue either in the home or in the office or restaurants (see Creeber, 2002: 132–3).

Sonic Environment

In today's television, the **soundtrack** has become increasingly important. As noted, the quality of **digital sound** is much improved and music has, perhaps in consequence, become an increasing part of the 'feel' or mood of drama series in a world where all human life seems to be played out to a soundtrack. In particular with the aim of attracting the elusive 16 to 25-year-old market, TV drama has increasingly used contemporary pop music over its images, emulating MTV. From *Heartbeat*'s (ITV, 1991–) use of pop music tracks from the 1960s for their nostalgic appeal to *Ally McBeal*'s (Fox, 1997–2001) use of popular songs interiorised to boost the personal confidence of each character – Ally's (Gladys Knight and the Pips) and John Cage's 'You're My Everything' (Barry White) – pop music serves many functions in contemporary TV drama. In *The Sopranos*, the soundtrack draws on pop and rock tracks which are used something like a film score to give the series overall its 'feel' and to underline, and occasionally to comment on, the mood of characters in moments of interaction.

The key point for studies of TV drama generally is that, far from the static theatrical product of the earlier multi-camera studio with its flimsy sets, today's output, shot with **cinematic** attention to detail and often with post-production digital treatment, affords high-quality images. When set to a range of pop tracks or a specifically composed score, TV drama becomes a form that can compete with theatre movies. It is not surprising, then, that the aesthetics and compositional principles of television drama are increasingly the subject for critical analysis.

3. THE RECEPTION CONTEXT: UNPACKING 'THE MESSAGE'

The Sopranos appears to tell us that the younger generation in America today has lost the plot. The old

values that bond a community together have been abandoned. The angst that typifies established professionals, notably Caucasian men of the older generation, and which leads Tony Soprano to the couch of Dr Melfi, is a symptom of this cultural malaise. If 'we' (as hailed by this TV series) do not resist the times, we shall fall prey to one of its debilitating designer diseases requiring counselling and even perhaps an endless infusion of Prozac. For the target market of *The Sopranos* is AB1 males, a key segment of audience for HBO which, as a subscription channel, needs to attract those with significant disposable income. AB1 males are likely to be '**appointment viewers**', busy professionals who work long hours and do not watch television habitually but who make a point of tuning into – or recording on TiVo (see Chapter 10). *The Sopranos*' emphasis upon strong bonds between males of the older generation not matched by the fecklessness of the younger men (e.g. Christopher Moltisanto) speaks directly not only to a particular subset of Italian Americans but more broadly to American men, and perhaps to men of a certain age across the globe, whose professional success and relative wealth have not brought them unmitigated happiness in a world which increasingly makes no sense and does not adhere to established values.

In the paragraph above, I am, of course, offering a reading from the imagined position of a member of *The Sopranos*' target audience. This is not the only possible reading but it will hopefully be recognised as an account of a key **discursive position** of the series as it might impact on key readers. I mean to indicate by 'discursive position', the discourse which is spoken through the text revealing where it is coming from, and I mean also to suggest that a text has a disposition to some meanings rather than others. Such an account does not deny that other readers differently situated might read the text very differently (see Chapter 2). Some women of mature years may identify with the long-suffering Carmela and read *The Sopranos* more as a soap opera concerned with the struggle to keep a family together in a situation where so many forces are pushing it apart. Younger males may identify with a character such as Christopher Moltisanto, who wants everything now, and share his frustration with the constraints of 'this thing of ours', since Moltisanto is quite unconcerned with matters of honour or how the end is achieved. Viewers, if any, in Islamic cultures might take *The Sopranos* to typify the violence and (hetero- and homo-) sexual promiscuity of American men and the Godlessness of America in general.

Ethnographic audience research (see, for example, seminal work on *Dallas*: Katz and Liebes, 1985 and Ang, 1985) has tended to support the idea that the meaning of the text is not fixed by the 'author' since its findings indicate a range of possible readings from **variant viewing positions** (see Chapter 6). The more television becomes a global phenomenon and (particularly American) programmes are beamed worldwide by satellite, the greater the number and variety of individual readers differently situated socially will engage with those texts (see Chapter 9). The empirical data that might be yielded by large-scale ethnographic research (thus far most studies have been based on very small samples), however, should always itself be subjected to sociological scrutiny. It is important to know something about the cultures and **microcultures** of the readers and something of their taste formations. Given the evident logistical difficulty and complexity of global audience study, then, a good starting point is to identify the target market and to note the '**preferred reading**' of the text from that specific point of view. If your own viewing position is located outside that, it is worth reflecting on your own reading and then trying to imagine how the text might be read by others situated elsewhere (differentiated by age, class, gender ethnicity etc.) as I have briefly indicated above.

What/Whom the Message Represents?

Finally, when studying a particular TV drama and probably getting very involved in it, it is worth stepping back to ask both who or what is represented by it and who or what isn't. The target market of *The Sopranos* favours, as noted, thirty-something and older males but the series also represents a range of women. Besides Carmela and Dr Melfi, there is Tony's college-student daughter, Meadow, his sister,

Janice (aka Parvati) and Tony's redoubtable mother, Livia, among a significant number of their friends and acquaintances. There is even a female boss of the Naples Mafia. Women are thus not effaced from the series, though commentators such as Martha Lauzen have criticised the 'thoroughly regressive portrayals of women . . . [arguing that] the show's writers give these psychologically and physically brutalized women no means of escape and no power' (cited by Akass and McCabe in Lavery, 2002a: 146). The series is located in an Italian-American subculture and the representation of this significant American group has also come in for harsh censure from critics located both within and outside the subculture. Lavery cites Camille Paglia's wrath at a 'buffoonish caricature of my people' (2002a: xiii). Though age and gender are broadly represented, albeit contentiously, the emphasis on Italian Americans draws attention to a notable absence from *The Sopranos*, black Americans.

One episode, 'Do Not Resuscitate', features a group of striking construction workers which happens to be predominantly black. The episode also features a black nurse in the rest home where Tony's mother is reluctantly staying and an apparently chance encounter between Tony and an old black man who dies in the course of the episode. Spiritual songs are heard at his funeral and there is a momentary identification between Tony and the man who leaves a son to grieve him. The dominantly memorable image, however, is of Tony's stooges wielding baseball bats and violently breaking the strike. Elsewhere in *The Sopranos*, black people are conspicuous by their absence. The focus of the series on the Italian-American community does not in itself explain either this treatment in – or this effacement from – the New Jersey–New York context.

SUMMARY

The academic study of television drama involves investigation of a force-field of influences and the production/distribution: text: reception model rehearsed above should not be seen as linear but as involving feedback loops. For example, the television industry's conceptions of audience taste feed back into the kinds of texts they produce. Similarly, the broader **socio–economic** culture affects the ways in which audience is constructed (as a mass or in fragmented microcultures). Some aspects of study are distinctive of TV drama but where others overlap with the broader concerns of Television Studies, the specificity of dramatic forms should be foregrounded in studies of TV drama, and detailed **textual analysis** undertaken (see Chapter 2). In the space this chapter allows it has been possible to offer a framework for study only. Lavery's (2002a) collection on *The Sopranos* includes examples of approaches ranging from psychoanalysis and linguistic theory to genre analysis and accounts of reception. Students are now invited to read, research, analyse and fill out the wider picture.

FURTHER READING

Brandt, George (ed.) (1981), *British Television Drama*, Cambridge: Cambridge University Press.

Caughie, John (2000), *Television Drama: Realism, Modernism and British Culture*, Oxford and New York: Oxford University Press.

Cooke, Lez (2003), *British Television Drama: A History*, London: BFI.

Creeber, Glen (2004c), *Serial Television: Big Drama on the Small Screen*, London: BFI.

Feuer, Jane (1995), *Seeing through the Eighties: Television and Reaganism*, Durham: Duke University Press.

Jacobs, Jason (2000), *The Intimate Screen: Early British Television Drama*, Oxford: Oxford University Press.

Nelson, Robin (1997), *TV Drama in Transition: Forms, Values and Cultural Change*, Basingstoke and New York: Macmillan/St Martin's Press.

Tulloch, John (1990), *Television Drama: Agency, Audience and Myth*, London and New York: Routledge.

CASE STUDY
Modernism and Postmodernism in Television Drama Robin Nelson

The complexity of cultural movements such as **modernity** and **postmodernity** and their related cultural products of '**modernism**' and '**postmodernism**' is such that any sharp delineation is likely to distort. History and its cultural products cannot be contained in neatly labelled boxes. Simply to cite, however, the well-worn adage about postmodernism (namely that it defies consensus and hence definition), is not helpful to readers aiming to get a handle on challenging concepts. The following account accordingly aims to offer a framework into which things might be placed to promote a conceptual grasp but it carries a warning about its inevitable oversimplifications.

In a seminal article on postmodern TV drama, Jim Collins asserts that '[t]elevision, unlike architecture, literature, or painting, never had a modernist phase' (1992: 330–1) since its products have not been marked with the distinctive, authorial signature of the creative artist. They are neither the products of the 'individual talent', to take the romantic individu-alist strain of modernism, nor do they wear the badge of 'authenticity' to resist capitalist commodification, to take the Marx-derived, Frankfurt School variant strain (see Chapter 2).

In stark contrast, John Caughie has recently sought to sustain the notion that, among the output of the television medium, television drama did, and perhaps still does, carry a modernist cachet. He argues that 'British terrestrial television, with its regulated duopoly operating in the public interest . . . seems to [him] still be rooted in modernity' (2000: 17). In the British television tradition, the medium itself claimed the **Reithian** (see Chapter 7) high ground from the inception of the BBC and, as Caughie puts it, '[t]elevision drama is, after all, the respectable end of television' (2000: 92). To understand these opposing claims about television, it will be helpful briefly to consider different perspectives on television culture from British and American standpoints. But first let us attempt a bold tabulation of modernist and postmodernist TV drama:

'Modernist' TV drama tradition (a line through time)		'Postmodernist' TV drama (dispersed through space)	
Authored single play	*Lena, O My Lena* (BBC, 1960) *Up the Junction* (BBC, 1965) *The Cheviot, the Stag, and the Black, Black Oil* (BBC, 1975)	Playful ironic distancing	*Moonlighting* (NBC, 1985–9) *Miami Vice* (ABC, 1984–9) *thirtysomething* (ABC, 1987–91) *Cop Rock* (ABC, 1990)
Authored series	*Bill Brand* (ITV, 1976) *Boys from the Blackstuff* (BBC2, 1982), *Our Friends in the North* (BBC2, 1997)	Genre hybridity	*Ally McBeal* (Fox, 1997–2003) *Six Feet Under* (HBO, 2001–) *Twin Peaks* (ABC, 1990–1) *The Sopranos* (HBO, 1999–)
Authored serial with frame-breaking features	*The Prisoner* (ITV, 1967–8) *Pennies from Heaven* (BBC2, 1978) *Edge of Darkness* (BBC1, 1985) *The Singing Detective* (BBC1, 1986)	Uncertainty of subject	*The X-Files* (Fox, 1993-2002) *Buffy the Vampire Slayer* (WB/UNP, 1997–2001) *The Kingdom* (Danish TV, 1994)
'Classic' adaptations	*The Jewel in the Crown* (ITV, 1984) *Middlemarch* (BBC2, 1994) *Brideshead Revisited* (ITV, 1981)	Self-reflexivity	*Twin Peaks* (ABC, 1990–1) *Northern Exposure* (CBS, 1990–5) *The Simpsons* (Fox, 1991–)

Figure 3. Modernist and Postmodern TV Drama: Examples and Types.

It is evident that the two sides of the table above do not match. On the right-hand side, 'postmodern' texts have been characterised by textual features to which we shall return, while the 'modernist' TV drama tradition merely list forms of texts. What the latter have in common is that they are all original, 'authored' works other than the 'classic adaptations' where original 'classic' novels (Paul Scott's *The Raj Quartet* [*The Jewel in the Crown*] and George Eliot's *Middlemarch*), re-worked for television by named writer–producer teams (respectively, Paul Scott–Ken Taylor and Andrew Davies–Michael Wearing) are the 'authored' equivalent (see Chapter 1).

It is impossible to characterise the textual features of 'modernist' arts, if only because the umbrella term shelters a rush of experiments with form. Thus a creative authorial signature becomes a very general defining characteristic. In the conservative, industrial medium of television drama, experiments with form such as 'frame-breaking, Brechtian devices' to interrupt the illusion of a real (though fictional) world is a 'modernist' feature of some, though not all, of the examples (see Cooke, 2003 for a discussion of each of the works cited). Formal means of drawing attention to the construction of the text, a feature apparently extended in postmodern textual **playfulness** have, however, a different purpose in modernism than in postmodernism.

Generally speaking the modernist aim was to create a shock into new awareness. A helpful way for drama students to understand the modernist inflection might be to remember that the devices in Brecht's **epic theatre** were aimed ultimately at making audiences conscious of the theatrical-political process in order that they might change things to improve the material conditions of their lives. *Ally McBeal*, in contrast, plays with form in a number of ways but merely with the aim of entertaining and, at best, making viewers quizzically thoughtful.

What the texts cited in the 'modernist' TV drama tradition have in common, whether they be explanatory 'grand narratives' like *Middlemarch* or formal experiments like *Pennies from Heaven* is an aim to offer an insight into the human condition or the real conditions of existence. Though their forms vary, they might all be located within the project of modernity as identified by Caughie (2000), since they share the aim of being analytically 'serious' in their accounts of the world. In contrast, postmodernity rejects linear, **'grand narrative'**, totalising accounts. Specifically, it rejects the sense of a progressive cultural trajectory to which the arts and TV drama might contribute. Furthermore, postmodernism questions any direct relationship between **signifier** and **signified** whereby the human condition might be revealed. Jane Feuer accordingly writes of 'a postmodern concern with images as images' (1995: 1). At its extremes, a postmodern approach denies access to any stable 'reality' (see Baudrillard) and thus foregrounds the idea that texts are formally related to each other 'intertextually' rather than metaphors for the real world (see Chapter 2).

Indeed, postmodernism's challenge to stability extends to the subjectivity of individuals. To some postmodernists, personal identity is a matter of lifestyle choice and can be changed almost at will. Accordingly, playfulness of all kinds, in the compositional principles of the text (**genre hybridity**, **irony**

and **self-reflexivity**) and between texts and viewers (subject identity and lifestyle choice), characterises the postmodern TV drama text and context. As style takes precedence over content, the breakdown of any clear distinction between art and popular culture is one of many blurrings of category boundaries. In the debate about modernity and postmodernity, however, this figures somewhat differently in the UK and the US.

BACKSTORY: TELEVISION TRADITIONS IN THE UK AND THE US

To make some simple historical distinctions between

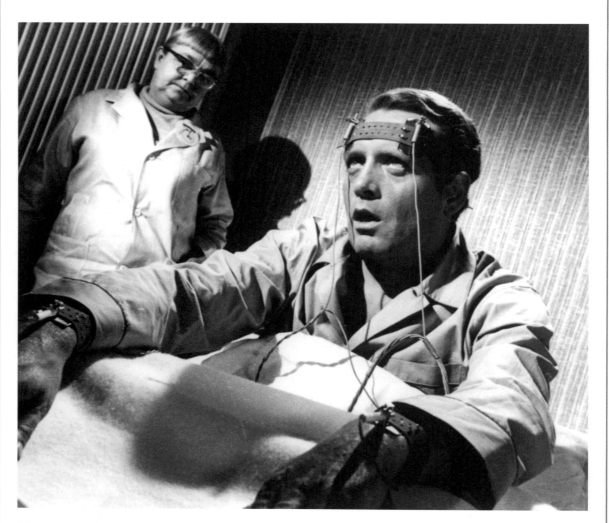

The Prisoner: authored serial with frame-breaking features

Twin Peaks: playful ironic distancing and general hybridity

the different cultures, the early strands of TV drama in the US based upon classics of the theatre (see the main part of this chapter) quickly faded out along with their attendant literary values. Television in America settled early into a cartel of the 'big three' commercial networks (CBC, NBC, ABC) who adopted an LOP, least-offensive programming, strategy from approximately the late 1940s to late 1970s to compete for shares of a mass audience (see Chapter 7). To maximise its audience share, each major network distributed a bland output of popular culture with which the majority of Middle America filled its leisure time. Industrial processes of production were developed to satisfy the demands of the schedules. Though, on exceptional occasion, distinctive programmes emerged, they are typically marked in television histories as 'not regular television' (see Thompson, 1996), departures, that is, from the televisual norm. The Public Service Broadcast channel in

America has from early on been a small minority interest.

In the UK, in contrast, **public service broadcasting** (PSB) dominated from the inception of the BBC in 1936. Though in 1955 commercial television was introduced in competition, the ethos of British television was already established and Independent Television (ITV), though somewhat more populist, took its cue in respect of drama from the BBC. As late as the early 1980s, Granada Television, an independent company, was making expensive, prestigious drama serials such as *Brideshead Revisited* and *The Jewel in the Crown* as flagship productions to illustrate their commitment to a PSB remit. George Brandt's brief account of the former illustrates the tradition of 'modernist' values in which the series wished to be located (1993: 11):

Scripted by John Mortimer [a well-known play-wright and barrister], handsomely directed by Charles Sturridge and Michael Lindsay-Hogg, it boasted a number of stellar performances, including those of heavyweights like Sir Laurence Olivier and Sir John Gielgud.

Such an account bears out Caughie's point that (2000: 3):

[j]ust as the notion of the 'legitimate' came to serve as a way of distinguishing culturally approved theatre from the popular theatre of melodrama and music hall, so 'serious drama' operates to mark off a 'legiti-mate' cultural territory within television from other areas which are not legitimated by the official dis-course of cultural approval.

Thus, precisely because it bears the '**high cul-ture**' strains of Lord Reith's philosophy and the traces of a literary theatre tradition particularly strong in English culture, television drama, and most notably 'serious drama', has arguably sustained in the UK something of a modernist sensibility. It is notable that Brandt's account of *Brideshead Revisited* above, stresses the individual talents of the '**authorial**' con-tributions of the writer–adaptor and the actors who have distinguished records in legitimate culture (see Chapter 1).

It is understandable, then, that Caughie fore-grounds the modernist strains of British television drama culture, while Collins, from an American per-spective, characterises the medium as postmodern. To throw further light on the debate, it will help to tabulate some broader characteristics.

The following table is offered as a conceptual aid and is intended to be neither definitive nor prescrip-tive. As noted in respect to television, the established time frames of the 'modernism' and 'postmodernism' cultural projects (themselves still open to debate) cannot apply directly to television which developed as a domestic medium only in the 1950s. If Caughie is right, however, strains of modernism remain trace-able in television today.

Perhaps because television is a domestic, popular medium, residual cultures take longer to displace. Older viewers may still watch with a realist disposi-tion taking the small screen to be a window on the world and its dramas to represent real life as it is lived by others. Younger viewers weaned on television and highly media aware, in contrast, may refract all tele-vision output through a typically postmodern irony, subverting the **preferred readings** proffered by any given text. Ultimately, there can be no neat division between one column of the table above and the other: examples of industrially produced output are evident in early television just as an authored single play may occasionally find a transmission slot today.

TV modernism	TV postmodernism
Authored 'serious drama'	Generic hybrids: 'flexi-narratives' (see Nelson, 1997)
Close to liveness and the authenticity of ephemeral theatre	Electronic culture, shifting from mass culture to microcultures
Distinctive product with meaning inscribed and underlined by an authorial signature	Polysemic text offering a range of pleasures to consumers; surface visual style: concern with images as images
Creation of individual talent *or* authentic product resisting capitalist commodifcation	Market-driven, led by market research; team-produced to ratings –effective template (e.g. *Heartbeat*, see Nelson 1997)
Each part integral to the whole in the author's overall design	Bricolage, the juxtaposition of (narrative or semiotic) fragments without any 'authorial' attempt at overall harmony
Universal meaning	Readings by individuals or microcultures in a pluralist semiotic democracy
Explanatory grand narratives Authored or hand-crafted by talented artist	Oblique storytelling with looser, less-motivated narrative drive Industrially produced, in later years by digital means

Figure 4. From Modernism to Postmodernism: Major Characteristics in TV Drama.

Analysing TV Fiction

91

Nevertheless the table offers an outline map which, if used with caution, should serve as a helpful guide.

In postmodern television drama, as with other popular cultural output, there is a marked disposition to hybrid products, refreshing one established genre by fusing it with another. Thus *Heartbeat*, in my own formulation is *Dixon of Dock Green* (BBC, 1955–76) meets *All Creatures Great and Small* (BBC1, 1978–90) (see Nelson, 1997) and *Twin Peaks* has been described as 'a cross between *Peyton Place*, the well-known 60s soap opera . . . and *Happy Days*, the 80s sitcom series set in the 50s' (see Chion 1995: 103–4). *Ally McBeal* mixes a courtroom drama with a workplace sitcom, soap opera romance and MTV (see Nelson in Creeber, 2001: 43). *Miami Vice* (BBC1, 1984–5) pioneered the use of pop music sequences which 'interrupt the continuity of the narrative' (Buxton, 1990: 140) and popular music has since then been used simply for its MTV-style pleasures. The intercutting of two or more modes of television contributes to an increased pace of combinations of narrative segments pasted together in a **bricolage** rather than linked through motivated plots, linear in construction, with a clear beginning, middle and end.

Turning to the reception context, the postmodern audience was no longer conceived as a mass who could be satisfied with one product (as in LOP above), but as an aggregation of **microcultures** with varying taste formations and, indeed, personal preferences within taste formations. The postmodern principle of composition affords pleasures to a more diffuse, segmented audience. No one authored, modernist play, inscribed with the singular meaning of the 'author-god' (see Barthes, 1977a) would suffice. Postmodern audiences in postmodern times are presumed to need at least the illusion of choice of something for them, personally. In a culture of consumer individualism, television pleasures must come thick and fast to avoid displeasure and channel-hopping at the touch of a button.

From this sketch, tendencies will be evident at each point on the production, text and reception spectrum. Postmodern cultural products reflect a spirit of the times which, having abandoned a linear trajectory of cultural progress, is dispersed through space rather than following a progressive timeline. Emphasis shifts away from the singular meaning of the work itself to the multiple readings of an **open text** which allows microcultures or individual viewers to construct their own 'meanings'. TV dramas such as *Northern Exposure*, through their sheer quirkiness as much as their ironic play, legitimise 'alternative' ways of seeing. The more fragmented approach to storytelling in postmodern television also reflects a scepticism about those 'grand narratives' which made singular sense of the world. Post-Watergate, the integrity and commitment to the greater good of figures of public authority and establishment institutions can no longer be taken for granted. Doubts in this domain are disseminated through popular television in dramas such as *The X-Files*. Though 'the truth is out there', we can 'trust no one'.

A shift in the 'postmodern' intellectual climate was centred in theories of language which emphasised the slipperiness of the relation between signifier and signified and afforded texts which were sometimes self-consciously playful. *Moonlighting* played with direct address to viewers, acknowledging the performers customarily concealed 'behind' TV characters. It showed an overt awareness of itself as a television text by referring to its generic origins while subverting those established genres. In a later example, *Ally McBeal*, digital distortions break the frame of the otherwise believable world of the Fish and Cage legal practice when, for example, Ally's tongue extends hugely if she does not like somebody. In *Twin Peaks*, there are so many '**intertextual**' references to other cinema and television texts, including numerous references to Hitchcock and other films (see Chion, 1995), that it appears to some readers a pastiche of popular culture (see Collins, 1992).

Finally, a few words about another possible shift in the early twenty-first century to a fully global digital television culture which Rogers *et al.* (2002) have dubbed **TV3** (see Chapter 7). Some dramas, particularly within the 'American Quality TV' output in recent years, appear to have aligned themselves with modernist theatre or European art cinema in emphasising that they are, as in HBO's headline, 'not

TV' at all. Programmes like *Oz* (HBO, 2001–3), *The Sopranos*, *24* and *Six Feet Under* variously deploy strategies such as bumpy narrative, oblique story-telling, dream sequences, direct address to camera which echo modernist devices. For a variety of reasons, these products cannot simply be termed 'modernist' but they function in significantly differ-ent ways from regular postmodern TV. In their modes of production, their address to the audience and their sense of individual signature, they con-sciously mark themselves as different with specific 'modernist' overtones. It may be, then, that from the American standpoint, a 'post-postmodernist' phase (building on postmodernism but echoing also some aspects of modernism) is now emerging or, from Caughie's point of view, such examples may affirm that the strains of modernism have never faded away completely and that postmodernism was merely a blip in the continuing project of modernity. A greater distance is perhaps needed in order for us to see this recent shift more clearly.

6 Television and Its Audience
Issues of Consumption and Reception
Matt Hills

> If you really want to know what the media means to people you have to ask them.
>
> Roger Silverstone, *Why Study the Media?* (1999): 64.

One might assume that studying television would necessarily involve studying its audiences and their behaviours, but the history of Television Studies has been rather more complicated. Audiences have generally been important, but despite this, the pendulum of TV theory has swung back and forth in a variety of ways, with audiences being thought about differently at different points in the debate, and with some scholars prioritising '**the text**' (i.e. the content of TV programmes) or the technology of television over and above studying how audiences actually interpret texts and use technologies. Text-based work has sometimes assumed that the scholarly interpreter of TV is a privileged 'reader' who can produce a 'true' and full interpretation of the text in question. What has been termed the '**structuralist**' approach to TV suffers from this belief: in structuralist work, academic 'readings' are assumed to uncover the 'deep structures' of TV texts (see Fiske, 1983; Silverstone, 1981; and Chapter 1). Against this type of work, which first became influential in the 1970s, latterday Television Studies has frequently taken the audience as its starting point, arguing that meanings of texts are not self-evidently 'just there', but have to be produced by audiences in their social/cultural contexts. And this necessitates studying audience activity in a variety of ways.

Audience studies in television can be divided into different phases, each being marked by certain assumptions. Although it may be tempting to argue for various progressions and developments across these 'phases' – so that audience theory today is automatically thought to be superior and more sophisticated than audience studies of, say, the 1940s or 1960s – we should remember that *all* theories of the audience are defined by the perspective they take, and the assumptions they make, and so all phases of audience work have their own specific uses and limits.

In what follows, I will set out chronological and conceptual stages in work on TV audiences, before then concluding with a few thoughts on likely future directions in this area of study. As Nicholas Abercrombie and Brian Longhurst point out, 'histories of [television] audience research divide up that history into phases, or periods – . . . a common analysis is of three phases – "**effects**", "**uses and gratifications**" and "**encoding/decoding**"' (1998: 4). To this, we can add the most recent, emergent phase in audience scholarship: the study of television audiences within '**media culture**' (see Alasuutari, 1999; Bird, 2003). Studying the interpretative **contexts** which frame and inform a viewer's understanding of the media is also known as **reception studies**. While audience and reception work often go hand in hand, it is sometimes important to distinguish between the audience itself and the *context* in which an audience *receives* the text (see Machor and Goldstein, 2001).

It is also worth noting that these different phases in audience and reception research tend to be linked to different **methodologies**, i.e. they have different ways of actually researching audience behaviour, as well as making different conceptual assumptions.

More recent work has usually (though not always) emphasised **qualitative** study. This involves trying to get access to how audiences themselves understand and interpret TV texts, either by doing **face-to-face interviews**, asking respondents to write reasonably open-ended accounts of their TV consumption, or by **observing** audience behaviour in its usual settings. By contrast, earlier audience study tended to be more **quantitative**, meaning that it sought to numerically quantify trends in audience behaviour, comprehending audiences **statistically** rather than interpretively, and through types of '**experiment**' or **questionnaire data**, rather than by considering audiences in their naturally occurring settings (see the Introduction).

However, it can also be pointed out that this separation of 'qualitative' and 'quantitative' methodologies is never total or final: recent academics still use statistical measures, for example, or combine the two methods (see Tulloch, 2000). Despite this, Television Studies is often – rather simplistically – depicted as a debate between **social-scientific** researchers who 'number-crunch' audiences, and **arts/humanities**-inspired researchers who are interested in audiences' qualitative, interpretive 'readings' of television texts (see Hartley, 1999; Ruddock, 2001; and Chapter 2). Although this representation of audience studies has more than a grain of truth to it – at least it captures the sense that TV and its audiences have been conceptualised within different academic disciplines such as literary theory, psychology, social psychology and sociology – it also tends to falsely turn audience studies into a kind of gladiatorial 'struggle' between scholars who are either labelled 'qualitative' or 'quantitative', and who are then viewed as proponents of 'arts' versus 'social-science' approaches. Just as no one phase in audience research has a monopoly on theoretical virtue or sophistication, so too does no stage have its own single, 'pure' methodology.

EFFECTS

Broadly speaking, much early work on audiences – taking place in the US 'mass communications' tradition – centred on the question of television's '**effects**'. Here, researchers were interested in how television 'affected' its audiences, and so they sought to determine the 'power' of television content to influence viewers. Much of this work was driven by the anxiety that television would have negative effects on people: that it could be used for propaganda purposes, or that representations of violence might corrupt and deprave audiences. Indeed, such work has even been characterised by some TV scholars as occurring within a '"fear" school [of thought which] . . . includes all those from behavioural psychologists to . . . "clean-up-TV" campaigners . . . who believe that television affects its audiences for the worse' (Hartley, 1999: 132).

Effects work has been much criticised by those proposing '**Cultural Studies**' approaches to TV (see Morley, 1992; Ruddock, 2001). Basic charges include the criticism that 'effects' or '**behaviourist**' paradigms deal with TV in artificial settings (Ruddock, 2001: 38), where for example clips from TV programmes may be shown to children or other experimental 'subjects' in a behavioural psychologist's lab. Furthermore, 'effects' work typically assumes that only 'other people', and never researchers or moral campaigners, are likely to be negatively affected by TV (see Gauntlett, 1998: 126).

In other words, effects researchers posited a '**passive audience**', one that was thought to be vulnerable to TV 'messages', almost as if these could be directly 'injected' into viewers' minds (see Chapter 3). Advertising sometimes formed the model for this style of argument: if companies pay vast sums of money to advertise on TV, and devote much time

Pushing products: advertisers clearly believe that TV has a direct effect on its viewers

and effort to this enterprise, then obviously TV *must* directly affect people's behaviour – or so runs the argument. However, choosing to buy a certain product is not at all the same kind of moral action as 'behaving violently' (which may be fully justified in some situations, in any case), nor is it equivalent to thinking about the world in certain political ways. Instead, the notion of being a 'good' consumer is what modern societies are largely geared up to support and maintain. This is a matter of more general cultural values, and it is certainly not simply an 'effect' of TV texts. We hence cannot infer from advertising-based arguments that TV will affect us, or others, either in terms of producing 'copycat' violence, or by influencing our politics via 'propaganda'. One persistent difficulty in 'effects' work is that types of 'pro-social' behaviour (i.e. it is the norm to consume specific products advertised on TV) are used to prop up arguments over TV's promotion of anti-social behaviours. Another recurrent problem has been the impossibility of fully isolating one TV 'message' from the social-cultural context in which it is produced, circulated and interpreted by audiences. And as scholars cannot do this, then it is extremely difficult to state that specific texts will affect an audience in a particular way.

However, like any kind of audience study, effects work can be more or less sophisticated, and this approach has not been entirely superseded by other developments. There are still TV scholars who argue forcefully for the need to consider how television impacts on audiences' understandings of mediated issues and events. Jenny Kitzinger, in a recent (2004) study of how child abuse has been represented in the media, suggests that TV news coverage contributes to public understanding of this matter by repeatedly '**framing**' and '**branding**' news stories in specific ways. Even if audiences actively engage with such TV coverage by drawing on their own personal experience, or by filtering out certain media stories, they are still responding to a specific, and massively reiterated fixing or '**agenda-setting**' of reportage. Kitzinger, on the basis of detailed audience study, thus concludes that rather than 'effects' work needing to be consigned to history, there remains a press-

ing need for '**new influence research**' (2004: 192). This is called for as a way of relating audiences' actions to models of textual/media power, instead of seeing 'audience activity' and 'TV effects' as being opposing terms. Kitzinger's work continues in the tradition of two versions of 'effects' work which emerged in the 1960s and 1970s: George Gerbner's '**cultivation analysis**' (see Gerbner, 1970) and the work of the 'Glasgow School' on TV news. Like Kitzinger's work, cultivation analysis is interested in how patterns in TV coverage and content may, over time, influence people's perceptions. And the Glasgow Media Group (named after its base at Glasgow University), similarly explored and emphasised systematic patterns in news coverage in studies such as *Bad News* (1976; see Jeff Collins, 1992). It was argued that these patterns would impact on, and affect, audiences' interpretations and responses (see Chapter 3).

USES AND GRATIFICATIONS

A major rival to the 'effects' tradition has been work on TV audiences from a '**uses and gratifications**' perspective (see Halloran, 1970). This approach does not stress how TV affects its supposedly 'passive audiences', but begins from the inverse assumption: namely, that audiences *actively* use TV in order to derive specific psychological 'gratifications' such as belonging to a community of viewers, or building up '**cognitive**' knowledge of the world. Like the effects tradition, this too has been critiqued by Cultural Studies scholars, who have alleged that 'uses and gratifications' work is 'insufficiently sociological' (Morley, 1992: 53). It assumes that television audiences can be analysed as purely psychological 'individuals', somehow divorced from their social contexts. Although the way in which 'uses and gratifications' scholarship thinks of audiences as being aggregations of individuals is probably close to how we think about TV audiences in everyday life, its stress on individual psychology somewhat weakens it as a theoretical model. However, this approach also has some strengths – in fact, ironically these are pretty much the same as its difficulties, given that 'uses and gratifications' has the virtue of considering audience members at the level of their individual identities, rather than reducing viewers to a series of category memberships (race/class/gender). We could suggest that sociologies of the audience are, albeit in a different way, as 'reductive' as psychologies of TV viewing. That is, both leave out certain dimensions of the viewing experience and so reduce their model of the TV audience to a one-dimensionally 'social' or 'psychological' portrait.

ENCODING/DECODING

Histories of TV audience research tend to represent the 'third' phase of work – 'encoding/decoding' – as a triumphant progression beyond the artificiality of 'effects' work and the individual-psychology of 'uses and gratifications'. This third phase was ushered in by Stuart Hall's essay 'Encoding and Decoding' (Hall, 1980a; see Gurevitch and Scannell, 2003). Here, Hall argued for the need to consider different types of audience responses to TV texts. He suggested that audiences could 'decode' (i.e. interpret/understand) texts in one of three ways: they could produce '**preferred**' readings which fitted with the meanings 'encoded' or placed into a text; they could entirely reject these intended meanings, and so produce resistant or '**oppositional readings**'; or they could accept certain intended meanings and reject others, thereby producing '**negotiated**' readings. Hall's theoretical model was then applied in a range of audience studies (see Lewis, 1991; Jhally and Lewis, 1992; Morley, 1992; Jancovich, 1992), and it formed a key theoretical component of new audience '**ethnographies**' in the 1980s and 1990s (see also Chapter 3).

Audience 'ethnography' (the term comes from anthropology) meant studying how audiences interpreted and used TV by observing their actual practices in naturally occurring settings, then seeking to relate these practices to questions of cultural power (for good overviews see Moores, 1993; Nightingale, 1996; Brooker and Jermyn, 2003). Ethnographers sought to determine whether audiences were making 'preferred' readings in line with the socially dominant meanings 'encoded' in TV texts, or whether they were 'resisting' these meanings and their ideologies (views of the world favouring those in power)

(see Chapter 3). Abercrombie and Longhurst term this phase of audience research the '**incorporation/resistance paradigm**' (1998:15), since it examines whether audiences are 'incorporated' into dominant cultural norms, or whether they fight back, **semiotically** and metaphorically, against these viewpoints. An emphasis on the **fan cultures** surrounding various TV programmes arose within this type of audience theory (see below). Fans could be analysed as an especially 'resistive' audience, and one which had a tendency to oppose producers' preferred meanings by reading texts in line with its own **subcultural** interests and agendas (see Jenkins, 1992; Hills, 2002).

'Encoding/decoding' work generally suggested, in line with Hall's original (1980a) argument, that audiences didn't have full power over how they could 'decode' texts: they were necessarily constrained by producers' 'encoding' of certain meanings, which they had to take into account. The work of John Fiske (1987 and 1989) became controversial in Television Studies for its apparent neglect of this constraining force, as Fiske developed Hall's interest in different audience interpretations by arguing that the power to make meaning resided more fully on the side of television audiences. Fiske's work was then frequently condemned (as in Morley, 1992: 29) for missing out the 'question of power'. Fiske's extreme version of '**active audience**' theory championed audiences' ability to '**resist**' preferred readings, but it did so by ignoring the issue of who had the power to shape media texts in the first place. Fiske therefore massively underplayed the cultural power of media producers and professionals, who actually have the direct capacity to limit the possible meanings of TV programmes.

It is arguable that Fiske also underplayed the importance of the '**political economy**' of television: who owns and controls media outlets can also powerfully determine the types of content made available to audiences (see Chapter 8). The legacy of anti-Fiske commentaries is that his work has become synonymous with the 'excesses' of 'active audience theory': 'Fiske's work . . . sparked a controversy over the audience's immunity to . . . persuasion'

(Ruddock, 2001: 127). Whereas 'effects' work frequently went too far in its conceptualisation of audiences as 'passive', Fiske seemingly over-compensated by going to the other end of the spectrum, assuming that audiences were all-powerfully 'active'.

Some histories of audience research conclude with Hall's 'encoding/decoding' model (Morley, 1992), as if this is *the* answer to conceptualising TV audiences, but the model is not without its limits. It was formulated, and applied, in relation to TV news programmes (see Tulloch, 2000 and Chapter 10) where structured audience responses were perhaps more clearly discernible. In relation to much other TV output, such as drama and generic fictions, it is rather less clear what might count as 'preferred', 'oppositional' or 'negotiated' readings (Corner, 1999: 87). Here, matters of audience pleasure and generic knowledge are central as well as issues of 'decoding'. In addition to this, Hall's (1980a) three categories of reading were purely hypothetical, but they seemed to become fixed as totems of research in studies of TV audiences. What if types of response could not be readily fixed into these logical categories? And what if an audience member's reading of one text was 'oppositional', while that same audience member read another text in line with the 'preferred' meaning? Simply celebrating isolated acts of audience resistance misses the wider context within which these moments of interpretation occur (see Chapter 3).

AUDIENCES AND MEDIA CULTURE

Recent work on TV audiences has begun to generate a range of new approaches to such questions, and these can be characterised as dealing with television and **'media culture'**. 'Encoding/decoding' work has often taken audiences for specific programmes as its objects of study, meaning that audiences for *Dallas* (CBS, 1978–91) (Ang, 1985) or *The Cosby Show* (NBC, 1984–92) (Jhally and Lewis, 1992), or the long-defunct UK current affairs programme *Nationwide* (BBC, 1969–83) have been studied (Morley, 1980). By focusing on single texts, 'encoding/decoding' has replayed a version of the **'isolating out'** problem which has frequently afflicted effects work. Just as effects researchers assumed they

could isolate specific TV messages and their impacts, so too have Cultural Studies scholars studied discrete texts and their audiences, as if other forms of media consumption can be removed from what is academically framed as a singular text–audience encounter.

Reacting against this, a number of scholars have indicated the need to move towards **multitext** (or more **contextual**) theories of the TV audience. Nick Couldry (2000: 83–4) has argued that scholars need to pay attention to the **'textual environment'** which audiences inhabit, which means considering the whole range of texts that audiences navigate between and through, as well as considering how each audience member may pay close attention to certain texts while **'screening out'** or inattentively viewing others. Although this sounds like a massive task, it does at least mark out a distinctive re-thinking of what Television Studies can mean when it refers to audiences (see Chapter 2). Pertti Alasuutari has similarly noted (1999: 6):

> One does not necessarily abandon ethnographic case studies of audiences or analyses of individual programmes, but the main focus [of a new approach to media culture] is not restricted to finding out about the reception or 'reading' of a particular programme by a particular audience.

In place of this type of work, Alasuutari advocates addressing 'the role of media in everyday life' (ibid.). The focal point of TV audience research shifts significantly in these newer ways of thinking about television. Rather than accepting industry definitions of 'the audience', and so analysing specific audiences for specific TV shows, academics have become increasingly interested in what it means to be part of 'the TV audience' more generally, and how TV viewing in general is thought about and culturally valued/devalued. The diffuse cultural processes through which **audience identities** are adopted are thus deemed to be as important, if not more so, than analyses of watching specific shows. It is the media saturation of society which has provoked such a turn towards studying **'TV culture'**, with both Abercrombie and Longhurst (1998) and S. Elizabeth Bird (2003) pointing out that in today's 'media world' we are constituted as TV audiences almost constantly. Abercrombie and Longhurst also argue that consumers of TV are becoming more **fan-like** in their engagements with texts, since the 'media are becoming more important in social organisation for everybody' (1998: 140). Whereas, in the past, only self-professed fans would have been socially organised as a group on the basis of their 'love' for a specific TV show, TV's cultural predominance implies that more and more consumers – who would not term themselves 'fans' – can now use TV-based knowledges and competences to structure their **social interactions** with others.

Our identity as part of the TV audience now stretches far beyond any specific moment of watching television. When we read consumer magazines, or talk to friends about what we saw on TV last night; when we post to online message boards or study TV at university; when we glance at a newspaper or read a book recommended by Richard and Judy or Oprah; when we download a leaked TV programme before it is even broadcast – all manner of cultural activities presuppose and reactivate our identity as a 'TV' audience. The challenge of studying audiences within 'TV culture' is therefore what confronts scholars at the turn of the cen-

Buffy the Vampire Slayer: researchers have examined its 'textual environments'

tury, and it is one which calls for **transmedia** and **transtextual** research. Television may be culturally important not just for 'quality' shows being hyped each year, nor for the qualities it has as a medium, but rather for the way in which it has begun to saturate the entire cultural field. In this context, 'studying television' and its audiences means, paradoxically, studying publicity and audience responses across the Internet, on the radio, and in magazines, as well as studying the transnational circulation of TV show 'formats' (see Chapter 9). Television is no longer a bounded 'object of study', and nor are its audiences.

What does all this suggest about possible future directions for audience studies? While it is impossible to anticipate exactly what theoretical turns may occur, it seems likely that fewer 'single audience–text' studies will be produced, as researchers seek to map more complex '**textual environments**' rather than isolating audiences for, say, *Buffy the Vampire Slayer* or *Doctor Who* (BBC1, 1963–). It also appears likely that fan studies will become more important within audience theory in general, given that fandom is moving towards the media-cultural 'mainstream' (see the following case study). And finally, it seems that assertions regarding audiences' 'passivity'/'activity' are now more likely to be avoided. Scholars have learnt from the excesses of past perspectives, seeking instead to analyse how TV audiences are always simultaneously 'active' and 'passive', displaying 'constrained cultural creativity' (Bird, 2003: 167; see Moores, 1993: 140).

FURTHER READING

Abercrombie, Nicholas and Longhurst, Brian (1998), *Audiences: A Sociological Theory of Performance and Imagination*, London: Sage.

Brooker, Will and Jermyn, Deborah (eds) (2003), *The Audience Studies Reader*, London and New York: Routledge.

Hall, Stuart (1980a), 'Encoding and Decoding in Television Discourse', CCCS Stencilled Paper no. 7; also in Stuart Hall, Dorothy Hobson, Andrew Lowe and Paul Willis (eds), *Culture, Media, Language,* London: Hutchinson; also in Simon During (ed.) (1993), *The Cultural Studies Reader*, London and New York: Routledge.

Hills, Matt (2002), *Fan Cultures*, London and New York: Routledge.

Machor, James and Goldstein, Philip (eds) (2001), *Reception Study: From Literary Theory to Cultural Studies*, London and New York: Routledge.

Morley, David (1992), *Television, Audiences, and Cultural Studies*, London and New York: Routledge.

Seiter, Ellen (1998), *Television and New Media Audiences*, Oxford: Oxford University Press.

Tulloch, John (2000) *Watching Television Audiences: Cultural Theories and Methods*, London and New York: Arnold.

CASE STUDY
Fandom and Fan Studies Matt Hills

'Fandom' is a form of enquiry that analyses those members of the TV audience known as '**fans**' (an abbreviation of 'fanatics') that appear to have an unusually '*intense*' relationship with television and its texts. A relatively recent area in the field of audience studies, fandom is gradually growing into an academic category (or 'subcategory') in its own right. As such, it is an area that is still clearly in the process of intense debate and intellectual formation. In order therefore to understand how '**fan studies**' is beginning to shed light on this particular type of audience it is important that the student first understand fandom's historical origins and gradual academic development.

PERFORMING AUDIENCES

Recent work on media audiences has sought to carve the field of research into distinct phases; for instance, John Tulloch's (2000) discussion of TV audiences draws on Pertti Alasuutari's (1999) definition of '**third-generation**' audience research, that is, research that does not focus on audiences as naturally occurring, but treats being an audience member as a cultural performance of identity. A similar map of audience research occurs in Nicholas Abercrombie and Brian Longhurst's (1998) book *Audiences*, which also separates the history of audience studies into phases such as the '**incorporation/resistance paradigm**' and the '**spectacle/performance paradigm**'. The former phase is concerned, in part, with whether audiences or media producers possess cultural power, and whether or not fans are able to 'resist' dominant media messages, while the latter sets aside issues of cultural power in favour of considering **fans-as-performers** operating within a media-saturated culture.

Abercrombie and Longhurst (1998) argue for a move towards thinking about audiences not just as present in front of the TV screen, but rather as **performing** their audience identities in a multitude of

ways diffused throughout everyday life – in talk, through wearing branded T-shirts or collecting DVDs, or by displaying knowledge of TV texts (see Lancaster [2001] for a related emphasis on 'fan performance' and Gauntlett and Hill, 1999: 149–52 on video collecting). In this perspective, it makes no sense to distinguish between TV and everyday life; TV is a constitutive part of everydayness (see Bird, 2003).

We can use these categories, or stories about broader audience research, to make sense of the appearance and development of fan studies. Given that its seminal academic works – Henry Jenkins' *Textual Poachers*, Camille Bacon-Smith's *Enterprising Women* and Lisa A. Lewis's edited collection, *The Adoring Audience* – were all published in 1992, fan studies as a distinctive subset of audience research is a relative newcomer on the academic scene. Pioneering studies such as Jenkins (1992) and Bacon-Smith (1992) seem caught on the cusp of a move into Alasuutari's 'third-generation' audience research (1999), or balanced on the dividing line between Abercrombie and Longhurst's 'incorporation/resistance' and 'spectacle/performance' paradigms. That is, both Jenkins and Bacon-Smith are concerned with issues of cultural power (the incorporation/resistance model in Abercrombie and Longhurst's parlance), but both also address fandom *as a type of performance*. For example, Jenkins focuses on fandom as an interpretive community with rules over how favoured TV shows should be appreciated (1992: 88–9), while Bacon-Smith analyses how female *Star Trek* fan communities use the 'mask of play' to shelter their serious, culture-building activities from critique (1992: 289; see also Bloustien, 2002 and 2004 on the 'serious play' of *Buffy the Vampire Slayer* fans).

As Garry Crawford has argued: 'the work of [Michel] de Certeau [1988], and in particular its application by Jenkins (1992) is far more subtle than

[Abercrombie and Longhurst's] . . . paradigm model allows' (2004: 139). Crawford goes on to spell out the way that Henry Jenkins' work considers (ibid.):

> how audiences draw on media resources to fuel their own production and performances, blurring the distinction between performer and audience. For instance, Jenkins (1992) suggests that fans are often dissatisfied with the character or story progressions of some cult media shows, or frustrated at the limited number of episodes or stories 'officially' produced. Hence, fans will 'poach' storylines or characters from these texts and produce their own narratives. These may take the form of stories, pictures, songs . . . for their own consumption, but also may create new texts to be publicly consumed by publishing these in fanzines.

Beyond this 'blurring' of audience/performer categories, more recent work on fans has stressed how they may go on to become professional (and thus 'official') producers of the show that they love (see McKee, 2004). And fans may also 'poach' – again, take selected meanings from – 'official' media theory as well as 'official' media texts (Hills, 2004b). Media fandom should be viewed with some caution, then. Its many different types of audience activity sometimes make it difficult to pin down, but these same problems also make it especially intriguing to study, and guarantee that fan studies' debates will roll on.

WHAT IS A FAN?

One of the fundamental problems that fan studies had to face in its academic development was the issue of what actually constitutes a 'fan'. When does somebody who enjoys watching a TV show move from being a viewer to being a 'fan'? What activities and practices can be taken to characterise media fandom?

Indeed, what I have elsewhere called media fandom's 'essentially contradictory' nature (Hills, 2002: 182) manifests itself in attempts at defining 'television fandom'. Despite the fact that both Jenkins (1992) and Bacon-Smith (1992) include the terms 'television fans' and 'television fandom' in the subti-

tles of their respective (1992) studies, the specificity of these fandoms immediately begins to recede. Jenkins notes that the type of cult media fans in his study are 'an amorphous but still identifiable grouping of enthusiasts of film and television which calls itself "media fandom"' (1992: 1), while Bacon-Smith similarly observes that the fans in her study tend to focus on 'their favourite television and movie characters' (1992: 3). The boundary around one medium – and thus around studying television through studying its fan audiences – begins to dissolve from the outset.

Defining fans as purely consuming TV fails to capture issues of transmedia consumption. Fans are likely to read specialist magazines about their favoured TV programmes (see Hills, 2004a) or to consume cult films alongside cult TV. Furthermore, we need to remember that as an 'object' of study, something called 'television' itself has rather porous boundaries (see the Introduction). Narratives 'in' TV shows are now increasingly extended or developed in other related media such as licensed novels, audio adventures, or on the web (see Chapter 10). It is this **'transmediality'** that has been explored by writers such as Janet H. Murray (1997), John Thornton Caldwell (2002 and 2003) and Will Brooker (2003), who has coined the phrase **'overflow'** to describe the phenomenon whereby TV narratives are supplemented with online material. Although fans may self-identify as liking a specific TV programme such as *Doctor Who*, or *Buffy the Vampire Slayer*, the televised text can be seen as the tip of a metatextual

Doctor Who: a serious and dedicated fan base

iceberg, or as the leading, canonical object within a surrounding series of 'more or less canonical texts' (McKee, 2004: 182) that are non-televised. The shifting boundaries around any 'TV text' thus need to be highlighted, as they are in Jonathan Gray's (2003) work. Gray argues that fans are often very much akin to academic readers, treating the TV text as a whole that has to be very closely watched for its minute details (ibid.: 70):

> As faithful viewers who know what happened last week and many weeks before, who likely shush those who interrupt a programme and/or who record it for subsequent (repeat?) viewings, and – simply – who watch the whole show, fans experience a proximity as close (if not closer) to the producer's text . . . as any researcher.

However, the image of the **fan-as-close-reader** masks the fact that television's fan audiences may well count themselves as 'fans' and yet still occasionally miss episodes in a series, or choose not to follow tie-in series of novels, or decide not to read official tie-in magazines, nor participate in online fan discussion. Alternatively, self-proclaimed fans may stop watching 'their' show entirely, while still appreciating – and being extremely knowledgeable about – its earlier seasons. Thus, no absolutely common meta-text, or even TV text, can be assumed for all self-identified 'fans' of a particular show (see also Sandvoss, forthcoming). As Gray says (2003: 68):

> What . . . is wrong with fan studies? Or, rather . . . what important issues, audiences and textualities are hiding in its shadows? . . . [L]et us focus on television, for while books and movies may at least ask for a more fan-like proximity with the text, television offers multiple viewing positions and distances. . . . [Fixed] reader positions may make perfect sense when the text being reacted to is the same (the finished book or film), but television offers the added complication of partly . . . read texts.

Television is characterised here as an 'unfinished' medium, being rendered so by its **'segmented flow'** or by its continuing 'working through' of issues within serialised texts (Ellis, 1982 and 2000: 79; Chapter 1). By stressing different proximities and distances taken up by different (fan) audiences – with some fans being completists and others missing occasional TV episodes or choosing not to engage with non-televised texts that they construe as non-canonical – Gray's work refuses to conceptualise TV as something that *has* to be watched either distractedly or concentratedly by its audiences (this is what has been termed the **glance/gaze debate** in Television Studies: Caldwell 1995: 25; Chapter 1). Although fans may generally tend to be close readers, it cannot always be taken for granted that they will be absolutely completist readers of all the associated texts circulating around a TV show. A subset of fans may be definable as 'TV fans' per se – valuing the TV text as the only 'true' and 'official' incarnation of a narrative – but this identification requires academics to study the precise range of texts that fans actually consume, something that fan studies has not tended to achieve to date. Many of its key works have typically assumed from the outset that there is a shared community and identity (and an absolutely shared series of texts) that constitutes, say, *Star Trek* (NBC, 1966–9) fandom or *Doctor Who* fandom (e.g. Tulloch and Jenkins, 1995). Countering such assumptions, Jonathan Bignell has recently pointed out that (2004: 291):

> For example, among *Doctor Who* fans some regard the original BBC television serials as 'genuine' *Doctor Who*, and perhaps also the paperback novels authorised by the BBC, but not spin-off merchandising products . . . or the two cinema films . . . produced at the height of the series' popularity. Even among fans who regard the BBC *Doctor Who* episodes as 'genuine', there are fans who regard some of these stories as not 'genuine' . . . Since television programmes are not coherent texts, it is possible to draw boundaries around episodes and groups of episodes that fans wish to include in or reject from the corpus.

These differential boundary-drawing exercises carried out by different factions of fans can be further complicated by the re-issuing of TV episodes on

DVD, where variant versions of texts can be created, and where DVD extras can introduce 'deleted' or previously untelevised scenes. Staying with the example of *Doctor Who*, the story 'Curse of Fenric' exists in two different forms on DVD – as broadcast, and with deleted scenes edited back in. And other *Doctor Who* DVD releases such as 'Ark in Space', 'Dalek Invasion of Earth' and 'Earthshock' include CGI-enhanced scenes which can be dropped into the version to be viewed (this was also the case for 'enhanced' episodes of the BBC's sci-fi-comedy series *Red Dwarf* [BBC2, 1988–97]). Rather like many film releases on DVD, TV shows can now take on an extended cultural afterlife through the creation of 'alternative' versions. And fans can also watch episodes of their favourite TV shows complete with audio commentaries from writers, producers, and assorted auteur figures as well as actors, altering the experience of the programme concerned, and allowing its creators a chance to 'anchor' specific meanings or to reinforce their own 'intended' interpretations. In his (2002b) online article 'Emotional Resonance and Rocket Launchers': Joss Whedon's Commentaries on the *Buffy the Vampire Slayer* DVDs', David Lavery emphasises the seeming co-presence of audience and media producer that DVD commentaries can engender (Lavery, 2002b):

> On the DVDs *Whedon talks in real time accompanying the pilot*, and in the process we learn a great deal about the realities – technical and economic limitations, on-set exigencies, ambitions and frustrations, actor proclivities – of television production. Whedon was making television for the first time and had much to learn about the process, and *thanks to . . . DVD we learn along with him* (emphasis in the original).

The emergence of DVD audio commentaries also blurs academic concepts of '**primary**' and '**secondary**' texts (i.e. 'the TV texts themselves' and surrounding commentaries/forms of publicity: see Fiske 1987: 84–5). This blurring can lead to another set of questions as to exactly where the boundaries are around 'the TV text'. As M. Keith Booker has commented: 'the development of new recording technologies [video and latterly DVD] introduces further complications, allowing television series to be viewed in a number of different ways, calling into question the very definition of the artifact under consideration' (2002: 21).

DIFFERENT TYPES OF FANDOM

John Fiske has examined 'the relationship . . . of the fan to the more "normal" audience member', suggesting that 'the fan is an "excessive reader" who differs from the "ordinary" one in degree rather than kind' (1992b: 46). This slightly curious manoeuvre is possibly intended to stress how fandom cannot be entirely opposed to non-fan/'ordinary' TV viewers, but unfortunately Fiske leaves the impression that there is something inherently 'extra-ordinary' or abnormal about fan activities (see Jensen, 1992). Still, Fiske's aim is to define what is distinctive about being a 'fan'; he achieves this by relating fandom to forms of productivity, arguing that unlike 'ordinary' audiences, fans do not only make meanings from texts ('**semiotic productivity**'), they also make subculturally shared meanings ('**enunciative productivity**') and textual meanings of their own ('**textual productivity**' such as writing for fanzines: see Fiske, 1992a: 37–9). Fans' 'textual productivity' can extend to writing reviews of episodes, and compiling episode guides to an entire series, or even writing their own fan fiction or '**fanfic**' – original stories based around characters and events from the TV text. Some fans write what is called '**slash fiction**'; this particular type of fan 'poaching' (making new, selective meanings from the original TV series) involves rewriting male characters from a favoured show so that they are depicted in a romantic relationship. The term 'slash' comes from the way that male pairings are referred to, e.g. 'Kirk/Spock'.

Fiske also stresses the knowledge that fans accumulate, using the term '**popular cultural capital**' (1992b: 39) to describe how fans are highly literate and educated in relation to their favoured texts (for a further examination of fan distinctiveness using the term '**subcultural capital**', see Thornton, 1995: 11; and for an overview of this style of fan studies' work based on the oeuvre of French sociologist Pierre Bourdieu, see Hills, 2002: 50–8). Early studies of dedicated soap audiences, effectively fan studies *avant la lettre* (Hobson, 1982; Ang, 1985), also emphasised the knowledge that loyal soap viewers brought to watching their favourite shows.

A series of contrasts between 'fans' and 'ordinary viewers' has, then, tended to structure Television Studies' definitions of fandom (see McKee, 2002: 68). Indeed, Garry Crawford has argued that the distinction between excessive/ordinary consumption can also be mapped onto **types of fandom**, with academics tending to champion more extreme, spectacular types of fan practice, while excluding from discussion the more mundane, everyday aspects of fandom (Crawford, 2004: 105):

Studies of fan cultures tend to focus upon the 'exceptional' rather than the 'mundane'. This has been true for most studies of media fan culture/ For instance, . . . Jenkins (1992) . . . focuses primarily upon the activities and interests of the most dedicated and 'serious' of audiences . . . This has also been apparent within the majority of discussions of sports fans, and in . . . British sport research, which has tended to focus . . . on 'exceptional'. . . or the most 'dedicated'. . . types of supporters [hooligans or fanzine editors] at the expense of more 'ordinary' fans.

Crawford suggests that this 'oversight' – equally present in work on TV sports fans and cult TV fans – has to do with the ease with which 'exceptional' fans can be recruited to take part in research projects,

Star Trek produced its own 'interpretive community'

meaning that 'issues of access' lead researchers to focus on more dedicated fans (Crawford, 2004: 105–6; see also Gray 2003: 76–7). This type of distinction between forms of TV fandom has also been addressed in Jostein Gripsrud's work. Gripsrud distinguishes between '"proper" fandom in relation to TV programs', where 'an enthusiasm for some cultural object . . . takes on . . . a totalizing, defining role in people's lifestyles and identities' and 'forms and degrees of viewer appreciation and devotion which do . . . not necessarily merit the tag . . . "fandom"' (2002: 119). Gripsrud concludes that 'proper' fandom, such as that surrounding *Star Trek*, is more serious in its outlook and enthusiasm (although it may well be playful on occasions), whereas '[o]ther shows may have produced similar phenomena, but for shorter times and possibly also with more irony and less serious devotion than in the *Star Trek* case' (ibid. – Gripsrud's example of an 'ironic' fandom is that attached to US soap *Dynasty* [ABC, 1981–9]).

Lyn Thomas, in her study of *Inspector Morse* (ITV, 1987–2000) fans, similarly argues that some viewers are '**mainstream fans**', sharing the values of the TV show and exhibiting an 'absence of irony' (2002: 89, 101), while other audiences display a 'feminist critique' of the show and 'develop . . . an ironic mode of talk' about it (ibid.: 101). Although this could potentially lead to an awkward equation between 'mainstream' fandom and 'incorporated'/dominant readings that accept *Inspector Morse*'s ideologies of gender and Englishness (versus 'subversive' readings equated with feminist fans), Thomas doesn't ultimately suggest that any one type of fandom – non-ironic or ironic – is more 'authentic' than the other. Her work thus resonates with recent tendencies in fan studies (witnessed in books such as Hills, 2002: xii on cult media fans and Crawford, 2004: 32 on sports fans) to avoid dividing fandom into fixed categories such as 'good, resistant, **active audiences**' or 'bad, passive **cultural dupes**'.

Work in Television Studies has therefore consistently stressed the distinctiveness of media fandom (Jenkins, 1992 and Fiske, 1992a), explored different types of fandom (Hills, 2002; Thomas, 2002) and even considered the different stages of 'becoming a fan' (Harrington and Bielby, 1995; Crawford, 2004: 42–51). Also, given the passionate and engaged nature of almost all fan activities (this being particularly evident in Gripsrud's 'proper' fandom) fans are one type of audience where **psychoanalytic theory** has begun to prove useful in understanding affective/emotional relationships with media texts. Psychoanalysis has allowed theorists to shed light on the ways in which some fan audiences retain an object of fandom from childhood, carrying this through into their adult lives (see Harrington and Bielby, 1995; Hills, 2002).

Through such methodological and theoretical diversity, fixed categories of fandom have become increasingly fluid, nuanced and differentiated, although some may want to suggest that this process has stretched the term 'fan' almost to breaking point, giving it a bewildering variety of different reference points. I view this movement positively, as it is now common for academic writers to stress that there is no 'one' version of what it means to be a fan (see Hills, 2002). It is also now more likely to be the case that academic work refutes simplistic analyses of **fan agency** (or simplistic analyses of fans' commercial exploitation), meaning that Simone Murray's suggestion that 'scholarly study of media fandom is out of touch with the contemporary lineaments of the phenomenon it seeks to analyse' (2004: 21) is highly questionable. Instead of an easy valorisation of fan activities, fan identity has recently been seen as context- and situation-specific: 'Fandom is never . . . a neutral "expression" or a singular "referent"; its status and its performance shift across cultural sites' (Hills, 2002: xii). Garry Crawford fleshes out this claim when he notes how (2004: 20):

[A] particular follower of a sport may consider themselves a 'fan', but their pattern of support (for instance, they may not attend 'live' games [watching only televised matches]) may see them deemed as not a 'real' fan by other supporters. However, in the company of others who have little or no interest in sport [such as watching TV with their family], this individual's interest may see them viewed as a 'true' and 'dedicated' fan.

THE FUTURE OF FAN STUDIES

In passing, I have already picked out a number of strands and developments in fan studies, particularly the move towards an emphasis on fandom and theories of identity 'performance' or **performance studies** (Lancaster, 2001; Hills, 2002; Crawford, 2004). There has also been a revitalisation of work on fans' **'serious play'** (Bloustien, 2002 and 2004). And Jonathan Gray (2003) has pushed theorists to study **'anti-fans'** (those who detest certain TV programmes) as well as fans. The field of fan studies would currently seem to be in a healthy state of growth and innovation, especially as writers are now returning to the key works of the 1990s with fresh eyes (Hills, 2002; Sandvoss, forthcoming).

Recent writings have also suggested that fandom itself may be becoming increasingly 'mainstreamed' (e.g. Pullen, 2004: 80), with the rise of the Internet meaning that it is now easier for new fandoms to form, for fans to find like-minded audience members, and even for media corporations to attempt to generate fans for a TV show prior to its broadcast (see Chapter 10). If this is so, and fandom is in the process of 'moving from cult status towards the cultural mainstream' (Jenkins, 2002: 161), then we can only expect fan studies to become a more important wing of Television Studies (and beyond). And perhaps the now-classic distinction between 'fan' and 'ordinary' audiences that marked the emergence of academic work on fandom (Jenkins, 1992; Fiske, 1992a) will start to make less sense and appear even less clear cut.

7 Television and History

Investigating the Past

Jason Jacobs

The past and history are not stitched into each other such that only one historical reading of the past is necessary. The past and history float free of each other, they are ages and miles apart. For the same object of enquiry can be read differently by different discursive practices (a landscape can be read/interpreted differently by geographers, sociologists, historians, artists, economists, etc.) whilst, internal to each, there are different interpretative readings over time and space. . . .

Keith Jenkins, *Re-Thinking History*, 1991: 5.

History is the study of continuity and change. As Keith Thomas has observed, 'Those who study the past usually find themselves arriving at two contradictory conclusions. The first is that the past was very different from the present. The second is that it was very much the same' (Thomas, 1992: 10). For example, there were no reality game shows in the 1950s but there were many game shows such as *Double Your Money* (ITV, 1955–68) that involved ordinary people as contestants (see Schwartz, *et al*. 1999). Similarly, there were many single plays in the past whereas now we have many more TV drama serials – the form is different, but the reliance on discrete fictional narrative remains much the same (see Creeber, 2004c). By investigating how television changed in the past and how it remained the same we can grasp why the present **television ecology** is the way it is; understanding the past is a crucial aspect of understanding the present.

Since history is always written from the present it is likely that the contemporary concerns of the historian will colour their approach. For example,

Asa Briggs' study of the history of the BBC was very much concerned with **managerial policy** and its relationship to government (Briggs, 1979); whereas the essays collected in *Popular Television in Britain* (Corner, 1991) demonstrate the interests of Cultural and Media Studies in the early 1990s, and its concern with **cultural** and **textual** matters. So while Briggs is interested in the BBC's policy on measuring audiences in the 1950s, Tim O'Sullivan's essay in *Popular Television in Britain* is concerned with the memories of actual audience members during the same time (O'Sullivan, 1991).

The moon landing: it is estimated that 465 million people watched it live on television

The television historian should also note that television has emerged over the past half-century as the one of the most important means by which people derive their information and leisure in the contemporary world. The history of television, then, is clearly a crucial element in the wider history of how society communicates with itself. As such, the historical study of television is also inevitably tied up in the **social history** of modern society. As Michelle Hilmes puts it (2003: vii):

> Television often serves both as our window onto the past and as an artefact of past events: are programmes, images, and representations to be treated as historical evidence, as transparent (or semi-transparent) traces of the past? Do the paranoid sci-fi dramas of the 1990s, for instance, reflect something salient about our culture during that period? If so, then television history becomes a kind of social history, less important in itself than for the social trends it channels.

It is also important to recognise that television now plays an influential role in the cultural formation of society. For example, many would agree that the first moon landing in 1969 was an important historical event. However, the huge role television played in its coverage (it is estimated that its audience was around 465 million [see Edgerton, 2004: 135]) reveals that TV did not just reflect this piece of history, but also played a significant role in shaping its global presentation and reception. As this suggests, television history is not simply the history of a single medium but also part of the history of the society that is watching and consuming it.

WHAT IS TV HISTORY?

From the beginnings of experimental television in the 1920s, articles, pamphlets, books and papers have been written about its development. Television history starts with the imagining of television during this **experimental phase**. One of the earliest books is Alfred Dinsdale's *Television* published in 1928, eight years before the first scheduled television programmes were broadcast by the BBC. Dinsdale considers the various television technologies available at the time and ends his book with a confident optimism that predicts 3D colour television (Dinsdale, 1928: 179–80):

> Today we sit at home, turn a dial, and listen to speech, music, and native sounds from far-distant lands. Tomorrow we shall, by an equally simple action, be able to bring into our homes not only the sounds but also the sights of these lands, faithfully reproduced in their natural colours. Add to this the ability to witness these scenes in stereoscopic relief, and we may well rub our eyes and wonder if we have not, by some form of magic, been personally transported right into the very midst of the scenes which we shall see on the screen of our stereoscopic colour televisor, and the sounds of which we shall simultaneously hear through the medium of our loud speaker.

While Dinsdale does not mention surround sound and rather overestimates the appeal of 3D, this is a reasonably accurate prediction of the contemporary home theatre. At the same time, television itself has charted the history of the medium with typical narcissistic fascination with reruns, anniversary celebrations and special nostalgia programming. Only recently has the academic study of television history begun to expand rapidly, but the **popular history** of television, both written and broadcast has been a constant feature since the beginning of the medium.

While the popular history of television is important, the most respected accounts of television history tend to situate it as part of a wider account of broadcasting history or, indeed, media history (Curran and Seaton, 1997). Some scholars, notably Paddy Scannell, object even to the idea of a discrete 'television history' that can be neatly separated from broadcasting overall (Scannell and Cardiff, 1991). As television has been produced by organisations that were also responsible for making and transmitting radio programmes (such as the BBC or NBC), this does make some sense. However, since television has arguably come to dominate the **broadcasting industry** and is a medium that is sufficiently distinct from radio there is little problem in treating it as deserving of a history in its own right, while acknowledging the broadcasting contexts within which it operated.

Asa Briggs and Eric Barnouw are scholars of *broadcasting* history and their monumental multi-volume works on British and American broadcasting respectively are vital to the television historian who wishes to understand the industrial and policy-making mechanisms of the medium as well as its involvement in social, cultural and **political structures** (see Chapter 8). Briggs' *History of Broadcasting in the United Kingdom* is a five-volume work of scholarship that covers broadcasting history from the beginning of radio to the early 1980s (Briggs, 1961, 1965, 1970, 1979, 1995). Barnouw's three volumes cover the institutional history of US broadcasting from the pre-history of radio in the nineteenth century to the 1970s (Barnouw, 1966, 1968, 1970, 1975). While Briggs mostly concentrates on the BBC, Sendall and Potter have painstakingly researched the history of ITV (the first British commercial channel) in four volumes (Sendall, 1982, 1983; Potter, 1989, 1990); there is also a history of the most recent British terrestrial channel, Five (Fanthome, 2003).

These books, while enjoyable to read, are really reference books for the professional historian. A shorter and more accessible history of British television and broadcasting can be found in volumes like Andrew Crisell's *An Introductory History of British Broadcasting* (1997). In addition, a book like the BFI's recent collection, *The Television History Book* considers the key aspects of television history in the US and the UK (Hilmes, 2003).

Television historians have also gone back to look at particular moments or decades that have been seen as central to television history. For example, 1950s' and 1960s' television can be looked at from a number of different historical angles. William Boddy's book, *Fifties Television: The Industry and Its Critics* (1990) is a detailed account of the development of the US networks, and the policy and regulatory frameworks that shaped them (see Chapter 8). Meanwhile, Christopher Anderson's *Hollywood TV: The Studio System in the Fifties* (1994)

is an account of the relationship between the networks and Hollywood film, an important revision of the assumption that the two mediums where hostile to one another during this period. Other histories are interested in the relationship between television and the wider culture. For example, Lynn Spigel's work on 1960s' television demonstrates how particular television shows segued with wider cultural assumptions and resonance, such as space travel and the move to the suburbs (Spigel and Curtin, 1997; Spigel, 2001). Of course, there are also studies of programmes and **genres** such as David Marc's excellent account of the development of the US sitcom, *Comic Visions* (1997), Toby Miller's account of the reception and production of *The Avengers* (1998) and Lez Cooke's *British Television Drama: A History* (2003).

While this is only the tip of the iceberg, in regard to the scholarly publications on television history, it is important to remember that there are journal articles and book chapters that can also contribute to our understanding. For example, Roger Sales' little-known, 'An Introduction to Broadcasting History' (1986) is a polemical and witty exploration of the origins and practice of British public service broadcasting and one of the finest examples of historical writing in the field. There are also a number of essays in journals such as the *Historical Journal of Film, Radio and Television*, *Media, Culture and Society*, *Media History* and *Screen* that offer astute and well-researched accounts of particular moments and programmes in television history.

Outside academic publishing there are many books that also provide useful resources for the television historian. For example, Denis Norden's collection of **historical reminiscences** about early British television, *Coming to You Live! Behind-the-screen Memories of Forties and Fifties Television* (1985) contains material and opinions that are likely to be overlooked in serious 'official' accounts, while *Mrs Slocombe's Pussy: Growing Up in Front of the Telly* (Jeffries, 2001) is an account of the writer's memories of television in his childhood. There are also accounts by those who worked in television such as Peter Graham Scott's *British Television: An Insider's*

History (2000), Don Taylor's *Days of Vision: Working with David Mercer: Television Drama Then and Now* (1990) and David Attenborough's autobiography, *Life on Air: Memoirs of a Broadcaster* (2003).

Television criticism and **reviews** written at the time are obviously useful in providing a sense of the contemporary response to programmes that are lost and forgotten. Some reviews have been collected, most famously Clive James's work for *The Observer* (1977, 1981 and 1983), and also Philip Purser's account of his life as a TV reviewer in *Done Viewing* (1992). There are also several **non-academic** books that offer entertaining and well-illustrated accounts of television history both national and international such as Francis Wheen's accompaniment to the television series, *Television: A History* and a number of books for and about fans of 'cult TV' (Wheen and Fiddick, 1985; Lewis and Stempel, 1993). Tisa Vahimagi's *British Television: An Illustrated Guide* (1996) is a fine reference book for the serious as well as the casual reader. More scholarly, and with the advantage of including much of world television is the three-volume *Encyclopedia of Television* written by scholars from around the world (Newcomb, 1997).

However, written accounts can help the historian only so far. It is worth remembering that **TV tie-in merchandise** is not a recent phenomena but stretches back to the 1950s (as the film *Toy Story 2* [Lasseter, 1999] usefully illustrates). There is a huge range of television ephemera that can inform our understanding of how television impacted on the wider culture. These include such items as toys and tie-ins, television annuals and handbooks, annual reports, government reports, promotional, sales and PR material that is often difficult to find. In that respect, since the mid-1990s the **Internet** has become increasingly valuable as a research resource for television historians. Not only is it possible to locate this ephemera, but fans and others have produced websites that list episode guides, accounts of early television and databases that allow us to trace a single actor throughout their entire career in television. While the resources on the Internet are prone to unreliability and partiality, they can also provide

valuable information that is not conveniently collected elsewhere (see, for example, www. tvhistory.tv).

Last, but not at all least, there is television itself. **Nostalgic retrospectives** such as 'TV Heaven' (Channel 4, 1992), 'Cops on the Box' (BBC2, 1993) and 'Docs on the Box' (BBC2, 1996) offer an evening's viewing of archival material often with commentary and documentary interviews with the original actors, directors and writers. These broadcasts represent television's continuing interest in historicising itself, an attempt to invent what we might call television's traditions.

HOW TO STUDY TV HISTORY

As this suggests, there are a number of academic approaches one could take to television history, but we might start by looking at Robert Allen and Douglas Gomery's book *Film History: Theory and Practice* (1985), where they outline the following kinds of film history: aesthetic, technological, economic and social. Television history concerned with the **aesthetic** dimensions would use the programmes themselves as primary evidence, perhaps situating them within generic traditions and creative environments (see Chapter 1). A **technological** history would be more concerned with the impact of, say, videotape on the primarily live production techniques of the 1950s, or the way in which colour television was developed as part of the competitive struggle between the US networks. An **economic** history might be concerned with the effects of commercial television on public service broadcasting, or the way in which the high cost of sports coverage has transformed both the television and sporting industries (see Chapter 8). Meanwhile, a **social** history might be more concerned with audience and critical reception (see Chapter 6).

However, in practice, television historians tend to be more '**holistic**' and these apparent divisions between approaches are rarely policed. For example, Morley and Brunsdon's accounts of the *Nationwide* (BBC, 1969–83) magazine/news programme combined audience research with an astute account of the textual strategies deployed by the show, as well as a fine grasp of the institution that funded it (Morley and Brunsdon 1999) (see Chapter 2). Creeber (1998) offers a fine account of the thematic aspects of Dennis Potter's television drama, but takes care to locate these within cultural and institutional frameworks (see Chapter 5); Caldwell (1995) privileges the development of the television image in his history of 'televisuality' but nonetheless situates this within a detailed cultural and technological history (see Chapter 1).

Apart from reading the considerable literature cited above there are a number of ways to find out about television history. There are various national archives open to the public and researchers such as the BBC Written Archives Centre, the National Film Archive and the Museum of Television and Radio (located in New York and Los Angeles). However, it is increasingly the case that old television programmes are finding their way to DVD and video, for example The Prisoner (ITV, 1967–8) and Pennies from Heaven, the latter with a commentary from the producer Kenith Trodd. These developments are a boon for television historians who used to have to visit audiovisual archives in order to see such treasures. Having access to these texts allows us to study in detail the history of gesture, acting, of camera technique, of creative aspiration, of décor design, fashion, cultural attitudes, narrative and genre (see Chapter 2).

However, there are always problems associated with historical evaluations of the past. For example, a common issue is that of selectivity. How do we decide what information is relevant to our enquiry? Since history can encompass everything from conversation to large-scale structural changes we need some means to decide the mediating connections between each. If we are studying an individual programme it is always useful to provide an overall context, but the danger is that the context threatens to swamp the particularity of the programme itself. Equally, an account of an overall television industry may pass over aspects of programming that were crucial to the identity of the channel or industry under investigation. As always, relevance is a matter of judgment, but this is not a subjective matter. The aspiration to objectivity and truth should be uppermost in the historian's mind even as he/she acknowledges that total objectivity is impossible to attain (see Jenkins, 1991).

The difficulties over the claims of historical truth and objectivity are suitably made explicit in the invention of television itself. Although John Logie Baird is often cited as the sole inventor of the medium, there is a complex and controversial history behind this apparently simple historical claim. Depending on which account you believe, television seems to have been invented by a number of different people and nationalities (including Russian, Japanese, American, French, Hungarian and German). Just some of the leading contenders are Vladimir Kosma Zworykin, Paul Gottlieb, D. Von Mihaly, Charles Francis Jenkins, Édouard Belin (with Fernand Holweck and Gregory N. Oglobinsky), Kenjiro Takayanagi, Alexander Dauvillier and Philo T. Farnsworth (see Smith, 1995: 13–34). As the race to patent television was so intense, conspiracy theories abound about dirty tricks and unfair practices that apparently excluded some from gaining their rightful place in the history books. As Brian Winston points out, Baird had a flair for public relations (or 'publicity stunts' [2003: 11]), that may have gone a long way to securing his historical status. Consequently, the invention of television provides us with a good example of how the complexity of the past is often transformed and simplified by written historical accounts (see below). As Ian Sinclair puts it in The Birth of the Box: The Story of Television (1995):

The people whose work has contributed most to modern technology are virtually unknown. No-one could claim to have contributed more to television and to Hi-Fi sound than A. D. Blumlein, for example, but how many of those who enjoy the fruits of his work as embedded in our TV receivers and our stereo systems have ever heard of his name? Would you immediately name A. A. Campbell Swinton as the father of television as we know it? Are Paul Nipkow and Boris Rosing as familiar as the man who drew publicity to their work, John Logie Baird?

John Logie Baird: was he really the sole inventor of television?

Apart from the debates over its invention, there are other problems that are specific to the study of television. One major issue, particularly for those interested in television from the 1930s to the 1970s, is the absence of many programmes. Archival holdings of audiovisual material are not continuous or representative. In part this is a product of the technical limitations of television in the 1930s. There was no reliable or standardised means of recording television and it was not until after World War II that the US navy developed a means of recording live television pictures on film. Even then, very few programmes were recorded, since very few acknowledged that they might be of interest at a future date (see the Introduction). As noted above, for many in the industry, television's primary distinction as a medium was its **immediacy**, its **liveness**. Those

programmes that were recorded were done so for expediency rather than posterity, with many US programmes filmed in order to ship them to the different time zones in the North American continent. In the UK this was not necessary; but there were difficulties with the artistic unions which meant that recording was rare before 1955 (Bryant, 1989). Indeed, what does survive in the archives is not necessarily representative of what was popular or 'good' – the danger here is that television history gets reconstructed around what survives for viewing rather than what was actually shown. **Archival policy** often privileged news, drama and current affairs before other 'trivial' programming. But, taking the 1990s as an example, arguably the biggest changes and innovation in television were in the so-called 'popular' genres of reality television and daytime programming (see Bonner, 2003).

How can we approach programmes that no longer exist? How does one, for example, gain an insight into what television programming looked like in the 1930s? Jacobs tackled this problem by 'reconstructing' early British TV dramas (now missing) from programme files, scripts, shooting scripts and other contextual information such as press reviews and anecdotes (2000). This method of exploring the discursive 'thickness' of contextual material can be applied to other missing programmes as well. Another problem is the reliability of second-hand sources, where memories and anecdotes can be exaggerated or misremembered. Similarly the **political perspective** of the historian may colour the kinds of research they are drawn to. There has, for example, been a lot written about the 'golden age' of British television drama (in particular the work of Ken Loach and Tony Garnett), largely because of the interest of their work in **social realism** and political relevance – something that some Cultural Studies academics find attractive (see, for example, Caughie, 2000). However, the actual contribution of this type of drama to the overall output of television in the 1960s was relatively small (see Chapter 5).

The final problem is not that there are too few programmes remaining but that there may be too many. How can one reliably consider *Top of the Pops*

Cathy Come Home: have historians prioritised certain TV genres?

(BBC) with its weekly episodes dating from 1964 or *News at Ten* (ITV) dating from 1967? In the same way, writing about the sitcom genre or police genre would require a lifetime of viewing in order to be comprehensive. Does the historian have to consider all of this programming, or can we isolate moments and trends? Here, the constant issue of selectivity and judgment is particularly pressing.

THE FUTURE OF TV HISTORY

The study of television history has possibly emerged as the most dynamic area of Television Studies in the early twenty-first century. There are several emerging tendencies that can be identified in this field. The first is the move away from purely national history to thinking about comparative **international history**. Hilmes raises this as a particular issue in her introduction to *The Television History Book*, and several other scholars have begun to consider the international relationships between national broadcasters, and the intersections and 'conversations' between television creators and industries before contemporary '**globalisation**' (Hilmes, 2003: vii–ix) (see Chapter 9).

Second, there is a renewed interest in the historical development of particular **television genres**. Jacobs' *Body Trauma TV: The New Hospital Dramas* (2003) offers a revisionist account of the history of the medical drama and Johnson does much the same with science-fiction and cult TV (forthcoming). Brunsdon's historical account of the development of daytime television also signals the expansion of interest in hitherto 'trivial' genres (like gardening and cookery programmes) that have subsequently emerged as power genres (2004).

The relevance of television history at a time when we are seeing the continuing emergence of **new media** is obvious. Television was once itself the 'new media'. At the same time, PC screens, web screens, portable and home cinema and digital television on demand threatens the integrity of television as a medium at all. Noel Carroll argues that the differences between cinema and television and other screen media are at best superficial and instead we should consider 'the moving image' rather than the imagined – or fantasised – 'specificities of the medi-

um' (2003). Time may well prove Carroll correct, and there seems little sense for the historian to police the boundaries of this or that medium. Nevertheless, the extent to which 'television as television' was understood as just that by its creators, its managers and its audience means that for the historian 'television' will never go away, even as media **convergence** might make it less of a discrete medium (see Chapter 10).

To some extent television history is the study of loss. Some television programmes are lost forever – that is, unless scientists can discover a way of catching up with the entirety of broadcast signals from Earth that are at this moment travelling through space. That is unlikely to happen, but there are compensations. Scholars of ancient Greece have limited access to the experience of the Battle of Thermopylae, and no one can know for sure what it would feel like to see the first performance of *Hamlet*. Unlike these kinds of history, television history has the advantage of having entire programmes, sometimes entire seasons, that are intact and available for viewing exactly as they were originally transmitted. In this sense, the television historian has direct and immediate access to what was experienced on television ten, twenty, even forty years ago. When we watch the BBC's coverage of the Coronation in 1953 or Rod Steiger's tortured performance as *Marty* (NBC, 1953) in the same year we are seeing events as they happened, broadcast live to the audience at the time. We can experience the televisual past almost as directly as they experienced the televisual present. Although we can never go back, it is perhaps the nearest we can ever get to a time machine. This is one of the reasons that television history continues to be such a vibrant and exciting area of critical debate.

FURTHER READING
Abramson, Albert (1987), *The History of Television, 1880 to 1941*, Jefferson, NC: McFarland.

Barnouw, Eric (1975), *Tube of Plenty: The Evolution of American Television*, New York: Oxford University Press.

Briggs, Asa (1961–1995), *The History of Broadcasting in*

the United Kingdom: Volumes 1–5, Oxford: Oxford University Press.

Corner, John (1991), *Popular Television in Britain: Studies in Cultural History*, London: BFI.

Crisell, Andrew (1997), *An Introductory History of British Broadcasting*, London and New York: Routledge.

Ellis, John (2000), *Seeing Things: Television in the Age of*

Uncertainty, London and New York: I. B. Tauris.

Hilmes, Michele (ed.) (2003), *The Television History Book*, London: BFI.

Smith, Anthony (ed.) (1995), *Television: An International History*, Oxford and New York: Oxford University Press.

Wheen, F. and Fiddick, P. (1985), *Television: A History*, London: Century.

CASE STUDY
A (Very) Brief History of Television
Jamie Medhurst

In his history of the BBC in Wales, the historian John Davies quotes Asa Briggs who stated that to write the history of broadcasting was to write the history of everything else (1994: ix). Indeed, to attempt to provide an all-encompassing, complete history of television in such a short space would clearly be impossible. Therefore, the aim of this section is to simply provide students with a **critical framework** in the form of an overview of the historical development of television as a medium, taking into account technological, institutional and social/cultural changes. It is hoped that this short case study will simply act as a platform to allow the reader to follow up and develop the ideas expounded by consulting more detailed histories.

For the sake of clarity, television history can be frequently divided into a number of different and distinct phases. Most commonly it can be separated into three separate periods, sometimes referred to as **TVI, TVII and TVIII** (see Rogers *et al.*, 2002: 42–57). When each period starts and ends is notoriously open to debate, but generally it can be loosely organised in this way:

- TVI: (begins) 1930s–
- TVII: (begins) 1980s–
- TVIII: (begins) 1990s–

John Ellis (2000) goes further, bestowing names to these three particular historical periods, i.e. TVI = **Scarcity,** TVII = **Availability** and TVII = **Plenty**. While these categories are not the only structure by which the major developmental periods in television history can be organised and understood, they are a useful framework. Although I will not follow any rubric exactly, this broad historical breakdown will help aid the clarity of this very brief account.

TVI: SCARCITY

John Logie Baird set up the world's first television company in 1925 (see Briggs, 1961: 519), but he was unable to secure a transmission frequency as the BBC had already established a monopoly of broadcasting in the UK (see Chapter 8). However, by the end of the decade he had started making experimental programmes in conjunction with the BBC and by 1930 had even installed one of the first television sets in the country in the house of the Prime Minister (ibid: 549). The quality of these early images was extremely limited, comprising of only thirty lines. Inevitably, Baird's '**mechanical**' system would improve but faced heavy competition from around the world, particularly from EMI's '**electronic**' service which consisted of 405 lines (see Flichy, 1995: 140–4). Consequently, when the BBC first began its regular television service at 3pm on 2 November 1936 it alternated between Baird's and EMI's equipment on a weekly basis, but finally the superiority of the EMI system won out in February 1937 (see Abramson, 1995: 30). Although Germany had begun transmitting 180-line pictures in 1935, this was the first high-definition service in the world. Transmitted from Alexandra Palace in north London, it was received only within a radius of forty to 400 miles by approximately 400 households. (For a general overview of early television see Abramson, 1987.)

The television of this **experimental phase** was mainly the preserve of the affluent (a set cost approximately the price of a small car) and the programming itself (at first only two hours a day and nothing on the Sabbath) was limited and set within the strict boundaries of **public service broadcasting** (PSB) (see Creeber, 2003). Defenders of PSB argued that it was about protecting and educating the masses through a heavily regulated monopoly of broadcast-

ing (funded by a compulsory licence fee). However, its detractors saw it simply in terms of state control. Although the BBC was theoretically independent of the government, it knew that its approval was crucial to its continued survival (see Chapter 8).

The BBC's first Director General, John Reith, certainly had a strong moral control over the Corporation and its output. Although he left the BBC in 1939, his paternalistic ('**Reithian**') version of PSB influenced the high moral tone and stuffy style of British television for years to come (see Crisell, 1997: 10–45). The '**Reithian mission**' was based on maintaining high moral and social standards together with a sense of duty to promulgate the very '**best culture**' to the audience. In later years this stance would be heavily criticised, and was crystallised in a minority report within the Beveridge Committee Report on broadcasting published in 1951, where the Reithian plan was described as '**compulsory uplift**' (see Briggs, 1979: 358–9). What is interesting to note,

An early TV set: 18–20,000 sets were sold between 1936 and 1939

however, is that Reith's concept of broadcasting influenced the development of radio and television services in other countries such as Ireland and New Zealand, where reference was made from the outset to broadcasting sustaining and nurturing the respective nations' cultures (see Chapter 8).

Regular television programming only appeared in the US in 1939, a year when the total number of sets barely exceeded 10,000 (Barnouw, 1968: 128). US radio and television developed along different lines altogether to that of the UK. Although it would be inaccurate to suggest that the media developed in a completely chaotic and untrammelled manner, there were fewer regulatory restrictions and mechanisms than in the UK. As Michele Hilmes notes (2003: 27):

> . . . limitations on government intervention mandated by the First Amendment, a precedent of private ownership and competition set by other technologies . . . as well as the strongly defended tradition of localism and relatively open access to the airwaves established very early on by radio amateurs, led to an American radio [and later TV] situation far more diverse and uncontrolled than those of most other nations.

In its early years, American broadcasting was driven largely by the key players in the radio broadcasting business, notably the National Broadcasting Company (NBC) and the Columbia Broadcasting System (CBS). In many ways, therefore, the structures which existed for American radio broadcasting were carried over into the early years of television's development. Television programmes, like their radio counterparts, tended to be sponsored by a single company or corporation, and it is here that the main difference between the US and the UK models lies. As Rogers *et al.* (2002: 43) point out, American television was founded on a **Fordist** model of broadcasting that enforced a rigid economic order (Fordism is named after Henry Ford, the great American entrepreneur and advocate of mass production). In contrast to the UK's attempts to provide a 'public service', critics have argued that American television was mainly interested in promoting the ethic of **con-**

sumption (see Boddy, 1995: 37–40). Hence the different view each country had to advertising, the BBC rejecting both advertising and the ethos of commercialism that typified the US system of broadcasting.

Whatever the structures of broadcasting, all television before World War II was at an early **experimental phase**. TV was black and white and primarily live as recording techniques were both primitive and expensive. This meant that if a TV play was to be repeated later in the week all the cast and crew would have to be reassembled in the studio to perform it all over again. Television was also still regarded as residing in the shadow of radio, not taken seriously as a medium in its own right, with a great deal of its personnel coming from the rival service and conceiving television as simply '**radio with pictures**'. British television was finally closed down altogether during World War II, unceremoniously switched off in the middle of a Mickey Mouse cartoon (see Crisell, 1997: 72–3).

While the rest of the world gradually established their own television services, another model of broadcasting also became apparent, i.e. **dominant state control** (see Chapter 8). This was clearly the case in the Communist-led Soviet Union and it also characterised Germany's television service during the years of the Third Reich. Unlike the BBC, German television remained broadcasting during the course of the war, producing a highly specialised and influential form of propaganda for the Nazis. As other countries created their own TV services so they tended to adhere either to the model of broadcasting set out by public service broadcasting, the American commercial model, the state-controlled model or a mixture of all three (see Smith, 1995, for a good overview of international television developments).

The model of broadcasting that most of Europe embraced after World War II was the BBC's public service model. By adopting PSB, European states could maintain a degree of control over broadcasting, producing a form of programming that was nationally focused but also internationally approved. As Weymouth and Lamizet explain, PSB was never designed to be culturally or ideologically neutral and its mission after the war was clear (1996: 9):

In the West the radio and emerging television services were developed along the lines of the public service model inherited from the BBC whose wartime performance [on radio] had won it the admiration of liberated Europe. This need to rebuild nations and to stabilise the European community was reflected in the process of mediation which had now been reinforced with a new mode of communication, the television. In the immediate post-war years the media actively represented to the peoples of Europe a mediated image of themselves as nations existing in a new, more united Europe within a new world order dominated by the two superpowers of the United States and the Soviet Union.

However, there was not uniformity to how PSB was imposed throughout Europe. For example, in countries such as France, state control was more direct than in the UK which had an 'arm's length' relationship with the BBC while Spain's television service, which commenced in 1956, was state-controlled, but funded by advertising (see Noam, 1991 and Chapter 8).

The immediate post-war period saw the rapid spread of television throughout the world. Like in Europe, Asian television was traditionally state-controlled. Japan's NHK, for example, was established in 1953 as a non-commercial network similar to the BBC and funded by a television licence fee. Meanwhile, in countries such as India, China and the Middle East, dominant state control and heavy censorship was the norm. As this suggests, some countries were clearly suspicious of the new medium and some (particularly the less democratic) even tried to prevent it being established at all. For example, South Africa (under its racist/apartheid regime) did not begin television transmission until 1976.

The mid-1950s and early 1960s is often remembered now as television's '**golden age**'. Nostalgia inevitably plays a part in this conception, but also television was undoubtedly at an exciting moment in its historical development. As improvements in TV technology (greater recording techniques, lighter cameras, less studio-bound transmissions) meant that innovation and originality was rife. Television drama,

for example, rather than simply adapting plays from the theatre saw more original plays being written specifically for the new medium. The content of these plays also reflected a new audience, an audience that had never gone to the theatre before, i.e. the working-class, helping to produce a form of **radical drama** rarely seen before (see Caughie, 2000: 57–87). Because of the scarcity of channels (at least by today's standards) and the lack of home-recording, television was also seen as playing a large role in each country's 'conversation' with itself: individual nations 'culturally cemented' by the thought that they were all watching and sharing the same programmes at the same time.

Historians have argued that British and American television was clearly leading the way during this revolutionary period. According to Janet Thumim (2002), '[a]ll other national broadcasting systems were developed in the light of the British and American experiences – not only that, but also US and British programmes were systematically exported thus providing models for local production in other parts of the world' (8–9). This heavy bias towards British and American television clearly had strong ideological implications, arguably promoting Western values and Western (white) culture throughout the world in an unprecedented manner (see Miller, 2002: 116–130 and Chapter 9). American television was particularly influential internationally,

Bonanaza: an American Western distributed to sixty countries in 1960

establishing the formats for enduring genres such as the quiz show, the talk show, news programming, soap opera and so on. As Lisa Parks explains, such programmes were both economically and culturally important to the USA (2003: 115):

> In 1960 *Bonanza* [a Western] was distributed to 60 countries for viewing by 350 million people each week and such programmes were dubbed into Spanish, Japanese, Portuguese, German, Italian, French and Arabic. By cultivating the growth of television stations around the world, US networks NBC, ABC and CBS attempted to guarantee future exhibition outlets for US television and to assert spheres of influence during a time of Cold War politics.

Despite Europe's public service television ideal, it was not immune to American influence. Indeed, while the dominance of PSB in Europe during the post-war years needs to be emphasised, so too does European television's gradual shift (albeit a slow and often painful one) towards commercialisation. For example, the debate over whether or not a rival television service to the BBC should be set up in the UK stems back to the period of the Beveridge Committee on Broadcasting (1949–51). Following years of often heated debate, the UK's first commercial television service, Independent Television (ITV) was established under the terms of the 1954 Television Act and began to broadcast on 22 September 1955. ITV was different from the BBC in many ways. Unlike the monolith Corporation, ITV was based on a loose '**federal**' structure with the regulatory body, the Independent Television Authority (ITA), granting licences to companies to broadcast programmes to a defined geographical region (see Chapter 8).

Figure 5. Television History – A Brief Timeline.

1900	The word 'television' is coined by Constantin Perskyi at the International Electricity Congress in Paris.
1907	Boris Rosing transmits silhouette images of geometric shapes, using a Nipkow disc, mirror-drum and a cathode-ray tube receiver.
1925	John Logie Baird sets up the world's first television company (Television Limited) in the UK with £500 capital.
1926	On 26 January Baird gives the first public demonstration of mechanical television to members of the Royal Institution.
1929	The Baird Television Development Company begins experimental broadcasting in association with the BBC.
1930	Baird installs a television at 10 Downing Street, London, the British Prime Minister's residence. On 14 July, Prime Minister Ramsay MacDonald and his family use it to watch the first ever television drama, *The Man with the Flower in His Mouth*.
1935	First TV broadcasts in Germany.
1936	The BBC starts a regular public television broadcasting service in the UK.
1939	Regular programming begins in the US. The BBC suspends its television service owing to the outbreak of World War II.
1941	First commercial on American TV shown.
1943	The American Broadcasting Company (ABC) is formed.
1946	The BBC resumes television broadcasting after its suspension during World War II. RCA demonstrates an all-electronic colour television system.
1952	The first political advertisements appear on US television.
1953	Television begins in Japan. The Coronation of Queen Elizabeth II is seen by approximately 20 million TV viewers in the UK.
1955	Commercial television begins in the UK.
1956	Television transmission begins in Australia. Black-and-white portable TV sets hit the market.
1958	Ampex demonstrates their design for a colour videotape recorder.
1959	TV begins in India and Nigeria.

1960	American presidential candidates John F. Kennedy and Richard M. Nixon debate live on TV.	**1976**	Television begins in South Africa. Ceefax goes live in the UK with thirty pages of information.
1961	Television begins in Zimbabwe (then Rhodesia).	**1983**	Zanzibar introduces colour television into Africa.
1962	The first satellite television signal is relayed from Europe to the Telstar satellite over the US.	**1986**	The Fox Broadcasting Company becomes the United States' fourth commercial TV network.
1963	Television begins in Singapore.	**1989**	The UK's first commercial DBS service, Sky Television, is launched.
1966	Canadian television stations broadcast in colour for the first time, while colour is now the standard in all US television.	**1992**	Cable TV grows in Europe (92% of homes in Belgium and 87% in the Netherlands).
1967	PAL and SECAM standards introduced in Europe. Television begins in Hong Kong.	**1994**	Television begins in Tanzania.
1969	The first moon landing is televised, watched by an estimated 465 million viewers worldwide.	**1996**	Zenith introduces the first HDTV-compatible front projection TV in the US.
1973	The first domestic North American satellite to carry television (Canada's Anik 1) is launched.	**1998**	The UK's first digital television service is launched.
1975	Sony introduces the Betamax, a home videotape recorder.	**2010–12**	This is approximately when analogue TV in the UK is meant to be switched off. By then it is hoped that all households will have switched to digital television.

(Acknowledgments to Wilkipedia.org)

More importantly, ITV was funded by **advertising revenue** and not by a licence fee. ITV companies had to 'sell' advertising slots to national and local advertisers, guaranteeing them an audience at different times of the day. The most lucrative slots, therefore, were those in so-called peak viewing hours, between 7.00pm and 10.00pm on weekdays. It is worth noting at this point that the Conservative government that introduced the legislation, which eventually led to ITV, deliberately avoided adopting the US system of **sponsored programming** for fear that such a move would unduly influence the programming content. Instead, the government opted for a '**spot advertisement**' pattern which would allow advertisements to be shown during natural breaks in transmissions. While the funding arrangements were different from the BBC, it is important to underline that public service principles were applied to ITV as they were to the BBC. There were clear requirements for the commercial companies to produce a certain number of hours of locally originated programming, documentaries, religious programming, and news and current affairs (see Chapter 8).

TVII: AVAILABILITY

The 1960s and 1970s witnessed the growth of television as a truly **mass medium**. By the early 1960s, almost 90 per cent of US households and 80 per cent of UK households had television sets. By 1970, there were 231 million TV sets in the world as a whole (37 per cent of these in the US). Television also moved from black and white into colour, adding both glamour and heightened reality to the images that viewers could now receive. In particular, the age of availability witnessed a rise in the number of channels and broadcasting providers. During the 1980s and 1990s, the **cable and satellite** television sector expanded rapidly and began to pose a threat to the **terrestrial television** providers, particularly in terms of attracting large audiences, thereby reducing the viewing figures for terrestrial television's core programming.

Old media structure		New media structure
Broadcasting	Monopoly	Competition
Goals	Democracy	Survival/success/profit
Means	Programme production/selection of material	Selection of material/programme mix
Logic	Responsibility	Market/economic
Criteria for selection	Political relevance	Sale
Reference group	Citizens	Consumers
Focus	Decisions taken/power structure	Processes of policy-making/new conflict dimension
Perspective	Nation/system	Individual and global

Figure 6. Old and New Media Structures.

Source: Siune and Hulten, 1998: 36.

At the same time, the television industry itself became increasingly competitive. Advances in technology as well as an ideological shift away from public service broadcasting (in the form of **neo-liberal** thinking) led to the abandonment of Reithian principles and the adoption of a more **market-driven** approach to television. The debates about increased commercialisation in television are complex and will continue to rage. However, Figure 6 outlines some of the basic differences between the old and new media structures.

In the UK, the driving force behind this shift was the Prime Minister, Margaret Thatcher, who held office between 1979 and 1990. As Kevin Williams has argued, during this period, Reith's **citizens** were transformed into Thatcher's **consumers** (1998: 172). During Thatcher's tenure, the period of the duopoly in the UK came to an end when Channel 4 and the Welsh-language channel Sianel Pedwar Cymru (or S4C) were launched in 1982. Channel 4's remit was specifically aimed to promote programming for **minority audiences** (which, it was argued, had been neglected by ITV), while S4C provided peak-time Welsh-language programming for audiences for the first time (see Chapter 8).

Channels such as these reflected television's general and gradual move away from broadcasting to **narrowcasting**. Broadcasting was originally an agricultural term, meaning to scatter seeds over a large area. When applied to the media, it meant serving as wide a demographic as possible, frequently an entire nation. In contrast, 'narrowcasting' refers to programmes and channels made for and aimed at smaller communities and **niche groups**, increasing-ly the case when societies become more diverse and multicultural and when cable/satellite channels inevitably multiply (see Moores, 2000). Undoubtedly this proliferation of channels leads to greater **audience fragmentation** and the idea of the whole nation watching the same programme at the same time becomes increasingly unlikely (see Chapter 9).

The age of availability has also been characterised by fears of what can be viewed as increasing '**cultural imperialism**' on the part of **global television** providers (see Chapter 9). Although such fears have always been prevalent in television discourse (see, for example, the cultural debasement arguments that were put forward at the time of the Pilkington Committee on Broadcasting in the UK, 1960–2), they became more pronounced as '**media barons**' such as Rupert Murdoch tightened his hold on satellite television around the globe. At the same time, countries such as France countered the perceived threat to the indigenous culture posed by American television exports by introducing the *Télévision Sans Frontières* European Directive in 1989. This aimed to control the amount of imported American programmes that could be shown on television and ensure that European broadcasters allowed for the transmission of indigenous material (see Chapter 9).

TVIII: PLENTY

Television's most recent age ('**plenty**') is characterised by John Ellis as being 'full of new technologies, new challenges and new uncertainties' (Ellis, 2000: 162). In particular, critics like Patrice Flichy

(1999) have identified three major areas of development during the contemporary period (34):

- HDTV (high-definition digital television)
- Personalised, interactive television (push media)
- Multichannel cable and satellite television

These three major developments have certainly had a huge impact on the way that television is now made, distributed and consumed. The quality of the image and sound we now receive at home (aided by home cinema, plasma screens, widescreens, DVD recorders etc.) is transforming the nature of TV. Technology has also seen TV increasingly becoming part of life on the go, something we can now carry around with us in our pocket and on our mobile phones (see Chapter 10). The growth of satellite and cable since the 1980s (coinciding with an increasingly commercialised and **deregulated** market [see Chapter 8]) has certainly resulted in an ever increasing amount of television channels now available to the viewer around the world.

Perhaps one of the most startling changes in TV is that related to the way in which the audience **interacts** with the medium. No longer do the schedules have the hold over viewers they once did. The development of the video recorder (and now DVD) allows audiences to watch programmes when they want, and with further technological advances (in the shape of **TiVo**, for example, which allows the viewer to record programmes and avoid advertisements as well as rewinding and pausing live television). The concept of the 'television set' itself is fast disappearing with 'content' – as opposed to the increasingly outdated notion of 'programmes' – being made available via other media such as PCs. In this way, the audience's relationship with the medium has changed, and continues to change, in a dramatic way (see Chapter 10).

However, such changes have led to debates about '**dumbing down**' and fears that sheer quantity inevitably brings down levels of quality programming (Moseley, 2003: 103–7). America's highly successful subscription channel HBO is clearly showing how lucrative such technological changes can be for

individual (**pay-per-view**) television companies, but also revealing how the question of quality on contemporary television is a complex one. Indeed, some critics have argued that HBO's independence as a subscription channel allows it greater freedom to create more challenging and innovative programming (see Chapter 5). Whatever your perspective on this critical debate, it is arguable that **digital television** will change the television landscape forever, and not just in terms of the programmes and channels available to the viewer. As William Boddy puts it (2002: 242):

> The technological promise of digital television, in the form of higher-definition images, greater bandwidth and interactive services, has thrown into crisis, or at least historiographic relief, long-established industry practices, business relationships and textual forms. The uneven adoption of digital technologies across the fields of consumer electronics, programme production and delivery systems has exposed new fissures among sectors of the television industry and brought new economics players into the business, in the form of start-ups and well-established firms, with significant amounts of venture capital being raised . . .

This is not to say that all countries in the world are now at the age of 'plenty', some are still clearly behind others. However, at the turn of the millennium television is now a truly global phenomenon with channels such as the music-based MTV (412 million homes and eighteen languages), the documentary channel, Discovery, and twenty-four-hour news channels like CNN (Cable News Network) and BBC News 24 being transmitted in customised versions to hundreds of countries worldwide. Television markets are undoubtedly changing and aligned with this, issues of the thorny relationship between television and **national identity** inevitably dominate the discourse of Television Studies (see Chapter 9). The control of the medium throughout the world has certainly been eroded by the increasing availability of TV. In the Middle East, for example, the number of satellite channels in Arabic is second only to the number of satellite channels in English, the best known of which is the Qatar-based news service, Al-Jazeera (see Chapter 8).

Yet from the age of 'scarcity' to 'plenty' television has continued to evolve, adapting to new worlds, new audiences and new technologies. Although television audiences may decline when attracted to new technologies like the Internet, it is unlikely that television itself will quickly disappear from the cultural landscape. As television approaches its first centenary it is still in the process of transformation and is now clearly playing its own crucial role in the **new media** revolution (see Chapter 10).

TVI *1930s–1960s/70s*	*TVII* *1970/80s–1990s*	*TVIII* *1990s–*
Scarcity	Availability	Plenty
State control	Deregulation	Market-driven
Broadcasting	Narrowcasting	Niche programming
Limited terrestrial channels	Cable and satellite	Multichannel
National	National/international	Global
Analogue/black and white	Analogue/colour	Digital/HDTV
Live	Video	DVD
Passive viewers	Mass viewers	Interactive viewers
Restricted broadcasting	Rigid schedules	TiVo (do-it-yourself scheduling)
Experimentation	'Golden Age'	Debates around quality

Figure 7. TV History: A Brief Overview.

8 Television and Regulation

Examining Institutional Structures

Elan Closs Stephens

We have now become used to a situation in which broadcasting is a major social institution, about which there is always controversy but which, in its familiar form, seems to have been predestined by technology. This predestination, however, when closely examined, proves to be no more than a set of particular social decisions, in particular circumstances, which were then so widely if imperfectly ratified that it is now difficult to see them as decisions rather than as (retrospectively) inevitable results.

Raymond Williams, *Television, Technology and Cultural Form*, 1974: 23.

Anyone who thinks that media regulation is the boring bit of Television Studies should recall the extraordinary events in the UK at the end of January 2004. In particular, the scenes outside Broadcasting House when the chairman of the board of governors of the BBC (Gavyn Davies) and the Director General (Greg Dyke) resigned in a moment of high drama. Did the BBC take wrong decisions and regulate too partially? Or did the two men go, as Gavyn Davies was to say in *The Guardian*, because it was only the fourth estate that now stood up to government (see Gibson, 2004)? These unexpected events serve to remind us of the importance of the regulations that underpin broadcasting around the world.

To put such events in context, we need to understand how television is monitored and controlled. Television doesn't just happen; it is **regulated** by government **policy** (i.e. state legislation). Who makes certain that there are no children's programmes which show children playing with carrier

bags over their heads or Sellotape on their mouths, or opening a cupboard door to fetch some pills? Why did British television accept that sanitary towel advertisements were unacceptable twenty years ago and acceptable now? Why is *The Black and White Minstrel Show* (BBC1, 1958–78) no longer on British screens? Do the words 'Christ' or 'Jesus' (if used in profanity) offend a certain part of the population to the extent that they are unacceptable? What should viewers be able to see in terms of violence or sexual content on TV? (see Arthurs, 2004). These are all issues of **content regulation**. Then there is the **regulation of delivery**: who owns the television companies and does foreign ownership matter? Are there obligations put on those who make profits from the industry? Should there be rules for indigenous production and content and for indigenous languages and diversity (see Chapter 9)? All of these regulatory issues are fascinating because they mirror the constant change in society's values. And even that statement begs several questions including the most difficult of all: whose values?

REGULATION AROUND THE WORLD

Each country that has television has rules and policies for its control. Television is regarded as a powerful force, one that can sway an electorate and depose or sustain a president or a government. Most governments retain powers to broadcast on the airwaves in cases of national emergency or national danger. But each country also comes to its own wider regulatory accommodation with its broadcasters. These vary and tend to come in three main models i.e. the **state broadcaster** (e.g. the old Soviet Union), the **liber-**

alised marketplace (e.g. New Zealand during the 1990s) and the mixed economy of rights and responsibilities (e.g. the British model).

One of the fundamental aspects of regulation is its relationship with the state. Broadcasters can be regulated at arm's length by a regulatory body that publishes a set of rules. These rules are the manifestation of a government's broadcasting policy and there will therefore be opportunities to change them within the democratic process. However, some countries forego the arm's length principle in favour of direct state control, putting the interests of the state before the interests of the individual. Examples of these two models (plus a combination of both models) can be found across the globe.

For example, the television industry in China is expanding rapidly with television sets reaching near universality at above 95 per cent of households with 60 per cent of urban families connected to cable networks. Yet television in China (with the exception of Hong Kong) is still completely controlled by the ruling Chinese Communist Party. However, it will be interesting to see whether this tight control slackens as China enters increasingly into a world market and trades in content and advertising with other countries (see Man Chan, 2004).

This was also the case in the Soviet Union but, since the collapse of the Communist state in the 1980s, control of the country's television has left the hands of the state. We see now in Russia a movement

The Black and White Minstrel Show: why is it no longer acceptable?

PAS 2 3836(V)
Al Jazeera

Al-Jazeera: satellite television is now challenging the
hegemony of national broadcasters

from the old type of state control into a control by
the political and financial elite of the new Russia, a
movement from state control to state and corporate
control. For instance, during President Yeltsin's re-
election campaign in 1996, NTV (set up originally
as a commercial independent Western-style channel)
created a temporary alliance with the two national
channels to promote the President. Yeltsin's popularity rose from 5–50 per cent in the course of one year.
It is difficult to ascribe this increase in popularity
solely to the intervention of broadcasters but it is
interesting to note that Yeltsin in 1996, after his re-
election, gave significant further benefits to NTV. So
Russia's current regulatory situation is a complex
one, not completely state controlled but control is
clearly not at arm's length either (see Vartanova,
2004).

Neither is there a simple or unified system of
regulation in Europe. For example, the main commercial channels in Italy belong to the Mediaset
company owned by the current Italian president,
Sylvio Berlusconi. Even on its public service channels, Italy has never been averse to an overt political
link between broadcasting and government; the Rai
Channels (the **public broadcasting services**), are
answerable to a parliamentary supervisory committee that reflects the standing of political parties in the
polls. The board chair and members are directly
nominated by the presidents of the Chamber of

Deputies and the Senate (see Buonanno, 2004). At
the other end of the scale, Germany has strict broadcasting rules, upheld by the Federal Constitutional
Court, to prevent political parties and pressure
groups from exerting undue pressure. Hand in hand
with impartiality, **decentralisation** is an important
principle reflecting the cultural sovereignty of the
Länder, the regions that make up the federalised
nature of Germany's government. ARD, one of the
public service television channels, incorporates programming produced by regional broadcasters including the five new Länder of the former GDR thus
offering plurality of opinion and production (see
Burns, 2004).

Yet the recent rise of **satellite channels** also
means that regulatory control is a lot more difficult
to implement than it once was. For example,
throughout the 1960s and 1970s, Egypt's powerful
transmitters broadcasted the influential 'Voice of the
Arabs'. However, the rise of satellite transmission
challenged this hegemony and made space for one of
the most interesting broadcasters, Al-Jazeera. Based in
Qatar, Al-Jazeera broadcasts twenty-four hours a day,
in widely understood classical Arabic, to over thirty-
five million potential viewers. Not only does it challenge some Arab views, it has also challenged the US
by selling some of its unique footage worldwide at
high prices (see Noureddine, 2004).

As these examples show, policy and regulation is
a complex area of debate and legislation to understand internationally. However, put crudely – **direct
intervention** for the most part seeks to control
information on behalf of the state or a ruling individual; a more democratic arm's length regulatory
process seeks to preserve the right of the individual
to receive that information. Inevitably, there are
always tensions and preconceptions even in the most
transparent and seemingly democratic systems.

CONTENT REGULATION AND OWNERSHIP

Because of its potential influence on society, what
television should broadcast and who should broadcast it has always been of the greatest concern.
Certainly, one of the overarching concepts within
the British television ecology has been that of **rights**

and **obligations**. Within the United Kingdom there has always existed a relationship between the conditions imposed on broadcasters and the value of the space they are allowed on transmitters. This relationship is implicit in the renewal of the licence fee between the BBC and the government of the day. It has also been explicit in the conditions set down for licence agreements for the commercial sector where there is an economic compact between creating commercial wealth and providing socially desirable programming. Despite the fact that this concept has been understated within a relatively uncompetitive ecology of four channels, it has always underpinned the licensing decisions for ITV, and the remit for Channel 4. Also implicit within these contracts is the idea that the more rights you have as a broadcaster, the more obligations you have to society. For example, the old ITC (the Independent Television Commission) set out a number of guidelines for commercial television in the UK. These included (Holland, 1997: 15):

- *Advertising standards and practice*: Ensuring that advertisements are not misleading, offensive or likely to encourage dangerous or anti-social behaviour.
- *Programme sponsorship*: Protecting editorial independence and preventing sponsor credits from intruding unacceptably on programmes.
- *A programme code*: Giving detailed advice on matters including taste, decency, the portrayal of violence, impartiality, intrusion into an individual's privacy, charitable appeals and religious programmes.

The obligations to society that a television industry has are most often discussed (at least in the public domain) through programming content, where standards of taste and decency are hotly debated. **Content regulation** is certainly the area that provokes most passion in the viewing public. For example, the 2005 broadcast of *Jerry Springer, the Opera* on the BBC caused unprecedented outrage (see Armstrong, 2005). Similarly, when Janet Jackson's singing partner, Justin Timberlake, ripped

open the front of her leather outfit to reveal her breast for 1.7 seconds on prime-time television during the Super Bowl, an event watched by millions of unsuspecting American citizens, the Federal Communications Commission denounced it as 'a classless, crass and deplorable stunt' and the House of Representatives voted to increase the maximum fine for indecency on the airwaves from $27,000 to $500,000 (see Gumbels, 2005). By November of the same year, 2004, twenty American TV stations boycotted a Veterans' Day screening of *Saving Private Ryan* (Spielberg, 1998) for fear that they would be censured over the movie's violence and graphic language. Ironically, at the same time the aftermath of the real war in Iraq was still claiming lives.

The ownership of television is also important as it influences programme content. In particular, there are concerns that if ownership is not distributed equally and fairly, then a small minority of the population will have a huge control over public taste and opinion. This concern is also caught up with general fears about the notion of **cultural identity** and its relationship to **indigenous programming** (see Chapter 9). For example, in Germany these concerns have led to a 'share of voice' model that limits ownership to 30 per cent of the audience share (see Burns, 2004). Of course, underlying all this is the perceived strength of the US entertainment industry and its dominance in world markets.

Canada is the country where US dominance is felt and feared most to the extent that its government has opposed the inclusion of cultural goods in general free trade agreements. If it succeeds, it would not be anti-competitive to protect, promote and financially underpin cultural products including television content. This is a difficult argument to win in a global economy, especially when the Canadians now only spend 33.5 per cent of their time viewing Canadian broadcasters in comparison to 54.8 per cent in 1989 (see Tremblay, 2004). It comes as no surprise that France (home of the 'Académie Française' and of an emphasis on purity of language and cultural excellence), has also been active in trying to maintain its right to self-expression in film and television. It has been the keenest supporter of such European directives as 'Télévision Sans Frontières' and has sought to build a European film and television culture that could stand up to the dominance of the American industry (see Doyle, 2004).

Opposing views point out that astute commercial owners will always seek to satisfy home audiences with its product. Thus, if the home audience responds to indigenous product it will be safeguarded. Despite this optimistic assumption (which does not take into account the likely budget differentials), most European countries have in place rules on indigenous production whoever owns the channel. Currently in France the barrier is 60 per cent and in Sweden 70 per cent.

CONTEMPORARY REGULATION: A CHANGING ENVIRONMENT

These issues of ownership and content regulation are arguably the ones most under threat in a **globalised multichannel** market where it is increasingly difficult to monitor content adequately (see Chapter 9). The television system that had operated since the 1930s (analogue) is now giving way to digital transmission that brings with it new challenges for governments, public bodies and regulators (see Iosifidis *et al.*, 2005). For the first time, there is **convergence** between the way in which our personal computers work, the way in which our mobile telephony works, and the way in which our television service is delivered (see Marsden and Verhulst, 1999). This allows for **interactive television**, red-button options, content delivery on new mobile phones, radio to be listened to on television, television, film and radio to be available on our computers, music and games to be available almost everywhere (see Chapter 10).

In Britain, by 2004 almost 60 per cent of the population had **digital television** either through satellite, cable or terrestrial transmitters such as the UK's 'Freeview'. Thirty million people in Britain now have mobile phones compared to only one million in 1990. Text messaging has reached unprecedented levels. It took broadcast television thirteen years to reach fifty million users; personal computers took sixteen; the Internet four years. In the UK the

Internet has now overtaken television viewing as a leisure occupation for some age groups. Two-thirds of British households have more than one television; it can no longer be assumed that children watch television within a family setting, they are far more likely to be viewing their own set in their own bedroom. Increasingly we live in a world, and demand that we live in a world, where instant communications is all around us locally, globally and constantly (see Chapter 9).

Even more importantly in terms of television content and viewing habits, digital technology removed the one constant of British broadcasting: **spectrum scarcity** (see Chapter 7). In 1980, Britain had three television channels. Even when a fourth appeared in 1982, the Welsh-language S4C could only appear in Wales by displacing Channel 4 programmes in peak time because of the lack of available spectrum. Suddenly, by 2000, there were 250 channels and 400 by 2004. These new channels need to be licensed. They need to be seen to provide fair competition within the market. The growth of new platforms such as broadband is to be encouraged and **digital deprivation** avoided. The whole sector is seen as an economic driver. Can we sell our content abroad? Can we sell formats? Already the creative industries in the UK account for a substantial export earning of about £1,500 million and the media and communications industry is currently growing faster than the rest of the economy.

Perhaps the most significant feature of competition and innovation will be the eventual opening up of the whole television world to **broadband** technology. At that point, the role of vertically integrated broadcasters as a gateway to the viewer will be challenged. Thus the preservation of rights allows the independents to be in control of content for **multiplatform delivery** outside the main broadcasting channels.

These changes present increasing difficulties for regulators. For example, how possible is it to regulate 40,000 hours and more per week in the detailed and prescriptive way in which the old systems of television tended to work? If adults pay for subscription channels in the privacy of their homes, shouldn't they be allowed to watch what they want, when they want? **Public service broadcasters** have long worked under the system of a caring and regulated schedule: children's programmes in the early evening, followed by general viewing, news and current affairs and then slightly more difficult or challenging entertainment or factual programming after the '**watershed**' i.e. after nine o'clock. However, what will happen to this system as viewers put their own menu together with the aid of **niche channels** and personal video recorders (see Chapter 10)? The impossibility of imposing public service rules on a satellite service for which the viewer pays is already accepted. In Britain, Sky Cinema now has a watershed threshold of eight o'clock as opposed to nine. Soft pornographic subscription channels are also deemed to be paid for by consenting adults.

In Britain, the Government was determined to drive forward into this new digital world. Until December 2003 there were nine broadcasting regulatory bodies all concerned with maintaining standards of technical delivery and content, including accuracy of information, fairness and political neutrality. When the Labour Government, under Prime Minister Tony Blair, came into power in May 1997, one of its aspirations was to produce a new Communications Act, which would seek to merge some of these diverse regulators and to enhance the competitiveness of the British communications industry. By December 2000 it had brought out a well-written and ambitious White Paper called 'A New Future for Communications', published jointly by the Department of Culture, Media and Sport (which looked after the broadcasting and creative industries) and the Department of Trade and Industry (which had an interest in fair competition, consumer issues and competitiveness in the global market). It sought 'to make sure that the UK is home to the most dynamic and competitive communications market in the world' (Department of Culture, Media and Sport; Department of Trade and Industry, 2000).

After a period of widespread consultation, the Communications Act finally became law on 29 December 2003 and a wholly new body called

Ofcom (Office of Communications) came into being while some of the original regulatory bodies ceased to exist. Specifically, the Radio Communications Agency, the Radio Authority, the Broadcasting Standards Commission, the Independent Television Commission and Oftel merged; the BBC and S4C retained their governance but came under Ofcom for part of their activities; the British Board of Film Classification and the Office of Fair Trading remained outside Ofcom.

The 2003 Communications Act was seen as setting out a regulatory system more in tune with the contemporary ecology of television both in the UK and globally. In particular, it allowed for greater freedom to occur in broadcasting structures, while also monitoring and regulating this new digital landscape. There were two primary reasons for the creation of this new regulatory structure. One dealt with positive economic regulation: How does the UK grow a world-class communications business? How does the UK drive forward the new digital future? The other dealt with negative and positive content regulation: How do we impose some obligations and safeguards on the communications business? Ofcom was later to devise a term, '**the citizen–consumer**'. As citizens, most of us want safeguards for our children and for ourselves. As consumers, we want the best possible deal in a global market. Are the two aspirations compatible?

From its beginning, Ofcom was a very different body from its predecessors. It made explicit its determination to free the marketplace and to encourage growth in the communications sector. It also made known its determination to keep citizen issues to the fore by means of a content board answerable to the main board. For the first time, the concepts of checks and balances, rights and obligations were being put forward explicitly and explored analytically. At the same time, never had these concepts been under such strain.

In particular, the 2003 Communication Act put forward the idea of increasing media literacy so that the viewing public itself would be aware of issues of **self-regulation**. This is matched by a voluntary labelling system by the content providers. However, it is generally acknowledged, as in the case of other ideas such as the V Chip, that those people most likely to respond to self-regulatory signals are already categorised as responsible parents and viewers.

In a more **market-driven** television economy, the regulation of public service broadcasters certainly becomes increasingly complex. What is clear is that television regulation in the UK (as elsewhere in Europe) has become increasingly **liberalised** and **deregulated**, removing hurdles to the growth of the communications industry in a global environment. The new regulation also recognised the impossibility of imposing obligations on commercial companies if there was no corresponding gain. The Communications Act of 2003 therefore provided for:

- Possible joint ownership of radio and television stations.
- Non-European ownership of commercial channels, paving the way for large companies such as Viacom to own ITV.
- Single ownership of ITV, allowing Carlton and Granada to forge a single company which could potentially be more attractive to foreign buyers.
- The decrease of regional obligations on ITV, making it more attractive to outside ownership.
- A newspaper group being allowed to invest in terrestrial television, e.g. Rupert Murdoch's News Corporation.

These liberalising clauses were hotly disputed during the passage of the Bill. Consequently, a final amendment of the Act in the Summer of 2003 put forward a '**public service plurality test**' which allows Ofcom to determine whether a proposed acquisition or merger lessens the plurality of voices in British broadcasting to a significant degree. In addition to the fear that foreign ownership would not draw on a nation's cultural heritage or produce indigenous contemporary content, there is also the fear that children's programming could become merely a platform to open up new income streams for related goods.

In accordance with the Communications Act, Ofcom reviewed the whole ecology of public serv-ice broadcasting during 2004–5. Given the reduction of ITV's PSB obligations, Ofcom suggested an intervention in broadcasting in the UK: the creation of a **public service publisher**. A sum equivalent to the loss of ITV PSB content (£300 million) would be tendered in a single franchise which would cater for high-impact public service programming on multiple platforms, including mobile phones, aimed at drawing in younger viewers to PSB. The BBC would not be allowed to tender. At the present time, it is unclear who would provide the additional £300 million. Should the BBC's licence be top-sliced? Should the whole of the BBC's licence fee become contestable funding for large tenders, i.e. a public service fund rather than a BBC fund? Why not allow Channel 4 to become the new publisher? Would Channel 4 become less hard-edged and innovative if it were to receive public funding? The debate continues and is unlikely to be resolved before digital switchover is under way and the future usage of platforms by viewers becomes consolidated.

Other countries have already grappled with such broadcasting liberalisation. In New Zealand, the 1989 Broadcasting Act deregulated the channels substantially, allowing up to fourteen minutes per hour of advertising to sustain this marketisation. Public service broadcasting was cared for by an 'Arts Council of the Air' fund called 'NZ on Air' where programme-providers could ask for funding for public service content. Although this fund had some success in opening the gateways, it is also deemed to be beauraucratic and to lack impact.

These are the type of changes and challenges that TV regulation faces in the new communications age. In this multiplatform ecology, regulatory issues of control, ownership, content and carriage are arguably more complex than ever before, and remain a vital area for debate in Television Studies as a whole. As Raymond Williams pointed out in the quotation that heads this chapter, we chose to develop the new digital world. We have chosen to undermine the traditional gatekeepers and have freed up access to broadcast and narrowcast content. The question that remains unanswered is whether control is now necessary, unnecessary or just impossible.

FURTHER READING

Blumler, Jay G. (ed.) (1992), *Television and the Public Interest: Vulnerable Values in West European Broadcasting*, London and Newbury Park, CA: Sage.

Creech, Kenneth C. (2003), *Electronic Media Law and Regulation*, London: Focal Press.

Curran, James (ed.) (2000), *Media Organisations in Society*, London: Arnold.

Franklin, Bob (2001), *British Television Policy: A Reader*, London and New York: Routledge.

Graham, Andrew and Davies, Gavyn (1997), *Broadcasting, Society and Policy in the Multimedia Age*, Luton: University of Luton Press.

Iosifidis, Petros, Steemers, Jeanette and Wheeler, Mark (2005), *European Television Industries*, London: BFI.

Marsden, Chris and Verhulst, Steffan (eds) (1999), *Convergence in European Digital TV Regulation*, London: Blackstone.

Sinclair, John and Turner, Graeme (eds) (2004), *Contemporary World Television*, London: BFI.

CASE STUDY
The BBC and the State Tom O'Malley

This case study considers aspects of the relationship between the state and the BBC. It provides a short outline of key developments in UK broadcasting followed by a brief discussion of the state. It then outlines the contours of the relationship between the Corporation and the state, and the way in which changes in the state have affected the role of the BBC. It concludes with a comment on the relationship between public service broadcasting and the state in the UK at the start of the twenty-first century.

THE BBC: ORIGINS

The British Broadcasting Company was established in 1922. It became the British Broadcasting Corporation (BBC) in 1927. In its early years it transmitted radio programmes to the United Kingdom. In 1936 BBC television was established (see Chapter 7). The BBC's TV and radio services grew from the 1950s onwards and an extra BBC channel, BBC2 was started in 1964. The 1954 Television Act brought commercial competition with the advent of carefully regulated Independent Television (ITV). In 1972, the Sound Broadcasting Act established advertising-financed radio in competition with the BBC's Radios 1, 2, 3 and 4 and its local radio services, which had started in 1967.

During the 1970s the BBC and ITV dominated UK TV as the sole providers of television services. In 1981 the Broadcasting Act introduced two new commercially funded channels, Channel 4 and S4C for Wales. The 1990 and 1996 Broadcasting Acts opened up the UK industry to more, less-regulated, commercially driven competition, exemplified by the expansion of cable and satellite services, the most famous of which was Rupert Murdoch's Sky service. This expansion was given a further boost by the passing of the 2003 Communications Act, designed specifically to expand further the amount of commercially funded communications – radio, TV, telecoms in the UK. After 1990, the BBC remained as an organisation funded by a licence fee on TV-set ownership, ITV was funded by advertising and sponsorship, and the new cable and satellite services were funded by a mix of pay-per-view, subscription, advertising and direct sales in the case of shopping channels (Curran and Seaton, 1997; O'Malley, 2003)

The BBC's structure, funding and purpose have always been determined by the government. The government of the day is made up of elected politicians. These politicians oversee the structures that govern the BBC. Since 1927 the BBC's governance has been based on a Royal Charter. This is written by the government and civil servants, in liaison with the BBC and fixed for periods of ten to fifteen years, for example the BBC's Charter ran from 1981 to 1996 and from 1996 to 2006. The period before a Charter renewal is one of intense political debate (O'Malley and Treharne, 1993; Broadcasting Policy Group, 2004).

The Charter is supplemented by a Licence and Agreement between the Corporation and the government. The government retains, but rarely uses, the right to ban programmes. The people appointed as governors have generally been people whom successive governments consider politically trustworthy, and unlikely to stray too far from the dominant political orthodoxy of the day. This has not, however, prevented the Corporation from developing, over time, a tradition of critical independence from government, and has on occasions led to severe clashes between the Corporation and the politicians.

THE STATE

In the UK the BBC was established in the 1920s by politicians and civil servants who assumed that Wales, Scotland and Ireland could be subsumed under one overarching 'British' (for which read English) identity. The Irish Rebellion of 1916, the growth of Welsh and Scottish nationalism since the 1920s, plus the arrival after 1945 of immigrants from the Caribbean, India, Pakistan and Uganda, highlighted the lack of unity that existed within the UK state, a problem which the BBC, like other institutions in the UK, has had to adapt to over time. The point is that the cultural conditions and assumptions within which the BBC was framed by the people running the state were, almost from the moment of its inception, placed under great strain and over time contributed to major changes in the tone, programming and output of all broadcasters in the UK (Weight, 2002).

There are many ways of thinking about the state, but Ralph Miliband's approach is of particular interest to the study of broadcasting (Miliband, 1973: 46):

There is one preliminary problem about the state which is seldom considered, yet which requires

attention . . . This is the fact that 'the state' is not a thing, that it does not as such exist. What 'the state' stands for is a number of particular institutions, which together, constitute its reality, and which interact as part of what may be called the state system.

His concept of the state system (for the purposes of this discussion 'state' will be used for 'state system') provides a way of thinking about the various forces of the state which act on broadcasters. As will be argued here, all these forces interacted with broadcasting over time and have also changed, as has broadcasting, since the 1920s.

Miliband describes the state as including the elected government and the administrative arm of the state, the permanent civil service. Then there is the 'coercive' arm of the state: the military, and the police and security services, which are meant to be answerable to the elected government. Judges form the fourth element. These are meant to be formally independent of government and have the task of administering and interpreting the laws made by governments in a manner free from political independence. The two other parts of the state are local or national governments, such as the National Assembly of Wales, or the Scottish Parliament (ibid.: 46–50).

Following Miliband's model it is possible to see how the state has related and continues to relate to broadcasting. The BBC was created by elected politicians and unelected civil servants in 1922. It has always had a close relationship, in the upper reaches of the Corporation, with the military and the security services. Director generals with military backgrounds have included Cecil Graves (1942–3), Lieutenant General, Sir Ian Jacob (1942–59) and Charles Curran (1969–77), who served in the Indian army (BBC, 2004a). The BBC routinely vetted senior personnel in the post-war years. Yet there have been conflicts with the security services, for example when in 1987 the BBC decided not to show a film about a spy satellite in the *Secret Society* series. When, however, the details of the contents of the programme were made public, Special Branch officers raided BBC Scotland looking for evidence of a breach of Official Secrets legislation (O'Malley, 2003: 88).

The BBC has had to defend its journalism in the courts against attacks by politicians. In January 1984, the *Panorama* (BBC, 1953–) programme transmitted '*Maggie's Militant Tendency*'. It explored allegations of extreme right-wing influence within the Conservative Party. As a result, five Tory MPs issued writs against the BBC. The Director General of the BBC, Alastair Milne (1982–7), was forced to settle out of court in 1986, in part as a result of direct pressure from the governors (O'Malley, 1994: 34, 56, 61 and 153). The BBC has had to deal with the interests and campaigning of local authorities over coverage in their area, in particular over the adequacy of the provision of local radio and TV services and has historically been subjected to criticism by MPs of all parties who have used the privilege of Parliament to mount public attacks on the Corporation (Local Radio Workshop, 1983; O'Malley, 1994).

The BBC therefore was created by the state and has a continuing relationship with its various parts. This relationship has, on the whole, been harmonious, but it has also often been a matter of intense controversy. The relationship of the BBC with the state can be described broadly using three chronological periods, 1922–45, 1945–80 and 1980 onwards.

1922–45

This first period saw the BBC established as a monopoly radio broadcaster for several reasons. First, the government felt wary about losing control of the new radio technology for security reasons. Second, it wanted to avoid the emergence of monopoly commercial ownership, in particular by the major equipment manufacturer, Marconi. Third, the rapid and under-regulated growth of commercial radio in the US served as a warning to UK civil servants and politicians of the technical chaos and cultural consequences of allowing radio to develop without state regulation (see Briggs, 1961 and Chapter 7).

In 1926, the government decided to turn the British Broadcasting Company, as it had been since 1922, into a public corporation. The Corporation was to be overseen by a board of governors appointed by the government and managed by staff operating under a chief executive, latterly known as the Director General. John Reith was the first managing director from 1922 to 1938.

The device of using a public corporation to organise broadcasting was an example of state intervention which had become an increasingly common tool for policy-makers in the UK from the end of the nineteenth century. It was seen as a way of preventing the worst excesses of market competition in the provision of key industries, and part of a more general trend among political elites in the UK in the first half of the twentieth century in favour of increasing levels of state involvement in the economy (Curran and Seaton, 1997).

Under Reith, the BBC established the idea that broadcasting should be a public service. This meant ordering programming for social and cultural purposes rather than, as was the case in the US, for making profits out of the sale of advertising (see Chapter 7). This was made possible by funding the BBC

John Reith: the first Director General of the BBC

through the device of insisting every owner of a radio set bought a licence to listen to radio.

Reith interpreted the public service broadcasting remit to include raising the standards of popular taste, encouraging the intellectual development of listeners and supporting the King, the Empire and the social system. Reith's ideas were attacked at the time for being too highbrow and too limited (Curran and Seaton, 2003), but the very success of the BBC in the 1920s and 1930s rested on the Corporation's ability to deliver not only the high-brow diet advocated by Reith, but other types of programming, especially music-based shows.

It was, however, Reith's departure in 1938 and the outbreak of World War II in 1939, that forced the BBC to be more populist in its programming. Programme-makers and politicians became much more concerned to use the BBC to maintain morale during the war and as a result the Corporation placed greater emphasis on light-entertainment pro-gramming. BBC news, although carefully controlled, also built a reputation for its overall accuracy. Therefore, by 1945 the Corporation had established itself as a popular, non-commercial institution that was closely associated with the victory over Fascism (see Chapter 7).

1945–80

The period 1945 to 1980 saw the BBC's TV services expand (along with those provided by its commercial public service competitors, ITV), and become firmly embedded as part of the cultural furniture of every-day life. Its producers, writers and creative staff were given, especially under the Director Generalship of Hugh Greene (1960–9), increasing amounts of editorial and creative independence. Within the over-all framework of public service TV in the UK, the idea that journalists should act as independent, often critical voices, became firmly established (Doig, 1997; Briggs, 1995).

This situation led, inevitably, to periods of con-flict between the BBC and the state. In 1956, the BBC clashed with the Prime Minister, Anthony Eden. He objected to the way the Corporation gave airtime to domestic critics of his invasion of the Suez

Broadcasting House: the original home of the BBC

Canal. The satirical BBC programme, *That Was the Week That Was* (BBC, 1962) provoked tension between the government and the BBC. Two major controversies erupted in the 1970s. *Yesterday's Men* (BBC1, 1971) provoked fierce criticism from the Labour politicians who were the subject of the pro-gramme. *The Question of Ulster* (BBC, 1972) tried to cover the difficult issue of the war in Ireland and provoked the Conservative Government to attempt, unsuccessfully, to get the programme stopped (Briggs, 1995).

During the period after the election of the Conservative Government under Margaret Thatcher in 1979 the relationship between the BBC and the state shifted, as the attitude of politicians and civil servants towards public services changed. Political clashes over the coverage of Ireland and security issues continued (O'Malley, 1994), but there was a much more fundamental shift in the ideas of those governing the UK, which impacted on the BBC.

Under Mrs Thatcher (1979–90), her Con-servative successor John Major (1990–7) and the new Labour Prime Minister Tony Blair (1997–), governments began to take a much more hostile attitude to the idea that the state should intervene in the economy. This was because of a more general resurgence of right of centre, or neo-liberal, economic thinking, which emphasised the nineteenth-century model of allowing the economy to run with as little state interference as was possible. It was associated with a drive to privatise public services, such as telecommunications, gas, electricity and transport (Cockett, 1995).

The landmark document in this shift was the 1986 *Report of the Committee on Financing the BBC* (HMSO), known after its chairman as the Peacock Report. It took the view that in the long term the market, not the state or the idea of public service, should determine the shape and products of broadcasting in the UK. In the future, with the spread of new technologies like cable, satellite and digital transmission systems, all programmes could be accessed on a pay-per-view or pay-per-channel basis. In the long term there would be no need to have a licence fee-funded organisation like the BBC when producers and consumers could enter the electronic market cheaply and engage in one-to-one transactions – a producer offers a programme and a consumer decides whether to buy that programme. There might need to be a tax-funded organisation to provide a minority of high-quality programmes. However, state intervention, epitomised by the BBC's very existence, should, effectively, be allowed to decline.

The BBC, in this strategy, was to remain in place while new commercial entrants were encouraged by state policy. A succession of laws (the 1990 Broadcasting Act, the 1996 Broadcasting Act and the 2003 Communications Act) accelerated this process. Competition in the form of advertising, subscription and pay-per-view services grew, so that, by 2003, the combined income of these operations far outstripped BBC income.

Ofcom, the government-appointed regulator for the new and older commercial sector, which came into being as result of the 2003 Communications Act pointed out that, in 2003, total TV broadcasting revenues, including the licence fee, rose to £9,534 million from £8,987 million – a 6 per cent real terms growth. Stripping out the licence fee, commercial revenues rose by a greater proportion in 2003 from £6,763 million to £7,301 million or 8 per cent. Most of this growth was in the digital sector (a revenue increase of 17 per cent) and, for the first time, subscription revenue exceeded advertising spending. Subscription was £3,202 million and advertising £3,148 million. The proportion of the licence fee, which was £2.7 million in 2002/3, spent on TV was only up 0.4 per cent in real terms to £2,233 million (BBC, 2004a: 116; Ofcom, 2004: 22). In essence over the period 1979–2003, the BBC became a relatively smaller player, economically, in the UK broadcasting sector *because* of changes in state thinking about the role of markets in society as a whole, and communications in particular.

PUBLIC SERVICE BROADCASTING, MARKET ORTHODOXY AND THE STATE

At the start of the twenty-first century the dominant political orthodoxy in the UK was neo-liberal. Politicians of all the main parties (Labour, Conservative and Liberal Democrat) were wedded to the idea that the way to run the economy was to allow the maximum possible amount of freedom to businesses to provide goods for consumers (Leys, 2001). The BBC and public service broadcasting was the creation of an earlier period (1900–60) when the orthodoxy was different. Then, under the pressure of global economic failure, the economic depression of the 1930s, the rise of Fascism, and pressure from a strongly organised Labour and trade union movement, politicians in the UK adopted the view that on matters such as education, health and broadcasting individual freedoms could only be enriched through giving people access to these resources by making them free at the point of use.

For broadcasting this model brought some negative consequences. The BBC, and subsequently ITV, were set up to ensure that they did not step too far outside the boundaries of political and cultural debate over which the governments of the day presided (see Creeber, 2004b). Yet control in the US, where there was no comparable state-sponsored system, fell increasingly into the hands of corporations which displayed a high degree of political cultural conservatism and were as firmly, if not more firmly wedded to the US political system than the BBC (McChesney, 2000).

Yet public service broadcasting as exemplified, in part by the BBC, was a space, relatively free from commercial pressures, in which there grew up a strong tradition of critical and creative independence and innovation (Curran and Seaton, 2003). It was this internal culture, fostered by the economic and political structures created by the state, which allowed for a flowering of programming in the UK. For some, this tradition proved too stifling and economically constraining. For others, it was far too close to the state for comfort. For others still, it was, on balance, the product of a relatively fruitful rela-

tionship between a democratically accountable government and an influential cultural institution.

By 2004, the drift in UK policy was towards increasing the commercial sector in UK broadcasting (see Chapter 7). The state will always retain a strong role in supervising the political and cultural framework of broadcasting, but unless there is another change in the orthodoxies that dominate the minds of politicians and civil servants away from the current fashionable anti-statism, the BBC is likely to become less important as a broadcasting institution in the UK over the next few decades. However, the state has always (and for the foreseeable future will always) provide the basic framework governing the programming we watch.

9 Television and Globalisation

National and International Concerns

John Hartley

> Before satellites, fiber optic cabling, and digital compression, television was a local outlet sometimes attached to a national programming network. No more. Television – like all major forms of electronic communication has gone global.
>
> Tony Verna, *Global Television*, 1993: 2.

Narrowly defined, **globalisation** is the extension of cross-border economic ties, leading to greater integration of societies and economies around the world. More broadly, it is used as a proxy term for the market economy or euphemism for capitalism. In relation to television, globalisation of TV-set manufacturing and programming, as well as the global reach of media corporations like Time Warner, Viacom, Disney, News Corporation, Bertelsmann and Sony, has intensified since the 1980s. Perhaps more to the point, television is one of the key sites for debate and activism in relation to the broader definition of globalisation as 'capitalism'. TV is a convenient metaphor – and scapegoat – for many of the perceived ills of commercial democracies, particularly worries about the effect of popular media on national and cultural identity in different countries.

We would do better to think of 'globalisation' as a *concept* than as a description of historical *process*, because it is not in fact the case that once upon a time, economic or social life was city- or nation-based and then it began to go global. We are not faced with an evolutionary or developmental change so much as a change in the history of ideas. In other words, we have begun to *conceptualise* the global dimensions of phenomena we had previously thought of (or experienced) only in local or nation-

al settings. This way of conceptualising has now gained very wide currency beyond the world of intellectual specialisation, as globalisation has become one of the most dynamic terms in popular media and politics in recent years as well as in more formal academic theorising.

GLOBALISATION: A BRIEF OVERVIEW

The globalisation that we hear most about results from those 'in-your-face' outpourings of US consumer culture, for example:

- Globalisation of movies and TV – 'Hollywood' (Miller *et al.*, 2004).
- Globalisation of fast food – the 'McDonaldization of society' (Ritzer, 2004).
- Globalisation of fashion – e.g. the four most-worn items of clothing in the world are all American: baseball cap, T-shirt, jeans, sneakers (Sondhi and Tyagi, 2002 and see Sweatshop Watch).

Such media, apparel, entertainment and shopping phenomena are themselves products of globalised but still US-dominated commercial investment, internationalised production and marketing, 'global capital' to its critics.

Since the 1980s the world has experienced unprecedented levels of intensity in the international movement of investment and marketing, and also in the global reach of information, knowledge and communications. But even among fully globalised industries, **transnational** movement is often only one-way. It is easier for US companies than for African and Asian countries to globalise their operations and markets, which means in practice that such Western-originated products and services as pharmaceuticals, infant milk formula and entertainment formats find their way into African and Asian homes quite readily, while much of the agricultural, intellectual and cultural produce of those countries is effectively blocked from entry into the US or EU. Global movement of people (labour) has also remained more difficult than movement of capital, again, especially migration to the affluent West from the rest of the world.

Critical analysis of corporate globalisation has focused on analysing these unequal freedoms. Critics tend not to emphasise the real advantage to be reaped from international traffic in goods and services which, for advanced economies, principally takes the form of radically lower costs enabled by standardisation and modularisation of components, economies of scale, and the ability to source materials and labour wherever they are cheapest internationally. The manufacture of TV sets provides a good example (Mougayar, 2002):

> In 1956, an RCA color TV set was sold for $500, or $1,300 in today's dollars. That same year, the average car sold for $2,100 and average annual salary was $5,300. In 2002, it is possible to purchase a standard, no-name 20-inch TV set for $130. That's a ten-fold decrease in price in 46 years.

While benefiting from such cheap and ubiquitous technology, critics of globalisation focus on the increasing control of resources, labour and markets by locally unaccountable international firms (McChesney, 2000).

Criticism has also dwelt on the feared '**homogenisation**' – in practice the **Americanisation** – of culture in many countries or localities, to the perceived detriment of national identity and local diversity. Television has become a potent symbol of these issues in recent years, because TV so clearly links economic and cultural issues (see Barker, 1999; Lee, 2003; Tomlinson, 1999; Morley and Robins, 1995).

But the present-tenseness of entertainment and

the size of American corporations should not blind us to the fact that globalisation is as old as the media themselves. Printing, for example, was invented in its 'modern' form, using moveable type, over half a millennium ago, during the 1450s in the city of Mainz. Printing (technology) and the publishing trade (business model) were recognisably modern and fully international from the start, not unlike other 'creative industries' of the time such as acting and cathedral-building. Firms located in Germany and the Low Countries soon supplied the entire continent with published product. Venture capitalists like Johann Fust (and the long-continuing firm Fust and Schöffer), who took over Gutenberg's firm in Mainz, or entrepreneurs like Caxton in Bruges and Westminster, Plantin in Antwerp and later on Elzevir in Leyden, operated in different countries at once, building productive capacity, demand and local variation across a range of markets. Printing spread very quickly from the 1460s, being distributed throughout Europe by 1490. Globally, it reached Istanbul in 1503, Morocco in 1521, Iceland in 1534, Mexico in 1539, Goa in 1556, Cairo in 1557, Russia in 1564, Palestine in 1577, Lima in 1584, Macao in 1588, which was also the year that the first printed Welsh translation of the Bible was published, and Japan in 1591. Content too was truly global from the outset, with an expansionist craze for maps, travel stories, both fantastical and historical, and accounts of expeditions of exploration, that was at least as important as the equally transnational religious content of early printing in the West (Vervliet, 1972: 356, 397–8).

In case a period of just under a century – the time it took for print to globalise – seems leisurely, it is worth noting that television itself took nearly as long to spread across the world. TV started as practical system in the 1930s (J. Baird's mechanical TV had been trialled since 1926 – see Chapter 7). Germany commenced broadcasts in public TV halls in March 1935 and the Berlin Olympics of July 1936 were broadcast live (Uricchio, 2004; see also Early Television). In Britain, the BBC began a domestic TV service on 2 November the same year. RCA launched broadcast TV in the US at the World's Fair of 1939. Thereafter it took sixty years to reach the kingdom of Bhutan, which in 1999 had the interesting distinction of being the last country on earth to accept a television system (see Scott-Clark and Levy, 2003).

Imaginative content has also been expansive and international for centuries. Both music and drama had been itinerant professions since the Middle Ages, and actors, singers and acrobats crossed national boundaries long before the print and electronic media began to dominate popular culture. Many of Shakespeare's plays, for example, which premiered in London from the 1590s to the 1610s, were actually set in global locations including Athens, Bermuda, Denmark, Egypt, France, Illyria and Rome (see Bardware). Shakespeare used cosmopolitan sources too, raiding books from across the known world (see Shakespeare-W.com). And of course Shakespeare's own work was itself quickly globalised via both print and performance. In this case most commentators were full of praise for the outcome, rather than protesting at cultural imperialism, even as the very English worldview of the Swan of Avon conquered hearts, minds and box offices from Alma Ata to Zeffirelli (see Hartley, 2004).

News too was international from the moment of the earliest newspapers in the seventeenth century, although editors had to rely on couriers who travelled no faster than horse or sail could carry them. News content that was simultaneously available across the world had to wait until the mid-nineteenth century, when the Reuters agency, founded in 1851 to send stock prices from London to Paris, pioneered the transmission of news via telegraph cables that linked Britain to Europe, the Americas and the Far East. Reuters scooped the world in 1865 by being the first agency in Europe to report the assassination of President Lincoln (see Reuters).

These examples demonstrate that the technology, organisational form and content of media have been global for centuries, from which it is necessary to conclude that recent interest in globalisation, which has burgeoned since the end of the Cold War, was not caused by new human activities. Globalisation became a key term in the 1990s (almost entirely supplanting '**postmodernism**')

partly for political reasons, partly because of intellectual history. It was newly noticed as a political and intellectual problem. Social theorists began to think of it as a condition of contemporary society, not just as a feature of economic or communicative activity.

Politically, the adversarial ideological stand-off between Left and Right was reconfigured at the end of the Cold War when the international Communist movement collapsed as a formal opponent to global capitalism. Marxist, anti-capitalist and radical single-issue groups began to organise around '**anti-globalisation**' as a way of contesting the remaining superpower. Conversely, proponents of free trade and economic neo-liberalism promoted globalisation as the key to business growth and competitiveness. This in turn provoked further critical concerns about **US hegemony** and the influence of corporate-controlled market forces. Opposition was voiced (often spectacularly, in street demonstrations) to US cultural power as well as to its political, economic and military might.

It was in this cultural context that the idea of globalised *society* – understood as a mixed blessing at best – gained prominence. Journalistic and academic observers alike began to comment on the *experience* of globalisation for consumers and citizens, not just on the existence of global business operations. However, it was increasingly evident that the gap between corporate performance and consumer experience was rapidly closing, because the way consumers felt began to affect the bottom line. Across the world, citizen–consumers might easily express their political opposition to US power by resisting US brands. Such sensitivities needed to be taken into account by corporate analysts as they assessed the risks to American competitive advantage (Roberts, 2005):

The danger for US companies is that they will fail to appreciate the growing self-assurance of consumers in markets such as China or India. This increasing confidence could translate into a growing tendency to take offence at cultural slights. This month, China banned a Nike advertisement that depicted US basketball star, LeBron James, defeating a kung fu master and other Chinese cultural icons in a video-game-style battle. China said the advertisement was offensive. Advertising executives suggested Nike erred by not letting the home side win. BBH got a better response with a Levi's advertisement that showed an Asian man facing down a street full of mean-looking westerners. 'We have to be very careful about advertising in these countries', Mr [Maurice] Levy [chief executive of Publicis] said. 'We know cultural things are very touchy'.

Intellectually, in the sciences as well as the arts and humanities, there has been a growing willingness to consider global organisation as a defining property of various phenomena both natural and social. The idea of explaining things in terms of their global coherence, rather than by reducing them to their smallest units as in normal science, has an intellectual history that goes back at least as far as the late nineteenth century, when scientists began to observe and theorise various phenomena as *global systems*. Where previously there was just locally encountered air, or life, or culture, or media, now there was the atmosphere (Wikipedia), the biosphere or ecosystem (Wikipedia), the semiosphere (Lotman, 1990) and, more recently, the mediasphere (Hartley, 1996; Hartley and McKee, 2000).

MAPPING THE 'MEDIASPHERE'

Can we imagine something big enough to cover the planet, coherent enough such that each tiny part may interact with all the others, and small or local enough to interact with and affect each individual person? Evidently we can – global television has these characteristics, as Marshall McLuhan pointed out with his concept of the global village (McLuhan, 1964; McLuhan and Fiore, 1967).

But before we get to that, it is worth remembering that the very same characteristics apply to things other than TV, including the physical and natural environment. For instance, take the atmosphere – what is it? It's the air each of us breathes, the weather we live under, the smog we choke on. It is about as intimate to our own personal life and as crucial to our comfort as anything we know or experience. At the same time the atmosphere is as big as the planet, stretching all the way around the globe and many kilometres above it. It is hard even to imagine how big that is, and yet we have relatively little trouble thinking about 'the' atmosphere in the singular – it is just one object, spread thinly like skin, but like skin a coherent organ in its own right.

The fact that we can imagine the global atmosphere as a single object, while individually breathing little bits of it in and out again, has recently become a significant matter in political and public life, because of concerns about the effect of greenhouse gas emissions and global warming. In fact, pollution may be one way to glimpse just how big the atmosphere is, because the sheer weight of what we pump into it each year is itself mind-boggling. During the 1990s for instance, the countries of the European Union alone belted out about *four billion tonnes* of 'greenhouse gases' (mostly carbon dioxide) into the atmosphere each year. And yet carbon dioxide comprises only about 0.035 per cent of the atmosphere's volume (European Environment Agency; National Statistics Online).

Turning from the physical to the natural environment, the atmosphere itself provided a model for the biologist V. I. Vernadsky to propose the concept of the **biosphere** – comprising all the living organisms on earth, their interactions and the conditions for the continuation of life; thus 'biosphere' is a similar concept to the later term **'ecosystem'** (Wikipedia). And turning from nature to culture, again following directly from the model of the atmosphere and the biosphere, the semiotician Yuri Lotman coined the useful term **semiosphere**: the 'semiotic space necessary for the existence and functioning of different languages', without which neither communication nor language could exist (Lotman, 1990: 123–5; and compare Vernadsky's concept of the **noosphere** – sphere of the human mind, Wikipedia). Like the atmosphere and biosphere, the idea of the semiosphere is not simply that it covers the planet, but more importantly that this global organism is the *condition of existence* for all the differentiated parts and interactions that go on at local level. Life (or 'biota') cannot exist in detail (species by species) without the entire biosphere, not least because species A eats species B. Similarly, meaning cannot exist, language by language or even speaker by speaker, without the entire semiosphere as a structuring set of conditions for relationships and interactions within which any individual communication can occur.

Using the same model, and turning from meaning to media, the term **mediasphere** was coined (Hartley, 1996; Hartley and McKee, 2000) to encompass the idea of something big enough to cover the planet, coherent enough that each tiny part may interact with all the others, and small or local enough to affect each individual person. Like the semiosphere, it expresses the various forms, relationships and structural conditions for existence and interaction of a worldwide system of media communication. The mediasphere is of course 'multiplatform,' not confined to one medium like television but encompassing the entire variety of print, photographic, audiovisual and performative media, which interact with each other such that television shares technological, industrial and semiotic forms, and audiences, with other media like radio, theatre, movies and print. It cannot be understood without the global interactive system that has shaped it and which allows it to operate in any given local instance.

As noted above, the mediasphere is older than it may seem. There was an international traffic in mediated plays, poems and stories long before the modern industrial era. But it became 'visible to the naked eye', as it were, only during and following the great modern industrial and imperial expansions of the nineteenth century. This period took all manner of European media, including books and literate reading publics, newspapers, magazines, theatre, news agencies like Reuters, songs, stories and live entertainments, across the world. What was new about this was not so much the global reach but the narrow source of media. Suddenly it wasn't just the same technology (like the printing press) that was available across the world for producing local materials, it was the same *content*, expressing the desires, fears and energies of Western commercial democracies and

their military enforcers everywhere, all at once, apparently drowning out other voices. In other words, the mediasphere could now appear as unified to a single reader–consumer at a speed that had not been possible before. It was increasingly filled with the **monocultural** 'emissions' of industrialised and imperial media.

Such a unity of content at the point of reception was only possible via a 'broadcast' model of communication – one-to-many, one-way, with centralised, professional producers and dispersed, passive consumers. This was not orderly turn-taking transmission and reception by more or less equal communicative partners; it was not modelled on conversation but on the oratorical tradition of the preacher and performer. The potential for both political and commercial persuasion via such global one-way mediation became a continuing theme not only of national politics (will our own population be adversely affected by messages from abroad or from undesirable sources?) but also of **colonialism** ('subaltern' populations subjected to the media and meanings of the coloniser), experienced first within the countries of Africa, Asia, the Americas and Australasia that were directly ruled by European powers in the nineteenth and early twentieth centuries, but more recently by those powers themselves as American broadcast entertainment carried all before it (see below).

In the twentieth century the audiovisual and broadcast media – radio, cinema and television – came of age, overtaking but not supplanting print as the most pervasive media, and in the process intensifying transatlantic rivalry as American media ascendancy grew. The global reach of radio was first demonstrated by its inventor Guglielmo Marconi, who sent the first transatlantic radio signal on 12 December 1901. He topped this feat on 26 March 1930 by using radio-telegraphy to turn on the town hall lights in Sydney, Australia, by throwing a switch aboard his yacht *Elletra*, which at the time was moored on the other side of the planet in Genoa harbour (Marconi, 1999: 44–54; 57–61; see also Uricchio, 2004, for an account of the first global time signal, broadcast from the Eiffel Tower in July

1913). While Marconi was perfecting the global infra-structure, the BBC began to globalise content through the Empire Service (predecessor of the BBC World Service) from 1932 (see Chapter 7). It broadcast via shortwave radio from Bush House in London, whose massive portico bears the BBC's globalising motto: 'Nation Shall Speak Peace Unto Nation.'

But perhaps more to the point, 'across the pond', Hollywood was vying for global supremacy with European film studios like Cinecitta, Mosfilm, Ealing and Pathé, establishing a powerful but not uncontested dominance after talking pictures arrived in 1929. All these developments indicate not only that the broadcast mediasphere was understood to be global from the very start, but also that much of the current disquiet about the cultural impact of global media has its roots in European dismay at the Americanisation of what until then they had seen as 'their' mediasphere. In Lotman's terms, the European part of the semiosphere flipped from 'transmitting' to 'receiving' mode while America flipped from receiver to transmitter. Emblematically marking this decisive shift in strategic and semiotic power from Europe to the US (see Kagan, 2003) was the identity of the TV show that happened to be playing when the BBC unceremoniously pulled the plug on its television service upon the outbreak of World War II in September 1939. It was the same show that they used to re-launch television in 1946, after being so rudely interrupted, as it were. It was of course a Mickey Mouse cartoon from Walt Disney (but it does seem that Mickey Mouse was soon followed by the home-grown Windmill Girls . . . see xtvworld).

TELEVISION AS AN INSTRUMENT OF GLOBALISATION

Television grew up as a cultural form in an existing atmosphere of technological excitement and international competition. To begin with it was established very much on a national basis, especially in Germany, Britain, the US and the USSR. Each country tried to develop their own system under their own legislation, using their own programming. There was little chance for viewers to see programmes from another country unless they visited it,

an experience that could lead to 'culture shock,' as happened to Raymond Williams when he first saw US TV (Williams, 1974; see Chapter 1). International traffic was restricted to filmed materials, including newsreel footage, documentaries and movies. Made-for-TV drama series were also exportable if they were made on film. But the special strength of television – liveness – could not be shared among the nations. Europe pioneered international television exchange via the Eurovision network in the 1950s. Eurovision's technical capabilities were popularised via the all-too-live *Eurovision Song Contest* from 1956 (BBC). But international live TV didn't really take off until it could cross the Atlantic, which the launch of the Telstar satellite made possible on 10 July 1962 (see NASA).

Meanwhile content had begun to be traded and some of the later features of globalisation could be discerned, not least the business of 'dumping'. For example, when television was introduced into Western Australia in October 1959, the local commercial licensee needed a lot of content. What better way to achieve this than buying a package from the US? Some of it may have been of dubious aesthetic or entertainment merit and of zero relevance to the home viewer's local culture or experience, but it was incredibly cheap. Old TV Westerns could go out for literally a few dollars an hour, when making the programme might cost hundreds of thousands of dollars per hour and require resources and talent that

The *Eurovision Song Contest*: an international event since 1956

Dallas: an American soap opera with a global reach

Who Wants to be a Millionaire?: seen in over a hundred countries

were simply not available to local producers. The costs of US TV shows were entirely recouped in their home market, releasing for export high-quality (technical), easily understood, commercial entertainment that was effectively cost-free at the point of export. Sales agents could therefore set whatever price would undercut local providers. Small wonder then that global commercial TV began to rely on US programming. At the same time, public TV stations were borrowing wholesale from the British, especially the BBC, for the same reason.

Commercial good sense and an international market in TV shows, which is still based in Los Angeles, thus inadvertently resulted in a distinct mismatch between popular programming and national or cultural specificities. People who had little in common with one another and even less with California all ended up watching *Hopalong Cassidy* (ABC, 1949–51) and later *Dallas* (CBS, 1978–91) (Liebes, 1990). By such means, American and British TV programmes were effectively global by the end of the 1950s.

The global coherence of the 'mediasphere' as an organised system of communication was not apparent to most individual viewers until they could see it on their own screens. Two separate developments have promoted this trend; global TV channels and global TV formats (Moran, 1998).

- The launch of CNN (1 June 1980) and MTV (1 August 1981) heralded global TV channels.

- Endemol's *Big Brother* (1999–) and Celador's *Who Wants to Be a Millionaire?* (1998–) are exemplary global TV formats. *Millionaire* is seen in over a hundred countries; *Big Brother* in twenty (see Endemol; Celador).

The novelty of 'reality' format shows from the business point of view is that a single (global) concept or format can be reproduced or '**re-versioned**' in different (local) markets. The production company can profit from global distribution while the local audience actually sees a show that is to all intents and purposes their own. Contestants on Australian or Brazilian *Big Brother* are Australians and Brazilians, not Dutch. The flexibility of this concept is such that different versions of the same show can develop distinct national characteristics, for example with more sexual activity and plotting and conniving in some countries (the UK), more female winners in others (Sweden), contestants who like each other (Australia), or a different eviction regime (in the US contestants are voted out by housemates not viewers) (see Mathijus and Jones, 2004). Also, the local reproduction of global formats increases the scope for multiplatform and interactive elements, bringing phone, fast-food and Internet companies into the game, and allowing viewers greater levels of personal interactivity with the show, including attending live events. It seems also that audiences like the idea of a successful global format. In 2005, for instance, viewers of FOX8 TV in Australia were able to enjoy a re-run of Tyra Banks' *America's Next Top Model* (NBC, 2003–) while at the same time trying out a new local re-version, *Australia's Next Top Model* (FOX8, 2004–). One advantage of the local show over its global parent was that it was made for pay-TV. As host Erika Heynatz commented, hinting at candid moments and tensions: 'The beauty of cable is we don't have that censorship' (*Courier Mail*).

GLOBAL TELEVISION: FOR BETTER OR WORSE?

Does the globalisation of television production, technology and content have an adverse effect on cultural identities, and does US-led media entertainment impoverish media culture in less favoured countries? The early flood of publications on globalisation, themselves representative of an internationally influential US left-academic activism, tended to answer both of those questions resoundingly in the affirmative. US TV companies ruled the world; US TV entertainment '**coca-colonised**' the planet. But latterly more measured judgments have come to the fore. It has been noticed that Latin American *telenovelas* are hugely popular in Eastern Europe, for instance – there's a global counterflow of media content among countries as various as Brazil, India, Egypt, Japan and increasingly China (see Morley and Robins, 1995). Todd Boyd has made the point that it is not just US culture but specifically *black* culture, represented in music, sports, fashion and style, that is exported around the world (Boyd, 2003). And it is self-evident that even the most intense global consumption of American media does not turn the people of the world into Americans, no matter which way round they wear their baseball caps. Indeed, since the Iraq War it has become evident that prolonged exposure to US media can create aversion rather than conversion. Furthermore, identity is often felt to be more important in small, hard-pressed nations than in more populous, heterogeneous ones: e.g. Wales or Scotland rather than England (though that's changing); Norway or Croatia rather than Germany; or indigenous people rather than settlers in Australia; and on a larger scale, France or Canada rather than the US. Being 'inundated' by another culture, not least via television programming, may actually provoke sharper and more defined local or indigenous cultural identity, not destroy it.

A more recent tragic event has shown that positive as well as negative outcomes can result even from the *globalisation of disaster*. The so-called 'Asian tsunami' (as the newsbars called it although it reached Africa) of 26 December 2004 was – among other things – a global television event. It demonstrated how television's global system of newsgathering resources, transmission networks and audience responses could be mobilised for humanitarian and public good. It showed the full *integration* of:

- **Sources of TV images and stories**: All channels relied on amateur footage of the event, and used general Internet/email traffic as a reliable news source. This disaster was reported as much by the audience/consumer as by professionals, especially in its early moments, integrating producer and consumer in the production process more visibly than is common in mainstream TV. It showed how the pervasion of digital cameras, mobile phones and computers among the general population has permanently altered what can be seen and said on TV, which is no longer the only 'window on the world', looking out on viewers' behalf, but

an extension of their own sense-making activities.

- **Media**: The event attracted immediate blanket coverage from media across the globe, which in previous times, before global television was fully integrated, would not have occurred. Compare the international coverage of the 1976 earthquake in China, where comparable numbers, perhaps 250,000 people, died. Access to that event was restricted by the Chinese government, of course, but so was interest in the event among Western media organisations and audiences. Many people in the West will never have heard of it, any more than they had heard of the troubled Indonesian province of Aceh before December 2004.

- **Populations**: Among the enormous toll of dead and missing people were many thousands of Western tourists, including a number of prominent people and celebrities. At one point it was reported that more Swedes lost their lives that day than in World War II (see also *Sydney Morning Herald*). Every country that covered the event could focus on its own nationals as well as local victims, thereby forging instant common cause with populations that are usually not thought of as neighbours by Western audiences.

- **Response**: It quickly became clear that the tidal wave itself was being followed by a no less remarkable wave of fellow feeling and generosity from the global viewing public. The speed and amount of donations to help victims was itself a major TV news story. Spontaneous acts of generosity from sports personalities like Russian tennis star, Maria Sharapova (who was in Thailand at the time), and speedy responses from organisations, like the gift of £50,000 from each of Britain's Premier League football clubs, soon shamed governments and international brands into following suit. A multinational bidding war was duly reported on CNN and BBC World, with the US, European countries, Australia and Japan vying to outdo each other. Norway alone contributed over one billion kroner – the equivalent of US $40 for every person living in that country. In Beijing, students braved the cold of Tiananmen Square to collect personal donations. The Chinese government, not to be outdone by Taiwan or its own citizens, pledged the largest aid package in its history.

Across the world, governments, firms, organisations and individuals were integrated in an active and practical desire to help. As so often, it took the worst of circumstances to bring out the best in a system of television production, organisations, content and audiences. Globalised TV came of age as a part of a 'mediasphere' where the smallest individual elements could clearly be seen to interact with all of the others around the planet. This was a globalisation not so much of technology, economics or even content, but of humanity. And television played the central enabling role. Certainly, the issue of global television is a complex debate and one that can be viewed from a number of critical perspectives.

FURTHER READING

McChesney, Robert (2000), *Rich Media, Poor Democracy: Communication Policy in Dubious Times*, Champaign: University of Illinois Press.

Moran, Albert (1998), *Copycat Television: Globalisation, Program Formats and Cultural Identity*, Luton: University of Luton Press.

Parks, Lisa and Kumar, Shanti (eds) (2002), *Planet TV: A Global Television Reader*, New York: New York University Press.

Sinclair, John, Jacka, Elizabeth and Cunningham, Stuart (eds) (1996), *New Patterns in Global Television: Peripheral Vision*, Oxford and New York: Oxford University Press.

Sinclair, John and Turner, Graeme (2004) (eds), *Contemporary World Television*, London: BFI.

Tomlinson, John (1999), *Globalization and Culture*, Cambridge: Polity Press.

Verna, Tony (1993), *Global Television: How to Create Effective Television for the Future*, Boston, MA: Focal Press.

CASE STUDY
Indigenous Television Faye Ginsburg and Lorna Roth

This case study deals with the way television has been used by indigenous communities around the world to communicate and support their own culture, customs and language. By 'indigenous' we simply refer to the native inhabitants of a territory who have now become marginalised by a power and a culture that did not originate in that region. Examples of indigenous communities would include the Aboriginals in Australia, the Maoris in New Zealand and the Native Americans in the US. The very presence of indigenous TV might suggest that rather than television simply being an aid in the gradual **homogenisation** of a global (possibly **Americanised**) culture, that the medium can also be used to promote and develop the cultural resurgence of smaller nations and communities. Roland Robertson refers to the possibility of this cultural and national resistance as '**glocalisation**', i.e. how the impact of globalisation may have actually forced

threatened communities to re-examine and re-invigorate their own cultural and national identities. According to Robertson, the very process of globalisation has also 'involved the reconstruction, in a sense the production, of "home", "community" and "locality"' (1995: 30). Similarly, Anthony Smith describes such a process as the 'globalisation of nationalism' (1991: 143), resurgent nations and communities seeking to position themselves in this new global space, sometimes using the media (frequently television) to do so. Certainly, indigenous television provides an interesting case study around which the global impact of television can be re-examined and understood.

INDIGENOUS TV: ARGUMENTS FOR AND AGAINST
Over the last three decades, television has spread from centres to peripheries, part of the rapidly changing landscape of global television – what some

call '**Planet TV**' (Parks and Kumar, 2003) – as media technology expanded from terrestrial TV to the more flexible range of satellite and small-format video and, increasingly, **convergence** with the Internet (see Chapter 10). The localised possibilities in this form of **globalisation** are especially apparent in the uptake of such media forms in First Peoples' communities throughout the world, creating 'Something New in the Air' (Roth, 2005); and undoubtedly have much longer histories that range from 'Songlines to Satellites' (Molnar and Meadows, 2001) or 'From Birchbark Talk to Digital Dreamspeaking' (Buddle-Crowe, forthcoming). The capacity of such media to communicate the concerns of these indigenous people to many audiences has created, some argue, a discursive space for an emergent **indigenous public sphere** (Hartley and McKee, 2000); others have recognised that media

might offer a kind of 'Faustian contract' for indigenous producers (Ginsburg, 1991), while the most pessimistic suggest that these projects inevitably entail 'getting into bed with the state' (Batty, 2003).

These concerns about compromise haunt much of the early research and debate on indigenous television, echoing the suspicions of indigenous communities as they have struggled to imagine how they might turn the imposition of media technologies to their advantage. Generally, this has involved a recognition of the cultural possibilities of indigenously controlled media-making as a way of making the nations that encompass them more aware of indigenous concerns, while also strengthening local inter-generational and inter-community knowledge. When they can control the circumstances of production and circulation, indigenous activists (and fellow travellers concerned with the **democratisation** of media)

Television in India: TV is now a global phenomenon

have embraced television and other media recognised as potentially important assets, as technologies that have allowed indigenous and other minoritised communities some degree of agency to 'talk back' to **hegemonic** forms of representation, even if under less than ideal conditions (Ginsburg, 1991).

To some extent, indigenous concerns about compromise benefited from the fact that many of the communication technologies they wanted to use initially were regarded as experimental and marginal. Indeed, the very idea of indigenous television was regarded as somewhat of an oxymoron, in many cases allowing this work to unfold at its own pace, in line with indigenously based ideas of what constitutes appropriate production and circulation practices, as well as aesthetics (Leuthold, 1998). As indigenous television has started to play more of a role in the global **mediasphere**, some are concerned, once again, that it will be increasingly compromised.

A BRIEF HISTORY OF INDIGENOUS TV

While indigenous television projects first emerged in Canada in the 1970s, Australia in the 1980s and most recently (March 2004) in New Zealand/Aoteoroa, varieties of indigenous television can be found in the US, Brazil, Bolivia and Mexico. These include participation in highly localised low-power TV (such as Radio y Video Tamix in Mexico or PAW TV in Yuendumu, Australia), what one scholar of Mexican indigenous media calls 'Television Sin Reglas' (Wortham, 2002: 265); regional remote networks such as the Central Australian Aboriginal Media Association; units affiliating with national television (such as the Indigenous Production Units inaugurated in 1988 as part of Australia's ABC and SBS stations); as well as national stations underwritten by government support, as happened with the Aboriginal People's Television Network in Canada and Maori TV.

Following on the heels of broader movements for indigenous rights, activists in a number of locales pushed government bodies to allocate resources for their communities to produce and circulate representations of themselves, their histories and their worldviews. Of particular concern was the capacity to create programming for all age groups in their local languages, to combat the overwhelming effects of exposure to the dominant culture and its language through other forms of television, a debate that was active in the 1970s and has resurfaced in 2005 regarding language policy on Canada's APTN. Eventually, the indigenous appropriation of television has been recognised as an important technology in the development of **indigenous citizenship** for those living in both remote and urban areas, and for their recognition by the surrounding settler societies as well.

Scholars and researchers have been attracted to indigenous television since the mid-1980s, seeking in it the empirical evidence of a kind of embedded cultural critique, an aesthetic and political alternative to mass media beholden to government or late-capitalist interests. This sense of possibility was articulated most notably in the mid-1980s in 'The Aboriginal Invention of Television in Central Australia' (1986), Eric Michaels' report on the development of low power – and at the time illegal – television at the remote Warlpiri community of Yuendumu. Eventually, the Warlpiri Media Association, as it was known, and a similar project in South Australia, Ernabella Video and Television (EVTV), became exemplary for the government's Broadcast for Remote Aboriginal Communities Scheme (BRACS), which delivered small-format equipment to remote Aboriginal communities in the hope that they would also establish low-power television, a project that has had mixed results (Molnar, 1993). In 1980, a regional Aboriginal media association, the Central Australian Aboriginal Media Association (CAAMA) won the licence for the commercial satellite downlink to Central Australia; the group's celebration of its twenty-fifth year is indicative of its success as 'a world leader in indigenous media', as it claims on its website (www.caama.com.au/). CAAMA produces work by, for, and about Aboriginal issues and culture, focusing on the key cultural and linguistic groups in the area, while also successfully developing national and international co-productions. CAAMA is also involved in the management of programming for Imparja ('foot-print' in the Arrente language of that region), the commercial satellite downlink to Central Australia, for which it provides a modest amount of programming in four local Aboriginal languages as well as mainstream television.

In the US, Native American Public Telecommunications (NAPT), headquartered in Lincoln, Nebraska, is also in its twenty-fifth year of supporting the creation, promotion and distribution of Native American public media for all media including public television and public radio, training opportunities for American Indians and Alaska Natives, addressing policy issues and developing telecommunications projects across 'Indian country' (www.nativetelecom.org/mission.html).

If the 1980s witnessed developments in remote broadcasting, indigenous television expanded by the end of that decade and into the 1990s to include the development of Aboriginal units as part of Australia's national public service television, ABC, and its multicultural counterpart, SBS; work produced there includes everything from short fiction to documentary to talk shows, to news and entertainment, to music videos. Importantly, these units have also served as incubators of indigenous talent, as indigenous producers, directors, actors and editors have had opportunities made available to them that never before existed. While initially, some of these indigenous media-makers felt that their assertion of a more cosmopolitan claim to an indigenous identity is sometimes regarded as inauthentic, increasingly, this is not the case, particularly with more collaborations taking place between remote and urban communities.

As indigenous media productions have developed under these regimes, the work made for such purposes increasingly circulates beyond the televisual moment of broadcast to other native communities in the form of tapes and DVDs, as well as to non-Aboriginal audiences via regional, national and even international television. The capacity of this work to have a life after television, so to speak, helps overcome the potential isolation of indigenous media to a particular channel or programming slot, overcom-

ing the hazard that such cultural slots may in the end create 'media reservations' (Roth, 2000). More broadly, the telling and circulation of indigenous stories and histories through media forms that can circulate beyond the local has been an important force for constituting claims for land and cultural rights, and for developing alliances with other communities.

Since Aboriginal media activists in Canada have played a pioneering and exemplary role in the development of indigenous television, we want to focus on this work briefly in order to give a richer sense of how this work has evolved and where its future might be.

TELEVISION NORTHERN CANADA AND THE ABORIGINAL PEOPLES TELEVISION NETWORK

Television Northern Canada (TVNC) and the Aboriginal Peoples Television Network (APTN) (www.aptn.ca), inaugurated in September 1999, as the first nationally sponsored First Peoples' television service in the world, are historically rooted in Canadian pilot projects which began in the early 1970s in which First Peoples gradually gained television access time for a variety of local, regional and national development purposes, the result, originally, of an experimental project that followed the launch of the communications satellite, Anik B. The Inuit Broadcasting Corporation (IBC) is perhaps the most well known of these projects. In 1981, the Canadian Radio Television–Telecommunications Commission's (CRTC) Committee on the Extension of Service to Northern and Remote Communities argued for a formal Northern Broadcasting Policy and an Aboriginal production vehicle to reinforce local languages and cultures. In response, the Northern Native Broadcast Access Program (NNBAP, 1983) was federally structured to financially assist Aboriginal radio/television development costs for thirteen regional Native Communication Societies (NCSs), seven of which continue to be a main source of Northern television programming for APTN. Although the NNBAP still exists, cuts in federal funds mean that NCSs rely on advertising and product marketing to supplement their discretionary costs.

The misleading assumption embedded in the original NNBAP was that up to five hours of programming would be willingly carried at prime time by existing Northern broadcasters (Canadian Broadcasting Corporation's [CBC] Northern Service and CANCOM). When these indigenous programmes were put into marginal time slots, NNBAP producers demanded reliable technical infrastructures dedicated to pan-Northern service exclusively. Acknowledging the importance of Northern-based control over its own media, Aboriginal broadcasting rights were enshrined in Canada's Broadcasting Act revision (4 June 1991). Six months later, the CRTC licensed Television Northern Canada (TVNC) to become this pan-Arctic distribution service – a recognition of the broadcasting rights of Northern First Peoples. TVNC's pan-Arctic success and growth convinced its board of directors to lobby for a national Aboriginal network linking north and south. The result was APTN, which took over and expanded TVNC.

APTN launched its service on 1 September 1999, as a nationally mandated Aboriginal broadcasting network targeted to native/non-native audiences in Canada and available in the US by satellite. Its funding contributions and distribution access for indigenous producers potentially resolves the historical bias on the part of the federal government which favoured financing of Northern Aboriginal programming; now Southern (non-Arctic) indigenous producers are no longer excluded from support for their initiatives. APTN is the sole (inter)national broadcasting service in the world which carries exclusively indigenous-perspective programming (news, current affairs, comedy, variety, drama, children's programmes, cooking shows, documentary films, international programmes). As a hybrid model of public/private broadcasting with programming reflecting multiple Canadian Aboriginal cultures, as well as nations around the world, APTN is both local and global in perspective.

With headquarters in Winnipeg and branches in Ottawa, Iqaluit (Nunavut), Yellowknife (Northwest Territories) and Whitehorse (Yukon), APTN broadcasts 120 hours a week to eight million Canadian cable subscribers, as well as direct-to-home and wireless service customers. Its production staff and management offer a full spectrum of genres with approximately 70 per cent Canadian content; the other 30 per cent originates from international indigenous film and video markets (US, Australia, New Zealand, Greenland). APTN is free to Northern residents via a special Northern feed; in southern Canada, APTN costs $0.15 per household through cable, and is a mandatory service on Canada's second and third programming tiers. These fees go to APTN for programme production costs, film acquisition and to subsidise recruitment and training of Aboriginal talent.

APTN's linguistic politics have always been complex and are currently being challenged and debated by those in the independent production sector. Broadcasts are carried in multiple languages: 60 per cent English; 15 per cent French; 25 per cent in a variety of (fifteen to twenty-five) Aboriginal languages. Recently, APTN altered its language policy and has stirred controversy among the independent production industry. According to its most recent 'Call for Proposals' on its website (APTN.ca), APTN has opted to purchase films only if dubbed in either English or French, over and above their original language of production. Its board president claims to be doing this due to 'an upcoming improvement of its technology – to high definition and SAP (Secondary Audio Programming) that will allow the viewer to choose the language in which to watch the programme (Jean LaRose on http://www.isuma.ca/forums/February 23, 2005). In taking this approach, APTN's board of directors aspires to resolve the issue of broader linguistic access to programming, given that so many Aboriginal people have lost their ability to speak their own language. It is also being justified on the basis that many Aboriginal people cannot read subtitles. Dubbing, they claim, would make it easier for audiences to understand programming content.

The unpopular (and expensive) decision to extend (non)native audience reach has caused much

debate among supporters of the Aboriginal independent production industry – especially since it is
the only channel in the world which will require
producers to submit programming in **both** the original language of the production **and** in English or
French, two of Canada's national languages.
Independent directors and producers argue that this
exclusive policy will not only be cost-prohibitive,
but will negatively impact on the power of the
filmic/television verbal content, and will probably
erode one of the principal assets of APTN – providing the concrete sounds and the musicality of the
multiple Aboriginal languages of Canada to all who
watch the network. Ironically, a channel which originated to provide a dedicated venue for a range of
Aboriginal cultures and languages will be the first in
the world to demand parallel linguistic voices as a
requirement for all acquired film programming. This,
while opening up APTN programming to wider
(inter)national audiences, might mean the conse-
quent loss of a sense of locality and linguistic distinction.

It is not all that surprising that APTN has taken
this route. In light of its evolution, it seems rather
clear that its intention is to become an international
indigenous channel of record, much like that of
CNN or the BBC World Service, although its focus
will be 'shared indigenous perspective around the
world', rather than news and documentary. If this is
one of the directions APTN is planning for the
future, then a dual language policy such as it is currently advocating, is quite predictable as a preparato-
ry moment preceding its entry into the international mediasphere.

Following the inaugural work of APTN, Maori
TV was launched in March 2004, the culmination of
thirty years of attempts to bring to air a Maori television network in Aotearoa/New Zealand. The gov-
ernment-sponsored network seeks to air programming that reflects (and creates) Maori interests and
cultural practices, yet is 'ma tatou', for everyone. As
has been the case for APTN and other initiatives,
language issues have been key. The bilingual network
was created explicitly to promote the revitalisation of
the Maori language (te reo), and at least 50 per cent
of the programming is broadcast in Maori. Maori TV
airs a wide variety of original programmes, ranging
from shows that offer language instruction in Maori
to those that feature Maori news broadcasts, current
affairs, sport, music videos and children's programming. Often included are feature films and documentaries by or about other indigenous peoples
around the world deemed to be of interest to Maori,
with a particularly strong exchange occurring with
Aboriginal Australia as well as Canada
(www.corporate.maoritelevision.com/faq/faq.htm).

CONCLUSION

Since the beginnings of indigenous television in the
late 1970s, producers from remote as well as urban
areas have struggled to find ways to use televisual
technologies for their own purposes, asserting what
Tuscarora scholar Jolene Rickard has called '**visual
sovereignty**'. This highly localised development in
the globalisation of television ranges across an array
of indigenous concerns, from documenting the rapidly disappearing worlds of elders raised on the land
and with traditional knowledge, to the creation of
works targeting young people to teach them literacy
and numeracy in their own languages, and addressing more dire concerns such as drug and alcohol
abuse. Getting indigenous histories into mainstream
media – as indigenous units situated in national
broadcasters have done – has been a critical goal, as
Aboriginal citizens feel their contributions to
national narratives have largely been erased or
ignored. As a case in point, a full-scale effort to bring
a series on the history of The First Australian
Nations to national television is currently in production in Australia. While activism and policy concerns
initially shaped much of indigenous media, it is
important to acknowledge the current range of genres being produced: drama, current affairs, political
analysis, humour, cooking shows, variety shows,
music videos and sport. As indigenous television has
grown more robust over the last two decades – in
part through the increasing convergence of media
forms that makes it hard to know where to draw the
boundary marking television from film from web-
based work – a remarkably diverse array of genres

suggest that this synthesis of media technology with collective self-production has much to offer indigenous communities as they redefine themselves and future generations in the twenty-first century.

ACKNOWLEDGMENTS
Thanks to April Strickland for her help on Maori television. This article grew out of an earlier piece entitled 'First Peoples' Television', in Toby Miller (2002).

10 Post TV?

The Future of Television

Kyle Nicholas

The key to the future of television is to stop think-ing about television as television.

Nicholas Negroponte, *being digital*, 1995: 48.

In the sci-fi series, *Sliders* (Fox, 1996–2000), young Quinn Mallory invents a timer that opens vortices between alternate universes. In the opening episode the timer is broken, leaving its characters unable to control when the vortices open, or which universe awaits them. *Sliders* ran from 1996 to 2000, begin-ning on the Fox Network and finishing on the Sci-Fi Channel. Although the series attracted only a cult following before its broadcast demise several years ago, I know about it because it remains 'alive' on the web. Fans circulate images and alternate stories. **Wikipedia**, the great, untethered web-based ency-clopedia, lists an entry including some production details. *Sliders*, cancelled after its first season and revived, in part, by fan enthusiasm, exists in *Earth 62*, *Gate Heaven* and the *TransDimensional Station* – all websites where fans create their own fiction and art, share reviews, swap digital images and lovingly retell episodes. The series that explored aspects of quantum physics exemplifies the parallel universe of the web, where '**old media**' goes not to die, but to be recir-culated and reimagined.

Television, too, has alternate futures. On the one hand, consumers appear to be buying television sets in record numbers. More than 300 million sets have been sold since 2003. Europeans continue to replace their old sets at a rate that will triple the number of **digital TV** sets in the EU to about ninety million by 2007. The combination of digital terrestrial and satellite signals will also enter more than 80 per cent of European homes in a similar time frame (Holden, 2004). Television channels, both terrestrial and satel-lite, are proliferating. New technical standards and new technologies continue to extend the global reach (and eventually the interoperability) of televi-sion. As television networks increasingly become part of **multimedia** behemoths, the sources of pro-gramming and the opportunities for **cross-promo-tion** rapidly expand.

On the other hand, the notion of television we have grown used to over the last fifty years appears to be changing beyond recognition. Will the future recognise the technological and cultural contours of television in more nimble and manoeuvrable alter-natives? Or will it see the old 'tube' as a quaint media distraction, on a par with the Zogroscope or the

New technology: the quality of sound and image has altered dramatically in recent years

player piano? This may depend on how loosely we continue to apply the term 'television' to this rapidly changing medium. Television screens are both growing (wall-to-wall plasma screens) and shrinking (to fit neatly into our pockets). Programming is both more local and more global than ever (see Chapter 9). Television content is both driven by competitive strategies that emphasise brand expansion, and repurposed by **active consumers** who see televisual elements as the raw materials for participatory pastiche. Television is increasingly subject to the logic of user mobility. Physical mobility compels television producers to get their products in the hands of viewers who are constantly on the go. Cultural mobility, accelerated by the Internet and satellite systems, requires that programmes be both highly identifiable and globally acceptable. As television is digitised – whether at the studio, via cable or satellite system, or in the homes of consumers – it is subjected to modes of semantic mobility, as users dexterously manipulate its most precious signs. Peering into our dusty vacuum tube we may see the future of television in its multitudinous present.

iTV: INTERACTIVE TELEVISION

The shift to **digital broadcasting** and receivers clearly creates new opportunities for both producers and consumers of television fare. Dallas Smythe (1993) observed that television viewing is both a consumptive and productive activity; the act of viewing requires a kind of (unpaid) labour on the part of viewers, namely the activity of processing advertisements. More recently, Bolter and Grusin (1999) have discussed how the bargain between consumers and advertisers has become explicit on the web. They argue that effective communication in digital media requires a more active relationship with audiences than the old television model. The technologies of marketing are foregrounded or 'remediated' on the web; participants intentionally interact with messages as they click through links and icons. As television producers seek new dimensions for their products, viewers (like the cyberfans of *Sliders*) become active, tinkering with the video product and proselytising for old characters or new story lines. The synergistic evolution of digital technologies

and audience activity may be the most telling portent for the future of television.

For many years observers have been predicting that new technologies will particularly mean increased personalisation of media content; some have predicted that we will craft insular worlds of information: the '**Daily Me**'. It was predicted that personalisation would **fragment audiences**, wiping out the notion of 'mass' media. 'No trend threatens the guardians of old media more than personalization', J. D. Lassica counselled in his Online Journalism weblog. 'The very notion challenges the philosophical underpinnings of traditional media . . .' (2002). But 'old media' have a tendency to adapt. Do they become new media in this process? Using web portals or mobile news services, or scanning the **blogosphere** (the online social and political sphere of weblog readers and writers), users today can tailor both their intake and output of information to construct intensely focused worlds.

Television, it appears, will be part of this media mix. For example, **MyTV** is a 'personalised interactive TV channel' that uses a variety of digital technologies to allow viewers to programme their own stations. Services like MyTV combine the flexibility of a **digital video recorder** (DVR) with some of the features of **video-on-demand** (VOD) services and interactive television (iTV). All of these predecessor services are enjoying success among television viewers. MyTV programming is stored at a cable head-end then pushed out to viewers according to an individual timetable. The cultural logic informing MyTV is that viewers want to personalise the flow of television: how and when it comes to them.

While MyTV has yet to catch on, television in general and digital TV in particular are being marketed as increasingly **interactive** and customised experiences. Global television satellite services, led by NewsCorp's Star, Sky and DirecTV, and the rapid expansion of broadband cable technologies (at least in Europe and North America) have vastly increased the number of channels available to television viewers wishing to pay for the services. Niche channels have popped up in such variety that the concept of **narrowcasting** so prevalent in the 1990s seems almost outdated. But even in the 300-channel universe, tailored programming will have trouble getting onto cable and satellite systems, let alone attracting an audience large enough for advertisers. The new strategy will be niche channels that launch through video-on-demand services; viewers will vote with their remote controls to choose who gets a lucrative cable slot and who remains on the fringes. While video-on-demand puts an extra economic burden on viewers, it offers them the promise of spending less time in the tedious murk of cable networks and more time attending to something that fits their desires.

Where digital transmission is available, television networks have the infrastructure needed to distribute interactive TV. But instead of providing rich two-way experiences, many have used their bandwidth to broadcast more channels of traditional television fare. For now, most viewers 'interact' with television by bringing their computer into the room. In the United States, more than forty-five million, or 50 per cent of Internet users, have a PC and a TV in the same room (Warley and Sheridan, 2004). Using their Internet connection, users can play along with the Game Show Network, or check fantasy sports statistics, or chat online with devotees watching reruns of *Absolutely Fabulous* (BBC, 1989–). Fans connect on the net and form social ties around cultural products. They spend more time in more media channels with programmes if there is an interactive component. If

Convergence: the traditional distinctions between television and the computer are breaking down

broadcasters are hesitant to implement iTV, advertisers and programmers will demand it in order to capitalise on intense viewer activity. The logic of syndication in a **multichannel** universe, where one can view a *Seinfeld* (NBC, 1989–98) or *Xena: Warrior Princess* (Sky One, 1996–) at any time of day is a half-step to the future. As viewers migrate away from the synchronous, linear space of television into asynchronous, omnipresent and mobile media, traditional commercial television will eventually abandon the remnants of its principal flow and become a ubiquitous video server. Microsoft, among others, has jumped on the interactive bandwagon, refashioning the computer as a television set and working digital video recorder (DVR) technology into the latest versions of its Media Center software.

To date, the Media Center, a set of software designed to allow consumers to create, mix and distribute personal as well as commercial media has only slowly gained consumer credibility (although Microsoft introduced a new version in late 2004). Digital video recorders consist essentially of huge computer hard drives that connect to incoming cable or satellite services and allow viewers to programme their day, rewind and fast-forward live television, and skip commercials. The diffusion of DVRs is expected to increase rapidly from about 5 per cent of television households in 2004 to 41 per cent by the end of the decade. **Time-shifting** is the killer application of the DVR; US viewers say they watch recorded material about two-thirds of the time.

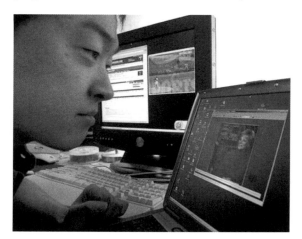

Interactive TV: how people watch television is now changing

THE NEW ECONOMIES OF TELEVISION

The use of digital video recorders is contributing to the rapidly changing economics of television. Nine out of ten DVR users skip commercials, although some ads fare better than others. The recorders have 'forced the ad business to admit the obvious – that most people will avoid commercials whenever possible' (Rose, 2003). Television executives speculate that while the demise of the thirty-second commercial is not imminent, the end is near: 'There is a freight train coming at us, and the only thing holding it back is the time it takes for consumers to bend this technology to the way they want to use it' (ibid). The time period is difficult to predict. While it is clear that web users employing digital technologies have promoted a rise in **participatory culture**, it is much less clear that television viewers are primarily seeking participatory experiences.

William Boddy compares the industry discourse surrounding the DVR to the network propaganda about 'pay-television' in the 1950s and 1960s. Networks claimed that pay-TV trod on the 'natural rights' of viewers of 'free', or network, television (Boddy, 2003: 194). Later, when they became major investors in cable and satellite networks and eventually developed their own pay-TV brands, networks proclaimed the need for choice as they staked out additional broadcast spectrum in the United States and market liberalisation around the globe. The DVR, like other electronic media arriving on the scene, 'carries with it an implicit fantasy scenario of its domestic consumption, a polemical ontology of its medium, and an ideological rationale for its social functions' (ibid: 191).

Skipping commercials and time-shifting programming is the 'fantasy scenario' of TiVo (currently [2004] the best-selling brand of digital video recorder) and other DVRs, but programme-length commercials, more conspicuous branding and the sale of viewer habits and preferences are also part of the future. TiVo sells space on the hard drive itself – the essential component of a DVR – for pre-programmed commercials. Computers at TiVo headquarters keep tabs on which commercials viewers skip through, which programmes they watch and how they configure their programme schedules. Programmers and the advertisers they love will come to see the DVR as the ultimate viewer ratings machine.

A television connected to a DVR is a hybrid of '**push**' and '**pull**' models of media reception. While broadcasting pushes television out to viewers, they also have an opportunity to programme the DVR to pull in particular programming (and to bar commercials). The expansion of channels and receiving technologies gives viewers more opportunities to pull content, but as a pull technology the DVR is only an intermediate step. The 'push' model of television really disappears as programmers take advantage of new services like **rich site summary** (RSS) coding to seed cable systems, DVRs and the web. Rich site summary codes carry a thirty-word phrase of keywords and teasers. They use web language and work by snagging 'content aggregator' software, as a hook with the proper bait will snag a trout. If a web developer wants her site to rank high when a seeker 'googles' it, she will create a set of keywords and phrases that correspond to popular, appropriate search terms and embed it in the site. RSS works in similar fashion, but potentially for all media. Political junkies and fan communities already use RSS to give them their daily fix without the hassle of extensive web searches. In the future, television stations will post RSS codes to the web, turning content aggregators into vast and detailed TV guides. As television continues to exploit the techniques of multimedia, users will programme their RSS software to pull programming in any medium into their devices of choice. As RSS evolves into a multiplatform utility, television will extend and morph accordingly. Television, like the web, will no longer be a place that viewers visit; it will come to the viewer when called.

The increased distribution of television programming and the demise of the push model exert new pressures on television producers to establish and extend network and programme brands. Television has used the web to create **branded communities**, online groups who use discussion lists and chat to involve themselves in programming

(Edgerton and Nicholas, forthcoming). Television grabs attention and multiplies its value to viewers by repackaging and repurposing content. Scripps' Food Network (the top-ranked ad-supported cable brand in the United States) revamped its websites into Web Marketing Association award winners in 2003. It promoted its web manager to senior vice president and began a public relations campaign touting its sites to potential advertisers. Requests for the Food Network website (www.foodnetwork.com) jumped nearly 60 per cent from the previous year. Nearly 120 million page views were generated in one month of 2004. Television and web producers at the network have created a digital repository of video content with a searchable database that allows viewers to go to the web for recipes and video demonstrations. People come to sites to interact in and through online resources that include discussion boards, chat rooms, game areas and ancillary stores. These sites are designed as a series of **nested infomercials**. As users navigate the sites, each click accentuates a different aspect of the brand-participant relationship. A variety of contests and instant polls characterise the basic level of interaction but all sites also feature well-populated discussion groups, as well as email connections with behind-the-scenes staff. While overall participation in these activities appears to be low compared with television viewership or page view ratings, these kinds of **horizontal communication** channels demonstrate the centrality of discursive practices in defining programme identities.

Online activities integrate **cyberspace** with the continuing trend towards 'productive leisure'. Channel expansion has provided the televisual complement to fitness, travel and do-it-yourself activities. Cable television – with brands like Food Network, HGTV and Outdoor Network leading the way – exploited the cultural trend by developing genre programming around commoditised activities and tying it to transmedia practices. For example, Food Network 'junkies' using mobile technologies stay connected while shopping. In one future scenario, viewers picking mushrooms in a supermarket will be able to call a network number (likely preprogrammed into their phone) and get recipes, serving suggestions, and even electronic coupons for other supermarket products. In the future, the Food Network may stay with them through the preparation of the meal, perhaps suggesting an appropriate, co-branded wine, and delivering a little mood music for dinner (from a programming partner), via their computer, digital set-top box, satellite dish or mobile device. Television, in this scenario, transcends traditional devices and context, becoming both more personal and more ubiquitous as viewers demand and technologies accommodate.

MOBITV: MOBILE TELEVISION

Television producers have been providing content for **mobile phones** for the past several years, but the explosion in wireless hand-held receivers of all types will change the way television is produced, marketed and used. More than 600 million mobile phones were sold in 2004. Virtually every major television firm has a mobile content division and joint ventures with mobile phone companies have become commonplace. The Cartoon Network and Sony Ericsson provide ring tones and downloads featuring 'Tom and Jerry' and the 'Powerpuff Girls'. But brand-driven sounds and icons that dress up teenagers' phones are already becoming passé as television and mobile phone services converge. The BBC World news service has teamed with Nokia to provide trial content for its new television phones. In South Korea, Skylife offers forty channels of satellite television to the 70 per cent of the population that owns mobile phones. Shanghai businessmen watch the Chinese Football League via the China Mobile network and Swedish Public Television joined with mobile phone carrier Telia to offer customers exclusive Athens Olympics coverage. Even Canada's now venerable web service, *Naked News*, has gone mobile, providing their unique blend of news and nudity globally via 'm-vision' (software designed to let you watch television on your mobile phone). In the US, mobile firms are moving in to create joint ventures with Hollywood or to launch new services of their own. MobiTV provides a mobile platform for Fox Sports, NBC news and Universal.

Developments like these underline the shift in

strategy for television producers. In addition to extending programming to the web and now mobile platforms, the 'content community' of information and entertainment producers will increasingly create programmes designed for viewing away from 'the tube'. Although animation, like the Cartoon Network's five-minute *Star Wars* miniseries, is optimal for low bandwidth Internet and the narrow mobile phone channel, new technologies developed in Asia and Scandinavia, and new technical standards developed in the EU, promise to make high-quality mobile television a reality. Complementing the roll-out of higher bandwidth phones, Sprint and AT&T will begin testing **HDTV phones** in 2006 capable of carrying 200 channels by the end of the decade. However, whether the television and mobile industries can develop a seamless, global network with desirable programming is still an open question. The European Commission's mGain (the strange acronym for the European Mobile Entertainment Industry and Culture project) preliminary report noted that users found present technologies difficult to use; fragmentation in the 'mobile entertainment industry' and the problems associated with the evolution of mobile networks also pose significant hurdles (mGain, 2003).

Conversely, the low-bandwidth functionality of most current mobile phones actually turns out to be an advantage for many users. As users add communication channels they also add social responsibilities. Rich communication channels, such as those provided by video-enabled mobile phones, require users to spend more time and thought (and more precious air minutes) on communication. Gesser predicts that 'customer demand for broadband phone transmissions are much lower than many optimistic telecommunications strategists . . . are currently assuming' (Gesser, 2004: 13). Gesser's important work underscores the dynamic and negotiated relationship between users and their media. Although mobile-phone screen size may be the most visible constraint on television, the physical and cultural context of mobile-phone use may exert the greatest influence on the format and content of television programming.

PARTICIPATORY CULTURE

The global nature of technological development and standardisation also means that we can expect televisual materials to circulate more broadly and in new directions. Commercial television currently exists as a professionally produced, centralised operation. Professionalism separates knowledge production from its users, a key distinction between current television and more participative media. The web provides for the distribution and display of amateur creations that in a previous era would only been seen by family and friends. It also enables insights into the creative process, as amateurs detail how they got ideas and what technologies they employed, and eagerly respond to questions no Hollywood producer would deign to answer. Henry Jenkins (2003) argues that web-based **digital cinema** – non-corporate creations posted to and publicised via the web – forms a kind of aesthetic middle ground between corporate, commercial media and strictly amateur productions. Web and mobile platforms will accelerate trends towards content globalisation and **decentralisation** i.e. the dissemination of media creation from highly centralised, professional corporations to multiple, amateur productions.

The proliferation of digital tools and networks (for now concentrated in relatively wealthy, educated sectors) has led to a rapid expansion of what it means to be an audience. For those who participate, using digital media skills to engage with information is now considered to be of equal importance as family and interpersonal interactions (Ross and Nightingale, 2003). Digital tools and the global networks that support them have blurred the boundaries between production and consumption, and call into question claims of ownership of cultural products at any particular stage in their development. As these tools continue to mature and diffuse, the role of an audience member will no longer be 'that of passive listener, consumer, receiver or target. Instead it will encompass any of the following: seeker; consultant; browser; respondent; interlocutor; or conversationalist' (McQuail, 1997: 129).

The synergy of emerging technologies and active audiences creates pinch points for global media companies both within programming divisions and between programming and telecommunication companies. The trick to competing in multimedia networks, on DVRs, or through 'pull' technologies is to create a prolonged relationship with fans across platforms. **Smart television** programme-creators design ambiguity and playfulness into content. They recognise that new digital technologies allow viewers to appropriate, alter, archive and recirculate media content. Writers and producers understand the importance of '**tertiary texts**' where viewers create meaning from texts through a process of interpretation rather than passively consuming the superficial story line (Ross and Nightingale, 2003: 130). They incorporate programme elements that enable and encourage fans to explore alternative meanings; they distribute programming elements in a way that allows fans to take pleasure in seeking, culling and sharing programme arcana and creating esoteric alternate universes of meaning (see Chapter 6). They recognise that extending programming and brand identity in multimedia means to some extent giving up control over the context in which it is used and manipulated. If a cheaply produced and little-watched show like *Sliders* cannot compete in prime-time broadcasting, it might still draw a dedicated audience (and potentially a profit) by allowing the meaning and purpose of its signs to drift in the flotsam of the web. But the business models, legislative and technical efforts of the television industry continue to assert intellectual property protection as the cornerstone of profitability.

The conundrum for television producers and other commercial media-creators is to fashion programming that can migrate through grassroots multimedia spheres without requiring the aggressive policing of copyright that alienates fans. Meanwhile, the very audience activities that impinge on intellectual property – appropriating, altering, archiving and recirculating – drive demand for telecommunication networks, like Time Warner's digital cable system, or News Corp's satellite systems. Promoting audience activity increases network traffic and the distribution – in multiple forms and formats – of media pro-

grammes. 'If media convergence is to become a viable corporate strategy, it is because consumers have learned new ways to interact with media content' (Jenkins, 2003: 286). So, Time Warner must find ways to get its HBO or Cartoon Network programmes into the interactive, interpretive realm, in a way that drives consumption of its high-speed cable and AOL Internet connections, while protecting its various property rights. News Corp may have to tolerate some blatant filching of characters from its Fox Network's *The Simpsons* (Fox, 1989–) to attract consumers to its DirectDVR and DirecWay Internet services.

CONCLUSION

The television device that Marshall McLuhan (1964) argued extends our eyes and ears is now one of many extensions, its primacy threatened by its own multiplicity and its absorption into newer, more direct media forms. In the fortieth episode of *Sliders*, the gang returns to Earth Prime, a title borrowed from the first *Sliders* fan website. Producers of the show were early fans of the site which offers a 'virtual sixth season' and Earth 211, an alternative future where the show became the successful cornerstone of Fox programming. 'Earth Prime' is part of a shadow cultural economy that will increasingly intersect with television's bottom line (Fiske, 1992a). The relationship between the television producer and consumer, between those who deliver TV signals and those who view them, is shifting as cable channels multiply, the Internet mediates and other technologies mobilise both reception and desire. Raymond Williams' (1974) notion of broadcast **flow**, with viewers floating along from programme to news bite to commercial, has morphed into a **hyperflow** in multiple media driven by the commercial needs for brand extension and new practices of consumption and production. Clearly, one of the alternate futures of television, particularly for those who are unable or disinclined to employ digital tools and conduits, will be much like the recent past. To that extent, we may recognise Williams' flow more as a strategy of reception, rather than production. The rest of us will actively alter the form of television, prying it loose from its mass-media past and tugging it in new directions. The concept of the broadcast, with its allusions to scattering seeds in the wind, will be replaced by something closer to genetic engineering: viewers working in their personal multimedia laboratories, splicing together programmes, channels, even networks from the televisual DNA offered by a variety of commercial and non-corporate contributors.

FURTHER READING

Bell, David (2001), *An Introduction to Cybercultures*, London: Routledge.

Berry, Chris, Martin, Fran and Yue, Audrey (2003), *Mobile Cultures: New Media in Queer Asia*, Durham, NC: Duke University Press.

Gitelman, Lisa and Pingree, Geoffrey (2003), *New Media, 1740–1915*, Cambridge, MA: MIT Press.

Harries, Dan (ed.) (2002), *The New Media Book*, London: BFI.

Noam, Eli, Groebel, Jo and Gerber, Darcy (2004), *Internet Television*, Mahwah, NJ: Lawrence Erlbaum.

Rabinovitz, Lauren and Geil, Abraham (2004), *Memory Bites: History, Technology and Digital Culture*, Durham, NC: Duke University Press.

CASE STUDY
Television and Convergence Jamie Sexton

Over the past decade, the television and the computer have become more dependent on each other, in line with an increase in '**media convergence**'. The convergence of media forms – hastened by, though not limited to, escalating digitisation – has led some media commentators and theorists to declare an imminent end to the television as a distinct medium (see Zielinski, 1999); others, however, have warned against such a hasty conclusion (see Bolter and Grusin, 1999). It will be the aim of this case study to explore these positions, as well as to look at some of the main trends that have led to the blurring of previous distinctions, and the new modes that such trends have given rise to.

MERGING MEDIA

It was once the case that the computer and the television set were seen as distinct media, with their own functions: the former, traditionally, a number-crunching machine, primarily used within industry and the military; the latter, a domestic, entertainment (as well as information) medium. While the computer was confined to use by a few specialists, the television set was firmly located within the domestic sphere of everyday life. This began to change in the early 1980s, as the computer gradually entered the domestic sphere, though at this point used only by a segment of the population (mainly young males using it for playing computer games and creating computer programs).

The introduction of the personal computer, with an easy to use **graphical user interface** (GUI) replacing the previously laborious system of entering commands, was an important step towards the domestication of the computer. Household penetration gradually increased as the 1980s wore on, with the computer's multifunctional capabilities (including word processing, graphic design, gaming) proving attractive to different types of people. The **Internet**, however, was undoubtedly the main force in enabling the medium to become fully 'domesticated'. This occurred as the 1990s unfolded, in line with increased connection speeds, falling monthly subscription costs, and the increased speed, power and affordability of computers.

Today, the computer is as much a medium of home entertainment as it is a numerical processor. This development has seen its functions both overlap with, and complement, television-watching and the ways in which people 'use' television in their everyday lives. This latter element has been most pronounced through the growth of the Internet, and its ability to allow people to talk about television in new ways, extending the reach of such televisual 'chat'.

In many studies of television and its place in everyday life, it has been found that television is not only home entertainment, but also acts as a platform for discussion with a number of other people, thus enabling people to 'make sense' of both their own selves and their relationship to the wider world (see, for example, Gillespie, 1995; Gauntlett and Hill, 1999). Traditionally, people have engaged in such talk with those that they live with (if they do not live alone), as well as a wider network of family and friends. Beyond this, attention has also been paid to **fans**, who form more intense attachments to certain programmes or genres of television, and who have often used television in a more *active* manner. (see Jenkins, 1992; Hills, 2002). Traditionally, fans have communicated through fanzines, magazines, letters and conventions (see Chapter 6).

There are a number of different ways in which people can extend '**televisual talk**' through the Internet, including the use of websites and e-zines (Internet magazines), email, newsgroups, discussion lists, as well as forms of synchronous online discussion (such as **Internet relay chat** groups). Websites and e-zines greatly extend the amount of information about television programmes, as well as being easy to access. Compared with traditional print media, information on the web can be produced and distributed with ease: there is no need to create multiple copies, or to send these copies to a number of spatially separate locations. This enables a much greater number of people to become involved in the production of information, thus exponentially increasing the amount of information available. Not only this, but it also enables more people to access such media.

Though access to the Internet is by no means universal, it is growing all the time, and this means that small publications can be read by a potentially much broader audience. The main problem with access to smaller-scale materials is, however, publicity; while costs are much lower to publish on the web,

it is still the case that larger-scale ventures can publicise their material much more extensively, which increases the chances of such publications being read. It is also the case that the navigational framework of the web favours larger corporate-owned sites, via the contractual alliances that search engines have forged (Caldwell, 2002: 141). Nevertheless, if a person is actively looking for information on a specific television show, or area of production, then they can – through patient searching – come across a range of material, which may be an 'official' site or a site developed by an enthusiastic individual.

Email communication increases the ability of a known network to extend their chat beyond copresence and telephone conversations. Though not primarily considered an important site of televisual talk, email can be used in this way. Its ease of use means that people, whether at work or at home, may choose to relay messages discussing a programme that they saw the previous day, for example, or for one person to recommend a programme that a friend may not be aware of. More importantly, newsgroups and discussion groups of various kinds are often established around specific television shows, or areas of television programming (such as '**cult television**'). As Nicholas states above, these types of Internet communication provide a ceaseless '**flow**' of information on television, much in the way that Williams conceived of the television set as providing a 'flow' of programming in the 1970s (Williams, 1974 and Chapter 1). They also characterise what have been termed the '**virtual communities**' of the Internet, in which a number of attachments are forged through the exchange of information over the computer (see Baym, 2000, for a study of 'virtual communities' based around soaps).

In many senses, the Internet begins to blur the boundaries between the 'ordinary' television viewer, and the television 'fan' (see Ross and Nightingale, 2003: 141–3). Traditionally, acts associated with fandom – such as the production of cultural material (**fanzines**, **slash fiction**), or the establishment of exclusive social networks – were seen as requiring a lot of monetary and temporal resources. (There was also an element of stigma attached to a fan.) Such

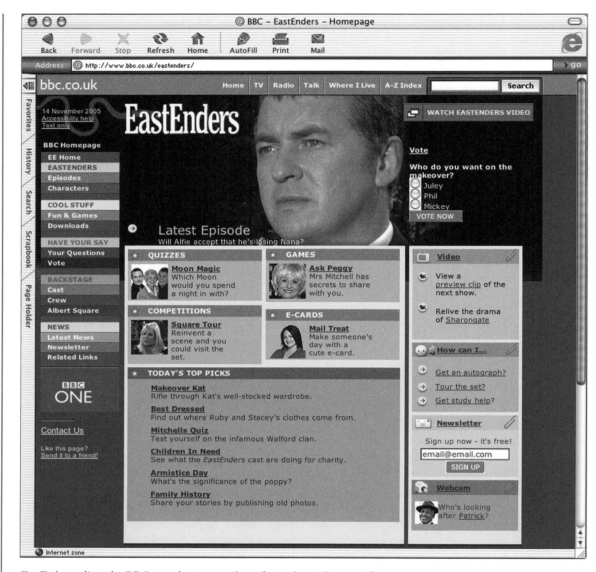

EastEnders online: the BBC now hosts a number of sites devoted to specific programmes

activities are now much easier to engage in, as people can anonymously engage in '**fan talk**' with like minds through the ease of clicking and entering text. Those who want to 'produce' texts inspired by television programmes can also do so more easily, as is testified by the glut of television sites produced by single individuals or small groups, as well as the increase of slash fiction (see Chapter 6).

Yet the computer is not limited to the exchange of information about programmes, or to the inter-vention of 'fans'. Television production companies and television channels, for example, are engaged in the production of websites, and these sites offer more than just information on programmes. In the UK, the main terrestrial television channels all have their own websites, offering extensive information on different programmes and related issues, as well as video and audio clips.

The BBC's web presence (www.bbc.co.uk), for example, is the most extensive of the UK terrestrial broadcasters' online operations. It offers a huge array of information on various issues, not all of these directly related to BBC programmes. However, as this chapter is focusing on the relations between the television and the computer, I will discuss those areas that are directly related to television. First, the BBC hosts a number of sites devoted to specific programmes, the most popular of which is the *EastEnders* (BBC, 1985–) site (www.bbc.co.uk/eastenders). These programme sites contain programme updates, message boards for viewers to discuss issues, competitions, downloads (of programme-related screensavers and wallpaper), games, as well as interviews with cast and crew (these are generally text interviews, but sometimes audio interviews can be accessed). Second, it also hosts sites devoted to types of television content – such as *Cult TV* (www.bbc.co.uk/cult) or *Comedy TV* (www.bbc.co.uk/comedy) – which also feature information on programmes that may have been shown on other channels. (This is something that has been heavily criticised by rivals, who claim that the BBC has spent far too much licence money [see Chapter 8] on content that falls outside its remit.) Third, it hosts sites for each of its channels, including its digital channels. These sites often include a number of audio clips and also some video clips. The

BBC News 24: the website streams broadcasts of the latest news, sport and weather

News 24 site (news.bbc.co.uk/1/hi/programmes/bbc_news_24) features the most extensive video footage, including streaming broadcasts of the latest news, sport, weather and business news.

The increasing amount of streaming video media on television websites is one particular feature that has seen the blurring of the television and the computer. With streaming video, Internet users can watch television on their computers. This can feature material that has already appeared upon the 'traditional' television screen or 'exclusive' material that has not been broadcast in any other format. The former includes, for example, the aforementioned news footage appearing on the BBC News 24 site, which is a digested version of footage culled from the rolling digital news channel. Or it can include clips from programmes that have already appeared on television. The 'exclusive' footage lets Internet users gain access to material that has not previously appeared. *Big Brother* (bigbrother.channel4.com/bigbrother) was an important show in this respect, because web users could access live streaming footage of the show, only portions of which would eventually make it onto the television highlights. This type of webcasting vastly complicated the pre-existing relations between television and the computer; for if, previously, the Internet provided a host of functions that *supplemented* the television programme, and extended its presence within the everyday, it could be argued that such a function was reversing. With *Big Brother* (Channel 4, 1999–), its edited format (and occasional, late-night live feed), could be seen as secondary to the twenty-four-hour Internet feed. While such a trend most definitely contributes to qualitative alterations in the status of the television set vis-à-vis the computer terminal, we should be cautious about jumping to any hasty conclusions. For the most part, television uses the Internet in order to broaden its audience, and it does so in a manner that prioritises the television programme, as opposed to exclusive Internet material. The manner by which television companies use the Internet as a secondary adjunct to their traditional broadcast functions is summarised in this quote by Siapera (2004: 167):

the older medium appears to accept, and even encourage, its audiences to venture further afield in cyberspace, but still wants to retain a connection with them while they are there, to help them orient themselves or navigate, but still to use the older medium as their compass.

It is also the case that the actual 'quality' of the streaming images on the computer may detract audiences from prioritising the Internet for viewing programme material. The relatively small size of the streaming frame, its position within the computer screen, its often unreliable character (streaming feeds are prone to interruptions), and the often jerky, poorly defined image quality (even via a broadband connection), often generates viewer dissatisfaction. It is also the case that the computer is merely a relay device for a text that has been especially designed for the aesthetics of television (see Chapter 1).

The popularity of *Big Brother* on the web (as well as a number of features tailored for mobile-phone access [see above]) has led to a growth in more 'exclusive', television-related material appearing on the Internet. Whether these will prove to be as popular, though, is a moot point. *Big Brother*, for example, is not a show that relies to a great extent on image quality: it was a show that, in the midst of a televisual landscape dependent on increasingly sophisticated visuals, was low definition. Its popularity stemmed more from the voyeuristic principles of viewing people interacting within artificial situations, rather than from any sophisticated formal organisation (at least on the pro-filmic level; it never-

Monthly charges with minimum terms. UK only.

'The tele-phone': TV is becoming increasingly mobile

theless required sophisticated planning of technological monitoring devices). The success of other online programming is less secure. In combination with RealNetworks, Channel 4 now features a **broadband channel** (www.channel4.com/broadband), which costs £4.95 per month, and which includes exclusive behind-the-scenes *Big Brother* material, as well as other programming (including *Wife Swap* [Channel 4, 2003–] and *Banzai* [Channel 4, 2003–]). The BBC, meanwhile, is currently developing its own Interactive Media Player (in combination with Microsoft), in order to allow online access to its previous week's programming. In addition, it plans to create an online 'archive' of previously screened material, though the details of such an ambitious plan have yet to be fully developed. There is no doubt that, as the quality of streaming media improves, more and more people will be watching television content online, though how quickly this might occur is open to question.

MYTV

Thus far, I have been primarily discussing the Internet, and how it has been used to both supplement and extend how people experience television and the role that it plays within their everyday lives. This focus, however, overlooks other important ways in which the television and the computer are converging; it also fails to take into account how the television set itself is becoming more and more like a computer.

One of the main ways in which the television set is becoming more like a computer is the development of the **personal video recorder** (PVR), a device that allows viewers to store programmes on a hard drive (see above). In the US, early PVR systems such as TiVo and Replay TV were launched on a wave of publicity, proclaiming viewer liberation from broadcast television schedules, as well as from having to sit through advertisements. PVRs extend the capabilities of the video cassette recorder: combined with an **electronic programme guide** (EPG), it is simple to key in what you want to record for the whole week ahead; the physical hard drive – currently able to store up to twenty hours of programming

– also obviates the need for videocassettes; while one can also use it to pause live broadcasts, and then continue the programme where you last left it. In a sense then, the PVR streamlines the pre-existing capabilities of the VCR, enhancing its ability to tailor the televisual flow into personalised, segmented chunks – what some commentators have referred to as **MeTV** or **MyTV**.

Early sales of the PVR were not high, which may have been due to its lack of obvious differentiation from existing VCRs, as well as the fact that their appeal seemed limited to a techno-literate, high-income group of males (Boddy, 2002: 247), thus preventing their prevalence within domestic spaces. Yet more recently, the PVR has begun to gain more widespread popularity in the home. In the UK, for example, the most popular type of PVR is the Sky+ service, which combines the television recorder with the satellite receiver. The Sky+ box currently costs £100, with an added subscription of £10 per month on top of programming subscription (a fee which is currently waived if you subscribe to more than one 'premium' service). In February 2004, Sky announced in its annual report that subscriptions to Sky+ had more than doubled between October and December 2003, rising from 121,000 to more that 250,000 (Dobson, 2004). In the US, sales of PVRs have also started to rise, in line with decreasing costs.

The Sky website highlights the customisation features of its PVR system, inviting potential customers to 'invent your own TV channel'. This 'saleable' element of the PVR stresses how it fits in with previous trends within domestic viewing activities. Cable, satellite and digital television systems, along with recording facilities such as the videocassette recorder and, more recently, the DVD player and recorder, have led to an explosion of the types of audiovisual material available in the home, which in turn has led to a breakdown of the historical distinctions between television, film and the computer (see Friedberg, 2002). This is in line with an increase in the **customisation** of home-viewing activities; the purchase of videos and DVDs, the recording of programmes and the advent of television channels devoted to specialist programming ('**niche-cast-**

ing'), all allow the viewer to pick and choose from a range of options. This is in stark contrast to an earlier age of terrestrial television, shadowed as it was by a public service ethos now under threat, which catered to a *mass* audience (see Chapter 7).

Yet, with the increase in choice, there arise new problems for the viewer, what John Ellis has termed 'time famine and choice fatigue' (Ellis, 2002: 169). Ellis argues that '**time famine**' is the feeling produced by the fact that not enough time exists to savour all the available choices. This results in a paralysis of the ability to choose – '**choice fatigue**' – which may result in a nostalgic hankering for pattern and habit, for 'an era when choices seemed few' (171). In light of such developments, it may be hypothesised that the attractiveness of the PVR, in addition to its falling costs, is that it is a device which, combined with the EPG, allows the modern television viewer to tackle such domestic anxieties. Automatic recording of 'favourite shows', combines with a search facility that – out of the mass of channel listings – catalogues programmes according to user preferences (such as genre, personality or other groupings), and can even recommend programmes in line with the profile of the user. While not everyone will want to take advantage of these features, there is no doubt that they enable an individual to pare down the glut of **multichannel** programming to a personalised, controllable diet.

The PVR is not limited to the television set, but is also increasingly a feature of personal computers. The personal computer has long been recognised as a 'media centre', with its ability to play streaming footage, as well as DVDs and CD-ROMs. These developments undoubtedly led to a blurring between the television and the computer; however, the fact that PCs were often situated on a desktop, alongside the often poor quality of streaming audiovisual material, meant that they were very seldom the machines that people relaxed in front of to watch television programmes or films. (Even the laptop, which is more mobile and can be placed in a comfortable viewing environment, is not an attractive alternative to the increasingly large, high-definition television sets, which often boast far superior sound capabilities.)

This situation is now beginning to change, as the television set can be hooked up to the computer in order to boost its own functionality. Computers can now receive television programmes and can record them to the hard drive; with a DVD burner, a television programme can be copied onto a DVD. Thus Sony GigaPocket technology is now being built into all Sony computers and enables users to pause and record television programmes, as well as to convert **analogue** signals into **digital**, so that a VHS tape can be recorded onto a hard drive and then transferred to a DVD. It is no surprise that the giants of the computer world, Microsoft, now have media-enhanced capabilities built into their operating systems: the Windows Media Centre is the system that Bill Gates believes signals the advent of the '**digital home**' (McIntosh, 2004). With wireless connections, computer-driven media content can be delivered to the television screen without any difficulty. In addition, with Internet connections, people can not only store televisual material on their hard drives, but also exchange these with friends over broadband lines.

Such developments may well mean that in the future the 'television set' as such will cease to exist. In its place, the domestic space will feature differently positioned screens that are compatible with a variety of machines. These screens will be used for gaming, watching films and television programmes, shopping, reading, word processing, listening to music and a myriad of other functions. To some extent, this has already happened: the television set, of course, is also a home cinema, as well as a screen for playing games upon. Satellite and cable digital services also enable people to send texts and email via their television set, as well as to use it as a home-shopping centre. Convergence is far from new phenomenon, but the rate at which previously distinct media are now overlapping and merging has undoubtedly accelerated, and this will impact (albeit often unpredictably) upon cultural and social arenas.

It may be, then, that the 'television screen' will only remain so when being used for watching television; at other times it may be referred to as a 'gaming screen' or an 'Internet screen'. The proliferation of screens that can be used for a variety of uses will not just be domestic. The rise of mobile technologies is now accelerating: many people have mobile phones and more people are acquiring mobile gaming devices, laptop computers and, to a lesser extent, Personal Digital Assistants (PDAs). Convergence will also lead to the multifunctional mobile screen, as small, portable devices increasingly incorporate computing, telecommunication and broadcast capabilities: the first mobile phones capable of receiving digital television are due to be launched at the end of 2004 (Shillingford, 2004).

THE END OF TELEVISION?

Will all this signal the end of television? In many ways, this question depends on how we interpret what television actually is. While industrial hype may sometimes signal the end of television, concrete evidence still points to the medium being an extremely important part of many people's everyday lives, even as other home entertainments compete for leisure time. Whether this will remain so in the future is difficult to predict, but it is certainly the case that, whether it is known as television or not, it will undergo significant changes. This in itself is not a big surprise: television has undergone many changes in its history, as have other media technologies, which is why it is notoriously difficult to characterise medium specificity. Bolter and Grusin make a forceful argument against the disappearance of television, asserting instead that it is in the nature of all media to *remediate* other media. They therefore avoid focusing on the changes of one medium in relation to other developments, but instead analyse how all media interact with each other. As they argue (1999: 224):

> Convergence is remediation under another name, and the remediation is mutual: the Internet refashions television even as television refashions the Internet . . . Not only will the new media landscape look like television as we know it, but television will come to look more and more like new media.

Comparing the CNN website and television channel, they demonstrate how each influences the other (also on this point, see Everett, 2003: 12). The CNN television channel, compared to around fifteen years ago, is much more like a webpage in its presentation of multiple windows, text and graphics combinations; yet the CNN website itself uses elements borrowed from television in order to attain an 'immediacy' (ibid.: 9–10).

It is, in some respects, no surprise that these mutual media interactions are increasingly occurring, as it is an aesthetic process that very much mirrors (and is in some sense constituted by) economic processes. It is no coincidence that the convergence of media has accelerated in tandem with the convergence of business sectors. The rise of large corporate takeovers has led to a situation where many of the biggest media companies are in charge of a range of different ventures: Murdoch's News Corporation, for example, owns a number of newspapers and magazines, book publishers, film companies and television companies, which operate in a global scale. It is also the case that many companies forge temporary connections in order to work on projects that may prove mutually beneficial (as was the case with Channel 4's partnership with RealNetworks in order to provide Channel 4 broadband).

In this economic climate it is not often in the interests of companies to eliminate particular media sectors. Rather, the logic emerging is that media content is being designed not for one specific media format, but for cross-platform multifunctionality. Content that is utilised for a television show is not only incorporated into websites, but can also be transformed into interactive television content, video game content and other formats. Thus *Who Wants to Be a Millionaire?* (ITV, 1998–) became embedded within the following formats: television show (including a specially commissioned interactive version), a series of board games, PC and video game, website, quiz book and interactive DVD. This type of cross-platform engineering is described by Will Brooker as '**overflow**' (2003: 325):

> The contemporary phenomenon of overflow . . . transforms the audience relationship with the text from a limited, largely one-way engagement based around a proscribed time slot and single medium

into a far more fluid, flexible affair which crosses media platforms.

This logic also arises from the fact that, while television is still popular, the rise in channels, as well as the rise of other competing media entertainments at home (and on the move), pressurises companies to capture audiences as they move between different media platforms.

At present, then and, at least in the near future, we will not see the disappearance of television as a medium. Instead, television will interact in a more marked manner with other media than previously, its content becoming increasingly '**leaky**'. At the same time, the boundaries of other media may also be seen as porous, so that both television form and content are adapted from 'external' environments. We should not see this as a radical alteration in the **media-sphere**, but rather an acceleration of previous trends (see Chapter 9). Television has never been totally distinct from other media, and when it commenced in Britain it was often dismissively viewed as a form of 'visual radio'. The intensified 'leakiness' of its boundaries then, in particular with computer technologies, should alert us to the fact that media distinctions are not essential or universal, but rather socially and historically contingent, containing the potential to interact and cross over with a variety of other media forms. In short: TV is dead, long live TV.

Bibliography

Abercrombie, Nicholas (1996), *Television and Society*, Cambridge: Polity Press.

Abercrombie, Nicholas, Hill, Stephen and Turner, Bryan S. (1980*), The Dominant Ideology Thesis*, Boston, MA and Sydney: Allen & Unwin.

Abercrombie, Nicholas and Longhurst, Brian (1998), *Audiences: A Sociological Theory of Performance and Imagination*, London: Sage.

Abramson, Albert (1987), *The History of Television, 1880 to 1941*, Jefferson, NC: McFarland.

Abramson, Albert (1995), 'The Invention of Television', in Anthony Smith (ed.), *Television: An International History*, Oxford: Oxford University Press.

Adorno, Theodor (1991), *The Culture Industry*, London: Routledge.

Akass, Kim and McCabe, Janet (eds) (2004), *Reading Sex and the City*, London and New York: I. B. Tauris.

Alasuutari, Pertti (1999), 'Introduction: Three Phases of Reception Studies', in Pertti Alasuutari (ed.), *Rethinking the Media Audience: The New Agenda*, London: Sage.

Ali, Tariq (2004), 'This Is Not Sovereignty', <www.zmag.org/sustainers/content/2004–07/03ali.cfm>.

Alia, Valerie (1999), *Un/Covering the North: News, Media, and Aboriginal People*, Vancouver: UBC Press.

Allen, Robert C. (1985), *Speaking of Soap Operas*, Chapel Hill: University of North Carolina.

Allen, Robert C. (ed.) (1992a), *Channels of Discourse, Reassembled: Television and Contemporary Criticism*, London and New York: Routledge.

Allen, Robert C. (1992b), 'Audience-Orientated Criticism and Television', in Robert C. Allen (ed.), *Channels of Discourse, Reassembled: Television and Contemporary Criticism*, London and New York: Routledge.

Allen, Robert C. and Gomery, Douglas (1985), *Film History: Theory and Practice*, New York: Knopf.

Althusser, Louis (1971), *Lenin and Philosophy and Other Essays* (trans. B. Brewster), London: NLB.

Anderson, Christopher (1994), *Hollywood TV: The Studio System in the Fifties*, Austin: University of Texas Press.

Ang, Ien (1985), *Watching Dallas: Soap Opera and the Melodramatic Imagination*, London: Methuen.

Ang, Ien (1991), *Desperately Seeking the Audience*, London and New York: Routledge.

Armstrong, Neil (2005), 'The Filth and the Fury', *Guardian (The Guide)*, 11 September: 4.

Arthurs, Jane (2004), *Television and Sexuality: Regulation and the Politics of Taste*, London: Open University Press.

Attenborough, David (2003), *Life on Air: Memoirs of a Broadcaster,* London: BBC.

Auslander, Philip (1999), *Liveness*, London and New York: Routledge.

Bacon-Smith, Camille (1992), *Enterprising Women: Television Fandom and the Creation of Popular Myth*, Philadelphia: University of Pennsylvania Press.

Bardware.com at: <www.bardware.com/bardware/med-big.jpg>.

Barker, Chris (1999), *Television, Globalization and Cultural Identities*, Buckingham and Philadelphia, PA: Open University Press.

Barker, Martin (1989), *Comics: Ideology, Power and the*

Critics, Manchester: Manchester University Press.

Barker, Martin with Thomas Austin (2000), *From* Antz *to* Titanic*: Reinventing Film Analysis*, London: Pluto Press.

Barnouw, Eric (1966), *A Tower in Babel: A History of Broadcasting in the United States, Volume One – To 1933*, New York: Oxford University Press.

Barnouw, Eric (1968), *The Golden Web: A History of Broadcasting in the United States, Volume Two – 1933 to 1953*, New York: Oxford University Press.

Barnouw, Eric (1970), *The Image Empire: A History of Broadcasting in the United States, Volume Three – From 1953*, New York: Oxford University Press.

Barnouw, Eric (1975), *Tube of Plenty: The Evolution of American Television*, New York: Oxford University Press.

Barrat, D. (1986), *Media Sociology*, London: Tavistock.

Barthes, Roland (1973) [1957], *Mythologies*, London: Vintage Classics.

Barthes, Roland (1975), *S/Z* (trans. R. Miller), New York and London: Cape.

Barthes, Roland (1977a), *Image, Music, Text* (trans. S. Heath), London: Fontana.

Barthes, Roland (1977b), 'The Death of the Author', in Roland Barthes, *Image, Music, Text*, London: Fontana.

Batty, Philip (2003), 'Governing Cultural Difference: The Incorporation of the Aboriginal Subject into the Mechanisms of Government with Reference to the Development of Aboriginal Radio and Television in Central Australia', Unpublished Ph.D. Thesis, School of Communication, University of South Australia.

Baudrillard, Jean (1988), 'Simulacra and Simulations', in Mark Poster (ed.), *Jean Baudrillard: Selected Writings*, Cambridge: Polity Press.

Baym, Nancy (2000), *Tune in, Log on: Soaps, Fandom, and Online Community*, Thousand Oaks, CA London and New Delhi: Sage.

BBC at: <www.bbc.co.uk/radio2/eurovision/2003/history/60s.shtml>.

BBC (2004a), 'Director Generals of the BBC' BBC at: <www.bbc.co.uk/heritage/resources>.

BBC (2004b), *Review of the BBC's Royal Charter. The BBC's Response to the DCMS Consultation*, London: BBC.

Bell, David (2001), *An Introduction to Cybercultures*, London: Routledge.

Bennett, Tony (ed.) (1981), *Popular Television and Film: A Reader*, London: Open University and BFI.

Bennett, Tony, Martin, Graham, Mercer, Colin and Woolacott, Janet (eds) (1992), *Culture, Ideology and Social Process*, London: Batsford and Open University Press.

Berry, Chris, Martin, Fran and Yue, Audrey (2003), *Mobile Cultures: New Media in Queer Asia*, Durham, NC: Duke University Press.

Bignell, Jonathan (1998), *Media Semiotics*, Manchester: Manchester University Press.

Bignell, Jonathan (2004), *An Introduction to Television Studies*, London and New York: Routledge.

Bignell, J., Lacey, S. and Macmurraugh-Kavanagh, M. K. (eds) (2000), *Television Drama: Past, Present and Future*, London: Palgrave.

Bird, S. Elizabeth (2003), *The Audience in Everyday Life: Living in a Media World,* London and New York: Routledge.

Bloustien, Gerry (2002), 'Fans with a Lot at Stake: Serious Play and Mimetic Excess in *Buffy the Vampire Slayer*', in *European Journal of Cultural Studies* vol. 5 no. 4, November: 427–50.

Bloustien, Gerry (2004), 'Buffy Night at the Seven Stars: A "Subcultural" Happening at the Glocal Level', in Andy Bennett and Keith Kahn-Harris (eds), *After Subculture: Critical Studies in Contemporary Youth Culture*, Basingstoke: Palgrave Macmillan.

Blumler, Jay G. (ed.) (1992), *Television and the Public Interest: Vulnerable Values in West European Broadcasting*, London and Newbury Park, CA: Sage

Boddy, William (1990), *Fifties Television: The Industry and Its Critics*, Urbana: University of Illinois Press.

Boddy, William (1995), 'The Beginnings of American Television', in Anthony Smith (ed.), *Television: An International History*, Oxford and New York: Oxford University Press.

Boddy, William (2002), 'New Media as Old Media: Television', in Dan Harries (ed.), *The New Media Book*, London: BFI.

Boddy, William (2003), 'Redefining the Home Screen: Technological Convergence as Trauma and Business Plan', in David Thornburn and Henry

Jenkins (eds), *Rethinking Media Change*, Cambridge, MA: MIT Press.

Bolter, Jay David and Richard Grusin (1999), *Remediation: Understanding New Media*, Cambridge, MA and London: MIT Press.

Bonner, Frances (2003), *Ordinary Television*, London: Sage.

Booker, M. Keith (2002), *Strange TV: Innovative Television Series from* The Twilight Zone *to* The X-Files, Westport, CT: Greenwood Press.

Bordwell, David, Staiger, Janet and Thompson, Kristin (1985), *The Classical Hollywood Cinema: Film Style and Mode of Production to 1960*, London and New York: Routledge.

Bordwell, David and Thompson, Kristin (1990; orig. pub. 1976), *Film Art: An Introduction*, New York: McGraw-Hill.

Boyd, Todd (2003), *Young, Black, Rich and Famous: The Rise of the NBA, the Hip Hop Invasion, and the Transformation of American Culture*, New York: Doubleday.

Brandt, George (ed.) (1981), *British Television Drama*, Cambridge: Cambridge University Press.

Brandt, George (ed.) (1993), *British Television Drama in the Eighties*, Cambridge: Cambridge University Press.

Briggs, Asa (1961), *The History of Broadcasting in the United Kingdom. Volume One: The Birth of Broadcasting*, Oxford: Oxford University Press.

Briggs, Asa (1965), *The History of Broadcasting in the United Kingdom. Volume Two: The Golden Age of Wireless*, Oxford: Oxford University Press.

Briggs, Asa (1970), *The History of Broadcasting in the United Kingdom. Volume Three: The War of Words*, Oxford: Oxford University Press.

Briggs, Asa (1979), *The History of Broadcasting in the United Kingdom. Volume Four: Sound and Vision, 1945–1955*, Oxford: Oxford University Press.

Briggs, Asa (1995), *The History of Broadcasting in the United Kingdom. Volume Five: Competition*, Oxford: Oxford University Press.

Broadcasting Policy Group (2004), *Broadcasting beyond the Charter*, London: Premium Publishing.

Brooker, Will (2003), 'Conclusion: Overflow and Audience', in Will Brooker and Deborah Jermyn (eds), *The Audience Studies Reader*, London and New York: Routledge.

Brooker, Will and Jermyn, Deborah (eds) (2003), *The Audience Studies Reader*, London and New York: Routledge.

Brown, Mary Ellen (1994), *Soap Opera and Women's Talk: The Pleasure of Resistance*, London and New Delhi: Sage.

Browne, Donald. R. (1996), *Electronic Media and Indigenous Peoples: A Voice of Our Own?*, Ames: Iowa State University Press.

Browne, Nick (1984), 'The Political Economy of the Television (Super) Text', *Quarterly Review of Film Studies*, vol. 9 no. 3.

Brunsdon, Charlotte (1990), 'Television: Aesthetics and Audiences', in Patricia Mellencamp (ed.), *Logics of Television: Essays in Cultural Criticism*, Bloomington: Indiana University Press.

Brunsdon, Charlotte (1997), 'Problems of Quality', in Charlotte Brunsdon, *Screen Tastes: Soap Opera to Satellite Dishes*, London and New York: Routledge.

Brunsdon, Charlotte (1998), 'What Is the Television of Television Studies?', in C. Geraghty and D. Lusted (eds), *The Television Studies Book*, London and New York: Arnold.

Brunsdon, Charlotte (2000), *The Feminist, the Housewife and Soap Opera*, Oxford: Clarendon Press.

Brunsdon, Charlotte (2004), 'Taste and Time on Television', *Screen* vol. 45 no. 2.

Brunsdon, Charlotte, D'Acci, Julie and Spigel, Lynn (eds) (1997), *Feminist Television Criticism: A Reader*, Oxford: Clarendon Press.

Bruzzi, Stella (2000), *New Documentary: A Critical Introduction*, London: BFI.

Bruzzi, Stella (2001), 'New Reflexive Documentary – "The Broomfield Film"', in Glen Creeber (ed.), *The Television Genre Book*, London: BFI.

Bryant, S. (1989), *The Television Heritage: Television Archiving Now and in an Uncertain Future,* London: BFI.

Buddle-Crowe, Kathleen (forthcoming), *From Birchbark Talk to Digital Dreamspeaking: A Partial History of Aboriginal Media Activism in Canada*, Lincoln: University of Nebraska Press.

Buonanno, Milly (2004), 'Italian Television', in John Sinclair and Graeme Turner (eds), *Contemporary World Television*, London: BFI.

Burns, Rob (2004), 'German Television', in John Sinclair and Graeme Turner (eds), *Contemporary World Television*, London: BFI.

Buscombe, Edward (1980), 'Creativity in Television', *Screen Education* no. 35, Summer.

Butler, Jeremy G. (1994), *Television: Critical Methods and Applications*, Belmont, CA: Wadsworth.

Buxton, David (1990), *From* The Avengers *to* Miami Vice*: Form and Ideology in Television Series*, Manchester and New York: Manchester University Press.

Caldwell, John Thornton (1995), *Televisuality: Style, Crisis, and Authority in American Television*, New Brunswick, NJ: Rutgers University Press.

Caldwell, John Thornton (2002), 'New Media/Old Augmentations: Television, the Internet, and Interactivity', in *Realism and 'Reality' in Film and Media*, Copenhagen: Museum Tusculanum Press.

Caldwell, John Thornton (2003), 'Second-shift Media Aesthetics', in Anna Everett and John Thornton Caldwell (eds), *New Media: Theories and Practices of Digitextuality*, London and New York: Routledge.

Capsuto, Steven (2000), *Alternate Channels: The Uncensored Story of Gay and Lesbian Images on Television: 1930s to the Present*, New York: Ballantine Books.

Cardwell, Sarah (2002), *Adaptation Revisited: Television and the Classic Novel*, Manchester and New York: Manchester University Press.

Carroll, Noel (2003), *Engaging the Moving Image*, New Haven, CT and London: Yale University Press.

Caughie, John (ed.) (1981), *Theories of Authorship: A Reader*, London and New York: Routledge.

Caughie, John (2000), *Television Drama: Realism, Modernism and British Culture*, Oxford and New York: Oxford University Press.

Celador at: <www.celador.co.uk/productions_history.php>.

Chandler, Daniel (2002), *Semiotics: The Basics*, London and New York: Routledge.

Chase, David (2001), *The Sopranos Scriptbook*, Basingstoke: Macmillan.

Chion, Michel (1995), *David Lynch*, London: BFI.

Clarke, Alan (1986), ' "This Is Not the Boy Scouts": Television Police Series and Definitions of Law and Order', Tony Bennett (ed.)*, Popular Culture and Social Relations* London: Open University.

Cockett, R. (1995), *Thinking the Unthinkable: Think Tanks and the Economic Counter-Revolution, 1931–1983*, London: Fontana.

Collins, Jeff (1992), 'Glasgow University Media Group, The *Bad News* Books', in Martin Barker and Anne Beezer (eds), *Reading into Cultural Studies*, London and New York: Routledge.

Collins, Jim (1992), 'Television and Postmodernism', in Robert C. Allen (ed.), *Channels of Discourse, Reassembled: Television and Contemporary Criticism*, London and New York: Routledge.

Cooke, Lez (2003), *British Television Drama: A History*, London: BFI.

Cormack, Mike (1992), *Ideology*, London: Batsford.

Cormack, Mike (2000), 'The Reassessment of Ideology', in D. Fleming (ed.), *Formations, A 21st Century Media Studies Textbook*, Manchester: Manchester University Press.

Corner, John (ed.) (1991), *Popular Television in Britain: Studies in Cultural History*, London: BFI.

Corner, John (1995), *Television Form and Public Address*, London: Arnold.

Corner, John (1996), *The Art of Record: A Critical Introduction to Documentary*, Manchester: Manchester University Press.

Corner, John (1999), *Critical Ideas in Television Studies*, Oxford: Oxford University Press.

Corner, John (2002), 'Sounds Real: Music and Documentary', *Popular Music* vol. 21 no. 3: 357–67.

Corner, John (2004), 'Television Studies: Plural Contexts, Singular Ambitions?', *Journal of British Cinema and Television* vol. 1 no. 1.

Couldry, Nick (2000), *Inside Culture: Re-imagining the Method of Cultural Studies*, London: Sage.

Courier Mail at: <www.thecouriermail.news.com.au/common/story_page/0,5936,11857635%255E28377,00.html>.

Crawford, Garry (2004), *Consuming Sport: Fans, Sport and Culture*, London and New York: Routledge.

Creeber, Glen (1998), *Between Two Worlds: Dennis Potter*, London and New York: Macmillan.

Creeber, Glen (ed.) (2001), *The Television Genre Book*, London: BFI.

Creeber, Glen (2002), 'TV Ruined the Movies: Television, Tarantino and the Intimate World of *The Sopranos*', in David Lavery (ed.), *This Thing of Ours: Investigating* The Sopranos, New York: Wallflower Press.

Creeber, Glen (2003), 'The Origins of Public Service Broadcasting', in Michele Hilmes (ed.), *The Television History Book*, London: BFI.

Creeber, Glen (ed.) (2004a), *50 Key Television Programmes*, London: Arnold.

Creeber, Glen (2004b), ' "Hideously White": British Television, Glocalisation, and National Identity', *Television and New Media* vol. 5 no. 1, February.

Creeber, Glen (2004c), *Serial Television: Big Drama on the Small Screen*, London: BFI.

Creech, Kenneth C. (2003), *Electronic Media Law and Regulation*, London: Focal Press.

Crisell, Andrew (1997), *An Introductory History of British Broadcasting*, London and New York: Routledge.

Curran, James (ed.) (2000), *Media Organisations in Society*, London: Arnold.

Curran, J. and Seaton, J. (1997), *Power without Responsibility*, London: Routledge, 5th ed.

Danaher, Geoff, Schirato, Tony and Webb, Jen (2000), *Understanding Foucault*, London, Thousand Oaks, and New Delhi: Sage.

Davies, John (1994), *Broadcasting and the BBC in Wales*, Cardiff: University of Wales Press.

De Certeau, Michel (1988), *The Practice of Everyday Life,* Berkeley: University of California Press.

Deming, Caren J. (1985), '*Hill Street Blues* as Narrative', *Critical Studies in Mass Communication* vol. 2 no. 1, March.

Department of Culture, Media and Sport; Department of Trade and Industry (2000), 'A New Future for Communications', Norwich: The Stationery Office <www.dcms.gov.uk>.

Derrida, Jacques (1976), *Of Grammatology*, Baltimore, MD and London: Johns Hopkins University Press.

Derrida, Jacques (1978), *Writing and Difference* (trans. A. Bass), London: Routledge and Kegan Paul.

Dinsdale, Alfred (1928), *Television*, London: Television Press.

Dobson, Sean (2004), 'Tailored Television', *The Guardian*, 26 February. Online at: <media.guardian.co.uk/newmedia/story/0,7496,1156849,00.html> [accessed July 2004].

Doig, A. (1997), 'The Decline of Investigatory Journalism', in M. Bromley and T. O'Malley (eds), *A Journalism Reader*, London: Routledge.

Dovey, Jon (2000), *Freakshow: First Person Media and Factual Television*, London: Pluto Press.

Dowmunt, Tony (ed.) (1993), *Channels of Resistance: Global Television and Local Empowerment*, London: BFI.

Doyle, Waddick (2004), 'French Television', in John Sinclair and Graeme Turner (eds), *Contemporary World Television*, London: BFI.

Dyer, Richard (ed.) (1977), *Gays and Film*, London: BFI.

Eagleton, Terry (1991), *Ideology: An Introduction*, London: Verso.

Early Television at: <www.earlytelevision.org/index.html>.

Eco, Umberto (1972), 'Towards a Semiotic Enquiry into the Television Message' (translated from the 1965 Italian original), *Working Papers in Cultural Studies* no. 3, Birmingham: University of Birmingham.

Eco, Umberto (1979), 'A Guide to the Narrative Structure in Fleming', in *The Role of the Reader*, Bloomington: Indiana State University Press.

Eco, Umberto (1986), 'A Guide to the Neo-television of the 1980s', *Framework* vol. 25.

Edgerton, Gary R. (2004), 'The Moon Landing', in Glen Creeber (ed.), *50 Key Television Programmes*, London: Arnold.

Edgerton, Gary and Nicholas, Kyle (forthcoming), 'I Want My Niche TV: Genre as Networking Strategy in the Digital Era', in Gary Edgerton and Brian Rose (eds), *Thinking Outside the Box: Television Genres in Transition*, Lexington: University of Kentucky Press.

Edwards, David (2004), 'Let Freedom Reign – the Big Lie', <www.zmag.org/sustainers/content/2004–0703edwards.cfm>.

Ellis, John (1982), *Visible Fictions: Cinema, Television, Video*, London and New York: Routledge.

Ellis, John (2000), *Seeing Things: Television in the Age of Uncertainty*, London and New York: I. B. Tauris.

Endemol at: <www.endemol.com/format_descriptions.xml?id=1>.

European Environment Agency at: <themes.eea.eu.int/Environmental_issues/climate/indicators/Kyoto_Protocol_targets/yir99cc5.pdf>.

Everett, Anna (2003), 'Digitextuality and Click Theory: Theses on Convergence Media in the Digital Age', in Anna Everett and John Thornton Caldwell (eds), *New Media: Theories and Practices of Digitextuality*, London and New York: Routledge.

Fairclough, Norman (1995), *Media Discourse*, London: Arnold.

Fanthome, C. (2003), *Channel 5: The Early Years*, Luton: University of Luton Press.

Feuer, Jane (1992), 'Genre Study and Television', in Robert C. Allen (ed.), *Channels of Discourse, Reassembled: Television and Contemporary Criticism*, London and New York: Routledge.

Feuer, Jane (1995), *Seeing through the Eighties: Television and Reaganism*, Durham, NC: Duke University Press.

Feuer, Jane, Kerr, Paul and Vahimagi, Tise (eds) (1984), *MTM: 'Quality Television'*, London: BFI.

Fiddy, Dick (2001), *Missing Believed Wiped: Searching for the Lost Treasures of British Television*, London: BFI.

Fiske, John (1982), *Introduction to Communication Studies*, London: Routledge.

Fiske, John (1983), '*Doctor Who*: Ideology and the Reading of a Popular Narrative Text', *Australian Journal of Screen Theory* nos 13–14.

Fiske, John (1987), *Television Culture*, London and New York: Methuen.

Fiske, John (1989), *Understanding Popular Culture,* London: Unwin Hyman.

Fiske, John (1992a), 'Television and British Cultural Studies', in Robert C. Allen (ed.), *Channels of Discourse, Reassembled: Television and Contemporary Criticism*, London and New York: Routledge.

Fiske, John (1992b), 'The Cultural Economy of Fandom', in Lisa A. Lewis (ed.), *The Adoring Audience*, New York and London: Routledge.

Fiske, John and Hartley, John (1978), *Reading Television*, London and New York: Routledge.

Flichy, Patrice (1995), *Dynamics of Modern Communication: The Shaping and Impact of New Communication Technologies*, London: Sage.

Flichy, Patrice (1999), 'The Construction of New Digital Media', *New Media and Society* vol. 1 no. 1: 33–8.

Flitterman-Lewis, Sandy (1992), 'Psychoanalysis, Film, and Television', in Robert C. Allen (ed.), *Channels of Discourse, Reassembled: Television and Contemporary Criticism*, London and New York: Routledge.

Foucault, Michel (1984), *The Foucault Reader*, (ed. Paul Rabinow), London: Penguin.

Franklin, Bob (2001), *British Television Policy: A Reader*, London and New York: Routledge.

Franzwa, Helen H. (1978), 'The Image of Women in Television: An Annotated Bibliography', in Gaye Tuchman (ed.), *Hearth and Home: Images of Women in the Media*, New York: Oxford University Press.

Friedberg, Anne (2002), 'CD and DVD', in Dan Harries (ed.), *The New Media Book*: London: BFI.

Gamman, Lorraine (1988), 'Watching the Detectives: The Enigma of the Female Gaze', in Lorraine Gamman and Margaret Marshment (eds), *The Female Gaze: Women as Viewers of Popular Culture*, London: Women's Press.

Gauntlett, David (1998), 'Ten Things Wrong with the "Effects" Model', in Roger Dickinson, Ramaswami Harindranath and Loga Linné (eds), *Approaches to Audiences: A Reader*, London: Arnold.

Gauntlett, David and Hill, Annette (1999), *TV Living: Television, Culture and Everyday Life*, London and New York: Routledge.

Geraghty, Christine and Lusted, David (eds) (1998), *The Television Studies Book*, London and New York: Arnold.

Gerbner, George (1970), 'Cultural Indicators: The Case of Violence in Television Drama', *Annals of the American Academy of Political Social Science*, 388: 9–81.

Gesser, Hans (2004), 'Towards a Sociological Theory of the Mobile Phone', University of Zurich, Release 30, March 2004. Online at: <www.socio.ch/mobile/t_geser1.htm>.

Gibson, Owen (2004), 'Greg Dyke Resigns', 29 January, *The Guardian*: 1.

Gillespie, Marie (1995), *Television, Ethnicity and Cultural Change*, London and New York: Routledge.

Ginsburg, Faye (1991), 'Indigenous Media: Faustian Contract or Global Village?', *Cultural Anthropology* vol. 6 no. 1: 92–112.

Ginsburg, Faye (1993), 'Aboriginal Media and the Australian Imaginary', *Public Culture* vol. 5 no. 3: 557–78.

Ginsburg, Faye (2002), 'Screen Memories: Resignifying the Traditional in Indigenous Media', in Faye Ginsburg, Lila Abu-Lughod and Brian Larkin (eds), *Media Worlds: Anthropology on New Terrain*, Berkeley: University of California Press.

Gitelman, Lisa and Pingree, Geoffrey (2003), *New Media, 1740–1915*, Cambridge, MA: MIT Press.

Gitlin, Todd (1994), 'Prime Time Ideology: The Hegemonic Process in Television Entertainment', in Horace Newcomb (ed.), *Television: The Critical View*, New York and Oxford: Oxford University Press.

Glasgow Media Group (1976), *Bad News*, London: Routledge.

Goddard, Peter (2004), '*World in Action*', in Glen Creeber (ed.), *50 Key Television Programmes*, London: Arnold.

Graham, Andrew and Davies, Gavyn (1997), *Broadcasting, Society and Policy in the Multimedia Age*, Luton: University of Luton Press.

Gramsci, Antonio (1971), *Selections from the Prison Notebook* (ed. and trans. Quintin Hoare and Geoffrey Nowell-Smith), London: Lawrence and Wishart.

Gray, Jonathan (2003), 'New Audiences, New Textualities: Anti-fans and Non-fans', *International Journal of Cultural Studies* vol 6 no. 1: 64–81.

Greenslade, Roy (2003), 'Their Master's Voice', *The Guardian*, 17 February: 2.

Gripsrud, Jostein (1998), 'Television, Broadcasting, Flow: Key Metaphors in TV Theory', in Christine Geraghty and David Lusted (eds), *The Television Studies Book*, London and New York: Arnold.

Gripsrud, Jostein (2002), 'Fans, Viewers and Television Theory', in Philippe Le Guern (ed.), *Les Cultes Médiatiques*, Rennes: Presses Universitaires de Rennes.

Gumbels, Andrew (2005), 'Sins of the Flesh', *The Independent Review*, 19 August: 2.

Gurevitch, Michael and Scannell, Paddy (2003), 'Canonization Achieved? Stuart Hall's "Encoding/Decoding"', in Elihu Katz, John Durham Peters, Tamar Liebes and Avril Orloff (eds), *Canonic Texts in Media Research*, Cambridge: Polity Press.

Hall, Stuart (1977), 'Culture, the Media and the "Ideological Effect"', in James Curran, Michael Gorevich and Janet Woolacot (eds), *Mass Communication and Society*, London: Arnold.

Hall, Stuart (1980a), 'Encoding and Decoding in Television Discourse', CCCS Stencilled Paper no. 7; also in Stuart Hall, Dorothy Hobson, Andrew Lowe and Paul Willis (eds), *Culture, Media, Language*, London: Hutchinson; also in Simon During (ed.) (1993), *The Cultural Studies Reader*, London and New York: Routledge.

Hall, Stuart, Hobson Dorothy, Lowe, Andrew and Willis, Paul (eds) (1980b), *Culture, Media, Language*, London: Hutchinson.

Hall, Stuart (1982), 'The Rediscovery of "Ideology": Return of the Repressed in Media Studies', in Michael Gurevitch, Tony Bennett, James Curran and Janet Woollacott (eds), *Culture, Society and the Media*, London and New York: Methuen.

Hall, Stuart and Whannel, Paddy (1964), *The Popular Arts*, London: Hutchinson Educational.

Halloran, James (1970), *The Effects of Television*, London: Panther.

Hardy, F. (ed.) (1966), *Grierson on Documentary*, London: Faber.

Hardy, Forsyth (1979), *John Grierson: A Documentary Biography*, London and Boston, MA: Faber.

Harries, Dan (ed.) (2002), *The New Media Book*, London: BFI.

Harrington, C. Lee and Bielby, Denise (1995), *Soap Fans: Pursuing Pleasure and Making Meaning in Everyday Life*, Philadelphia, PA: Temple University Press.

Hartley, John (1982), *Understanding News*, London and New York: Routledge.

Hartley, John (1996), *Popular Reality: Journalism, Modernity, Popular Culture*, London: Arnold.

Hartley, John (1999), *Uses of Television*, London and New York: Routledge.

Hartley, John (2002), 'Textual Analysis', in Toby Miller (ed.), *Television Studies*, London: BFI.

Hartley, John (2004), 'Kiss Me Kat: Shakespeare, *Big Brother*, and the Taming of the Self,' in Susan Murray and Laurie Ouellette (eds), *Reality TV: Re-making Television Culture*, New York: New York University Press.

Hartley, John and Alan McKee (2000), *The Indigenous Public Sphere: The Reporting and Reception of Indigenous Issues in the Australian Media, 1994–1997*, London: Oxford University Press

Hill, Annette (2005), *Reality TV*, London: Routledge.

Hills, Matt (2002), *Fan Cultures*, London and New York: Routledge.

Hills, Matt (2003), '*Star Wars* in Fandom, Film Theory, and the Museum: The Cultural Status of the Cult Blockbuster', in Julian Stringer (ed.), *Movie Blockbusters,* London and New York: Routledge.

Hills, Matt (2004a), 'Defining Cult TV: Texts, Inter-texts and Fan Audiences', in Robert C. Allen and Annette Hill (eds), *The Television Studies Reader*, London and New York: Routledge.

Hills, Matt (2004b), 'Strategies, Tactics and the Question of *Un Lieu Propre*: What/ Where Is "Media Theory"?', *Social Semiotics* vol. 14 no. 2: 133–49.

Hills, Matt (2004c), '*Star Trek*', in Glen Creeber (ed.), *50 Key Television Programmes*, London: Arnold.

Hilmes, Michele (ed.) (2003), *The Television History Book*, London: BFI.

HMSO (1986), *Report of the Committee on Financing the BBC*, London: HMSO, Cmnd. 9824.

Hobson, Dorothy (1982), *Crossroads: The Drama of a Soap Opera,* London: Methuen.

Hodge, Robert and Tripp, David (1986), *Children and Television: A Semiotic Approach*, Cambridge: Polity Press.

Hoggart, Richard (1960), 'The Uses of Television', *Encounter* vol. 76.

Holden, Windsor (2004), *Digital Terrestrial TV: Prospects in the Enlarged European Union*, Juniper Research: <www.juniperresearch.com>.

Holland, Patricia (1997), *The Television Handbook*, London and New York: Routledge.

Holmes, Sue and Jermyn, Deborah (2004), *Understanding Reality Television*, London and New York: Routledge.

Houston, Beverle (1984), 'Viewing Television: The Metapsychology of Endless Consumption', *Quarterly Review of Film Studies* vol. 9 no. 3.

Iosifidis, Petros, Steemers, Jeanette and Wheeler, Mark (2005), 'European Television in the Digital Age', in Petros Iosifidis, Jeanette Steemers and Mark Wheeler, *European Television Industries*, London: BFI.

Iser, Wolfgang (1974), *The Implied Reader*, Baltimore, MD: Johns Hopkins University Press.

Izod, John and Kilborn, Richard, with Hibberd, Matthew (eds) (2000), *From Grierson to Docu-Soap: Breaking the Boundaries*, Luton: University of Luton Press.

Jacobs, Jason (2000), *The Intimate Screen: Early British Television Drama*, Oxford: Oxford University Press.

Jacobs, Jason (2001), 'Issues of Judgement and Value in Television Studies', *International Journal of Cultural Studies* vol. 4. no. 4, December.

Jacobs, Jason (2003), *Body Trauma TV: The New Hospital Dramas*, London: BFI.

James, Clive (1977), *Visions before Midnight: Television Criticism from* The Observer*, 1972–76*, London: Jonathan Cape.

James, Clive (1981) *The Crystal Bucket: Television Criticism from* The Observer*, 1976–79*, London: Jonathan Cape.

James, Clive (1983), *Glued to the Box: Television Criticism from* The Observer*, 1979–82*, London: Jonathan Cape.

Jancovich, Mark (1992) 'David Morley, The *Nationwide Studies*', in Martin Barker and Anne Beezer (eds), *Reading into Cultural Studies*, London and New York: Routledge.

Jancovich, Mark and Lyons, James, (eds) (2003), *Quality Popular Television: Cult TV, the Industry and Fans*, London: BFI.

Jeffries, S. (2001), *Mrs Slocombe's Pussy: Growing Up in Front of the Telly*, Manchester: Flamingo.

Jenkins, Henry (1992), *Textual Poachers: Television Fans and Participatory Culture*, New York and London: Routledge.

Jenkins, Henry (2002), 'Interactive Audiences?', in Dan Harries (ed.), *The New Media Book*, London: BFI.

Jenkins, Henry (2003), 'Quentin Tarantino's Star Wars? Digital Cinema, Media Convergence, and Participatory Culture', in David Thornburn and Henry Jenkins (eds), *Rethinking Media Change*, Cambridge, MA: MIT Press.

Jenkins, Keith (1991), *Re-Thinking History*, London and New York: Routledge.

Jensen, Joli (1992), 'Fandom as Pathology: The Consequences of Characterization', in Lisa A. Lewis (ed.), *The Adoring Audience*, New York and London: Routledge.

Jhally, Sut and Lewis, Justin (1992), *Enlightened Racism: The Cosby Show, Audiences, and the Myth of the American Dream*, Boulder, CO: Westview Press.

Johnson, C. (forthcoming), *Telefantasy*, London: BFI.

Kagan, Robert (2003), *Of Paradise and Power: America and Europe in the New World Order,* New York: Knopf.

Kaplan, E. Ann (1987), *Rock around the Clock: Music Television, Postmodernism and Consumer Culture*, London: Methuen.

Kaplan, E. Ann (1992), 'Feminist Criticism and Television', in Robert C. Allen (ed.), *Channels of Discourse, Reassembled: Television and Contemporary Criticism*, London and New York: Routledge.

Katz, E. and Liebes, T. (1985) 'Mutual Aid in the Decoding of *Dallas*: Preliminary Notes from a Cross-Cultural Study', in P. Drummond and R. Paterson (eds), *Television in Transition*, London: BFI.

Kellner, Douglas (2002), 'Television and the Frankfurt School', in Toby Miller, (ed.), *Television Studies*, London: BFI.

Kilborn, Richard and Izod, John (1997), *An Introduction to Television Documentary*, Manchester: Manchester University Press.

King, J. C. H. and Lidchi, Henrietta (1998), *Imaging the Arctic*, Seattle: University of Washington Press.

Kirkham, Pat and Skeggs, Beverley (1998), '*Absolutely Fabulous*: Absolutely Feminist?', in Christine Geraghty and David Lusted (eds), *The Television Studies Book*, London and New York: Arnold.

Kitzinger, Jenny (2004), *Framing Abuse: Media Influence and Public Understanding of Sexual Violence Against Children*, London: Pluto Press.

Konczal, Lisa (2000), 'Content Analysis', in D. Fleming (ed.), *Formations, A 21st Century Media Studies Textbook*, Manchester: Manchester University Press.

Kozloff, Sarah (1992), 'Narrative Theory and Television', in Robert C. Allen, (ed.), *Channels of Discourse, Reassembled: Television and Contemporary Criticism*, London and New York: Routledge.

Lacan, Jacques (1979), *The Four Fundamental Concepts of Psychoanalysis*, London: Hogarth Press.

Lacey, Nick (2000), *Narrative and Genre: Key Concepts in Media Studies*, London and New York: Palgrave.

Lancaster, Kurt (2001), *Interacting with* Babylon 5: *Fan Performances in a Media Universe*, Austin: University of Texas Press.

Lassica, J. D. (2002), '"My News" to Digital Butlers: An In-depth Look at the Different Flavors of Personalization, in *Online Journalism Review*', 25 October.

Lavery, David (ed.) (1995), *Full of Secrets: Critical Approaches to* Twin Peaks, Detroit, IL: Wayne State University Press.

Lavery, David (1996), *Deny All Knowledge: Reading* The X-Files, New York: Syracuse University Press.

Lavery, David (ed.) (2002a), *This Thing of Ours: Investigating* The Sopranos, New York: Wallflower Press.

Lavery, David (2002b), '"Emotional Resonance and Rocket Launchers": Joss Whedon's Commentaries on the *Buffy the Vampire Slayer* DVDs', *Slayage: The Online International Journal of Buffy Studies* no. 6 available at: <www. slayage. tv/essays/slayage6/ Lavery.htm>.

Lazarsfeld, Paul (1948) (ed.), *The Communications of Ideas*, New York: Harper.

Lealand, Geoff and Martin, Helen (2001), *It's All Done with Mirrors: About Television,* Palmerston North, NZ: Dunmore Press.

Leavis, Frank R. (1930), *Mass Civilisation and Minority Culture,* Cambridge: Minority Press.

Leavis, Frank R. (1948), *The Great Tradition,* London: Chatto and Windus.

Lee, Chin-Chuan (ed.) (2003), *Chinese Media, Global Contexts*, London and New York: Routledge.

Leuthold, Steven (1998), *Indigenous Aesthetics: Native Art, Media, and Identity*, Austin: University of Texas Press.

Lewis, Justin (1991), *The Ideological Octopus: An Exploration of Television and Its Audience,* New York: Routledge.

Lewis, Justin (2003), 'Biased Broadcasting Corporation', *The Guardian*, 4 July: 27.

Lewis, Jon E. and Stempel, Penny (eds) (1993), *Cult TV: The Essential Critical Guide*. London, Pavilion Books.

Lewis, Lisa A. (ed.) (1992), *The Adoring Audience*, New York and London: Routledge.

Leys, C. (2001), *Market-Driven Politics: Neoliberal Democracy and the Public Interest*, London: Verso.

Liebes, Tamar (1990), *The Export of Meaning: Cross Cultural Reading of* Dallas, New York: Oxford University Press.

Local Radio Workshop (1983), *Capital: Local Radio and Private Profit*, London: Comedia/LRW.

Lockett, Andrew (2002), 'Cultural Studies and Television', in Toby Miller (ed.), *Television Studies*, London: BFI.

Lotman, Yuri (1990), *The Universe of the Mind: A Semiotic Theory of Culture*, Bloomington: Indiana University Press.

Lury, Karen (2005), *Interpreting Televison*, London: Arnold.

Lyotard, Jean-François (1984), *The Postmodern Condition: A Report on Knowledge*, (trans. G. Bennington and B. Massumi), Manchester: Manchester University Press.

Machor, James and Goldstein, Philip (eds) (2001), *Reception Study: From Literary Theory to Cultural Studies*, London and New York: Routledge.

Man Chan, Joseph (2004), 'Television in Greater China', in John Sinclair and Graeme Turner (eds), *Contemporary World Television*, London: BFI.

Marc, D. (1997), *Comic Visions: Television Comedy and American Culture*, Malden, MA and Oxford: Blackwell.

Marconi, Maria Cristina (1999), *Marconi My Beloved*, Boston, MA: Dante University of America Press.

Marsden, Chris and Verhulst, Steffan (eds) (1999), *Convergence in the European Digital TV Regulation*, London: Blackstone.

Masterman, Len, (1984), *Television Mythologies: Stars, Shows and Signs*, London: Comedia.

Marx, Karl (1982), *Critique of Hegel's 'Philosophy of Right'* (ed. Joseph O'Malley), London and New York: Cambridge University Press.

Marx, Karl (with Friedrich Engels) (1998), *The German Ideology*, New York: Prometheus Books.

Mathijus, Ernest and Jones, Janet (eds) (2004), Big Brother *International: Formats, Critics and Publics*, London and New York: Wallflower Press.

McArthur, Colin (1985) 'Historical Drama', in Tony Bennett *et al.* (eds), *Popular Television and Film*, London: BFI and Open University Press.

McChesney, Robert (2000), *Rich Media, Poor Democracy: Communication Policy in Dubious Times*, Champaign: University of Illinois Press.

McIntosh, Neil (2004), 'TV Meets PC in Microsoft's Digital Home', *The Guardian*, 9 January 2004. Online at: <media.guardian.co.uk/newmedia/story/0,7496, 1119422,00.html> [accessed July 2004].

McKee, Alan (2002), 'Fandom', in Toby Miller (ed.), *Television Studies*, London: BFI.

McKee, Alan (2003), *Textual Analysis: A Beginner's Guide*, London, Thousand Oaks and New Delhi: Sage.

McKee, Alan (2004), 'How to Tell the Difference between Production and Consumption: A Case Study in *Doctor Who* Fandom', in Sara Gwenllian Jones and Roberta Pearson (eds), *Cult Television*, Minneapolis: University of Minnesota Press.

McLuhan, Marshall (1962), *The Gutenberg Galaxy*, London: Routledge and Kegan Paul.

McLuhan, Marshall (1964), *Understanding Media: The Extensions of Man*, London: Routledge and Kegan Paul.

McLuhan, Marshall and Fiore, Quentin (1967), *The Medium Is the Massage*, New York: Bantam/Harmondsworth: Penguin.

McMurria, John (2003), 'Long-format TV: Globalisation and Network Branding in a Multi-Channel Era', (in Mark Jancovich and James Lyons, (eds), *Quality Popular Television: Cult TV, the Industry and Fans*, London: BFI.

McQuail, Denis (1997), *Audience Analysis*, London: Sage.

McQueen, David (1998), *Television: A Media Student's Guide*, London and New York: Arnold.

Meadows, Michael (1994), 'Reclaiming a Cultural Identity: Indigenous Media Production in Australia and Canada', *Continuum: The Australian Journal of Media and Culture* vol. 8. no. 2.

Metz, Christian (1982), *Psychoanalysis and the Cinema*, London and New York: Macmillan.

Meyrowitz, Joshua (1987), *A Sense of Place: Impact of Electronic Media on Social Relations*, New York and Oxford: Oxford University Press.

mGain (2003), 'Mobile Entertainment Industry and Culture: A European Commission User-friendly Information Society (IST) Accompanying Measures Project' IST-2001-38846, 30 April.

Michaels, Eric (1986), 'The Aboriginal Invention of Television in Central Australia: 1982–1986 Canberra', *Australian Institute of Aboriginal Studies*, Canberra.

Michaels, Eric (1994), *Bad Aboriginal Art: Tradition, Media, and Technological Horizons*, Minneapolis: University of Minnesota Press.

Miliband, Ralph (1973), *State in Capitalist Society*, London: Quartet Books.

Miller, David (2003), 'Taking Sides', *The Guardian*, 22 April: 19.

Miller, Toby (1998), *The Avengers*, London: BFI.

Miller, Toby (2002), 'Introduction', in Toby Miller (ed.), *Television Studies*, London: BFI.

Miller, Toby, Govil, Nitin, McMurria, John, Maxwell, Richard and Wang, Ting (2004), *Global Hollywood 2*, London: BFI.

Millington, R. and Nelson, R. (1986), Boys from the Blackstuff: *The Making of TV Drama*, London, Comedia.

Mittell, Jason (2004), *Genre and Television: From Cop Shows to Cartoons in American Culture*, London and New York: Routledge.

Molnar, Helen (1993), 'Indigenous Use of Small Media: Community Radio, BRACS and the Tanami Network', paper presented at CIRCIT seminar, Melbourne, December.

Molnar, Helen and Meadows Michael (2001), *Songlines to Satellites: Indigenous Communications in Australia, the South Pacific and Canada*, Leichardt: Pluto Press.

Moores, Shaun (1993), *Interpreting Audiences: The Ethnography of Media Consumption*, London: Sage.

Moores, Shaun (2000), 'Broadcasting, Narrowcasting and Broadcatching', in D. Fleming (ed.), *Formations, A 21st Century Media Studies Textbook*, Manchester: Manchester University Press.

Moran, Albert (1998), *Copycat Television: Globalisation, Program Formats and Cultural Identity*, Luton: University of Luton Press.

Morley, David (1980), *The* Nationwide *Audience*, London: BFI.

Morley, David (1986), *Family Television: Cultural Power and Domestic Leisure*, London: Comedia.

Morley, David (1992), *Television, Audiences, and Cultural Studies*, London and New York: Routledge.

Morley, David and Robins, Kevin (1995), *Spaces of Identity: Global Media, Electronic Landscapes and Cultural Boundaries*, London: Routledge.

Morley, David and Brunsdon, Charlotte (1999), *The* Nationwide *Television Studies*, London and New York: Routledge.

Morris, Meaghan (1990), 'Banality in Cultural Studies', in Patricia Mellencamp (ed.), *Logics of Television: Essays in Cultural Criticism*, Bloomington: Indiana University Press; London: BFI.

Moseley, Rachel (2003), 'The 1990s: Quality or Dumbing Down?', in Michele Hilmes (ed.), *The Television History Book*, London: BFI.

Mougayar, William (2002), 'Small Screen, Smaller World', *Yale Global Online*, Yale Center for the Study of Globalization, 11 October, at: <claudius. its.yale. edu/ globalization/display.article?id=204>.

Mulvey, Laura (1975), 'Visual Pleasure and Narrative Cinema', *Screen* vol. 16. no. 3, Autumn. Also in Laura Mulvey (1989), *Visual and Other Pleasures*, London: Macmillan.

Mumford, Laura Stempel (1995), *Love and Ideology in the Afternoon: Soap Opera, Women and Television Genre*, Bloomington and Indianapolis: Indiana University Press.

Murray, Janet H. (1997) *Hamlet on the Holodeck: The Future of Narrative in Cyberspace*, Cambridge, MA: MIT Press.

Murray, Simone (2004), '"Celebrating the Story the
Way It Is": Cultural Studies, Corporate Media and
the Contested Utility of Fandom', *Continuum* vol.
18 no. 1: 7–25.

NASA at: <roland.lerc.nasa.gov/~dglover/sat/
telstar.html>.

National Statistics Online at: <www.statistics.gov.uk/
cci/nugget.asp?id=366>.

Nelson, Robin (1997), *TV Drama in Transition: Forms,
Values and Cultural Change*, Basingstoke and New
York: Macmillan/St Martin's Press.

Nelson, Robin (2000) 'TV Drama: "Flexi-narrative"
Form and "A New Affective Order"', in Eckart
Voigts-Virkow (ed.), *Mediatized Drama; Dramatized
Media, Contemporary Drama in English*, vol. 7, Trier:
Wissenschaftlicher Verlag.

Newcomb, H. (ed.) (1997), *Encyclopedia of Television*,
Chicago, IL: Fitzroy Dearborn.

Nichols, Bill (1991), *Representing Reality*, Bloomington
and Indianapolis: Indiana University Press.

Nightingale, Virginia (1996), *Studying Audiences: The
Shock of the Real*, London and New York:
Routledge.

Noam, Eli (1991), *Television in Europe*, New York and
Oxford: Oxford University Press.

Noam, Eli, Groebel, Jo and Gerber, Darcy (2004),
Internet Television, Mahwah, NJ: Lawrence Erlbaum.

Norden, Denis (ed.) (1985), *Coming to You Live!
Behind-the-screen Memories of Forties and Fifties
Television*, London: Methuen.

Noureddine, Miladi (2004), 'Television in the Arabic-
speaking World', in John Sinclair and Graeme
Turner, (eds), *Contemporary World Television*,
London: BFI.

Ofcom (2004), *The Communications Market 2004 –
Overview*, London: Ofcom.

O'Malley, T. (1994), *Closedown? The BBC and
Government Broadcasting Policy, 1979–92*, London:
Pluto Press.

O'Malley, T. (2003), 'Satellite, Cable and New Channels
in the UK' and 'Zircon', in Michele Hilmes (ed.),
The Television History Book, London: BFI.

O'Malley, T. and Treharne, J. (1993), *Selling the Beeb:
The BBC and the Charter Renewal Process*, London:
CPBF.

O'Regan, Tom and Batty, Philip (1993), 'An Aboriginal
Television Culture: Issues, Strategies, Politics', in
Lisa Parks and Shanti Kumar (eds), *Australian
Television Culture*, Sydney: Allen & Unwin.

O'Shaughnessy, Michael (1990), 'Box Pop: Popular
Television and Hegemony', in Andrew Goodwin
and Garry Whannel (eds), *Understanding Television*,
London and New York: Routledge.

O'Sullivan, T. (1991), 'Television Memories and
Cultures of Viewing 1950–65', in John Corner
(ed.), *Popular Television in Britain: Studies in Cultural
History*, London: BFI.

Owen, Rob (1997), *Gen X TV: From The Brady
Bunch to Melrose Place*, Syracuse, NY: Syracuse
University Press.

Paget, Derek (1998), *No Other Way to Tell It:
Dramadoc/Docudrama on Television*, Manchester:
Manchester University Press.

Parks, Lisa (2003), 'US Television Abroad: Exporting
Culture', in Michele Hilmes (ed.), *The Television
History Book*, London: BFI.

Parks, Lisa and Kumar, Shanti (eds) (2003), *Planet TV:
A Global Television Reader*, New York: New York
University Press.

Perkins, Tessa (1979), 'Rethinking Stereotypes', in M.
Barret, P. Corrigan, A. Kuhn and V. Wolff (eds),
Ideology and Cultural Production, London: Croom
Helm.

Philo, Greg and Berry, M. (2004), *Bad News from Israel*,
London: Pluto Press.

Poster, Mark (ed.) (1988), *Jean Baudrillard: Selected
Writings*, Cambridge: Polity Press.

Potter, J. (1989), *Independent Television in Britain. Volume
Three: Politics and Control, 1968–80*, London and
Basingstoke: Macmillan.

Potter, J. (1990), *Independent Television in Britain. Volume
Four: Companies and Programmes, 1968–80*.
Basingstoke: Macmillan.

Probyn, Elspeth (1997), 'New Traditionalism and Post-
Feminism: TV Does the Home', in Charlotte
Brunsdon, Julie D'Acci and Lynn Spigel (eds),
Feminist Television Criticism: A Reader, Oxford:
Clarendon Press.

Propp, Vladimir (1968), *Morphology of the Russian
Folktale*, Austin: University of Texas Press.

Pullen, Kirsten (2004), 'Everybody's Gotta Love Somebody, Sometime: Online Fan Community', in David Gauntlett and Ross Horsley (eds), *Web.Studies*, 2nd edn, London: Arnold.

Purser, P. (1992), *Done Viewing: A Personal Account of the Best Years of Our Television*, London: Quartet.

Rabinovitz, Lauren and Geil, Abraham (2004), *Memory Bites: History, Technology and Digital Culture*, Durham, NC: Duke University Press.

Rampton, Sheldon and Stauber, John (2003), *Weapons of Mass Deception: The Uses of Propaganda in Bush's War on Iraq*, London: Constable and Robinson.

Reuters at: <about.reuters.com/aboutus/history/>.

Rimmon-Kenan, Shlomith (1983), *Narrative Fiction: Contemporary Poetics*, London: Methuen.

Ritzer, George (2004), *The McDonaldization of Society*, rev. edn, Thousand Oaks, CA: Pine Forge Press/Sage.

Roberts, Dan (2005), 'Is the World Falling out of Love with US Brands?', *Yale Global Online*, Yale Center for the Study of Globalization, 5 January, at: <yaleglobal. yale.edu/display.article?id=5109>.

Robertson, Roland (1995), 'Glocalisation: Time-space and Homogeneity–heterogeneity', in M. Featherstone and S. Lash (eds), *Global Modernities*, London: Sage.

Rogers, Mark C., Epstein, Michael and Reeves, Jimmy L. (2002), 'The Sopranos as HBO Brand Equity: The Art of Commerce in the Age of Digital Reproduction', in David Lavery (ed.), *This Thing of Ours: Investigating* The Sopranos, New York: Columbia University Press; London: Wallflower Press.

Rose, Frank (2003), 'The Fast Forward, On-demand, Network Smashing Future of Television', *Wired News* 11.10, October.

Ross, Karen and Nightingale, Virginia (2003), *Media and Audiences: New Perspectives*, Berkshire: Open University Press.

Roth, Lorna (1998), 'Television Broadcasting North of 60', in Leen d'Haenens (ed.), *Images of Canadianness: Visions of Canada's Politics, Culture, Economics*, Ottawa: University of Ottawa.

Roth, Lorna (2000), 'The Crossing of Borders and the Building of Bridges: Steps in the Construction of the Aboriginal Peoples Television Network in Canada', Special Issue on Canadian Communications, *Gazette International Journal of Communication Studies*, vol. 62 nos 3–4: 251–69.

Roth, Lorna (2005), *Something New in the Air: The Story of First Peoples Television Broadcasting in Canada*, Montreal: McGill-Queens University Press.

Ruddock, Andrew (2001), *Understanding Audiences: Theory and Method*, London: Sage.

Ruddock, Andrew (2002), 'Uses and Gratifications Research', in Toby Miller (ed.), *Television Studies*, London: BFI.

Sales, Roger (1986), 'An Introduction to Broadcasting History', in D. Punter (ed.), *Introduction to Contemporary Cultural Studies*, London and New York: Longman.

Sandvoss, Cornel (forthcoming), *Fans and the Mirror of Consumption*, Cambridge: Polity Press.

Sarup, Mandan (1988), *An Introductory Guide to Post-Structuralism and Postmodernism*, New York and London: Harvester Wheatsheaf.

Scannell, P. and Cardiff, D. (1991), *A Social History of British Broadcasting*, Oxford and Cambridge, MA: Blackwell.

Schroder, Kim (1992), 'Cultural Quality: Search for a Phantom', in M. Skovmand and Jeffrey Scource (eds), *Haunted Media: Electronic Presence from Telegraphy to Television*, Durham, NC: Duke University Press.

Schwartz, David, Ryan, Steve and Wostbrock, Fred (1999), *Encyclopaedia of TV Game Shows*, New York: Checkmark Books.

Sconce, Jeffrey (2000), *Haunted Media: Electronic Presence from Telegraphy to Television*, Durham, NC: Duke University Press.

Scott, Peter Graham (2000), *British Television: An Insider's History*, Jefferson, NC: McFarland.

Scott-Clark, Cathy and Levy, Adrian (14 June 2003), 'Fast Forward into Trouble'. *The Guardian* at: <www.guardian.co.uk/weekend/story/0,3605,975 769,00.html>.

Seiter, Ellen (1992), 'Semiotics, Structuralism and Television', in Robert C. Allen (ed.) (1992), *Channels of Discourse, Reassembled: Television and Contemporary Criticism*, London and New York: Routledge.

Seiter, Ellen (1998), *Television and New Media Audiences,* Oxford: Oxford University Press.

Selby, Keith and Cowdery, Ron (1995), *How to Study Television*, London: Macmillan.

Sendall, B. (1982), *Independent Television in Britain. Volume One: Origin and Foundation, 1946–1962*, London: Macmillan.

Sendall, B. (1983), *Independent Television in Britain. Volume Two: Expansion and Change, 1958–1968*, London: Macmillan.

Shakespeare-W.com [The Bard of Avon] at: <www.shakespeare-w.com/english/shakespeare/source.html>.

Shillingford, Joia (2004), 'Broadcast News . . . on the Mobile', *The Guardian,* 4 March. Online at: <media.guardian.co.uk/newmedia/story/0,7496,1 161857, 00.html> [accessed July 2004].

Shinar, Dov (1996), ' "Re-membering" and "Dis-membering" Europe: A Cultural Strategy for Studying the Role of Communication in the Transformation of Collective Identities', in Sandra Brahman and Annabelle Sreberny-Mohammadi (eds), *Globalization, Communication and Transnational Civil Society*, Cresskill, NJ: Hampton Press.

Shukor, Steven (2005), 'From Feminist to *Big Brother* Housemate', *The Guardian*, 7 January.

Siapera, Eugenia (2004), 'From Couch Potatoes to Cybernauts? The Expanding Notion of the Audience on TV Channels' Websites', *New Media & Society* vol. 6 no. 2: 155–72.

Silverstone, Roger (1981), *The Message of Television: Myth and Narrative in Contemporary Culture*, London: Heinemann.

Silverstone, Roger (1999), *Why Study the Media?*, London: Sage.

Sinclair, Ian (1995), *The Birth of the Box: The Story of Television*, London: Sigma Press.

Sinclair, John, Jacka, Elizabeth and Cunningham, Stuart (eds) (1996), *New Patterns in Global Television: Peripheral Vision*, Oxford and New York: Oxford University Press.

Sinclair, John and Turner, Graeme (eds) (2004), *Contemporary World Television*, London: BFI.

Siune, K. and Hulten, O. (1998), 'Does Public Broadcasting Have a Future?', in D. McQuail and K. Siune. (eds), *Media Policy: Convergence, Concentration and Commerce*, London: Sage.

Smith, A. D. (1991), *National Identity*, Harmondsworth: Penguin.

Smith, Anthony (ed.) (1995), *Television: An International History*, Oxford and New York: Oxford University Press.

Smythe, Dallas (1993), *Counterclockwise: Perspectives on Communication*, Boulder, CO: Westview Press.

Sondhi, M. L. and Tyagi, K. G. (eds) (2002), *Asia-Pacific Security Globalisation and Developments*, New Delhi: Menas Publications.

Spigel, Lynn (2001), *Welcome to the Dreamhouse: Popular Media and Postwar Suburbs*, Durham, NC: Duke University Press.

Spigel, Lynn and Curtin, M. (1997), *The Revolution Wasn't Televised: Sixties Television and Social Conflict*, New York: Routledge.

Storey, John (ed.) (1993), *Cultural Theory and Popular Culture: An Introductory Guide*, London: Harvester and Wheatsheaf.

Strinati, Dominic (1995), *An Introduction to Theories of Popular Culture,* London and New York: Routledge.

Sweatshop Watch at: swatch.igc.org/global/index.html.

Sydney Morning Herald at: <www.smh.com.au/news/Asia-Tsunami-braces-for-death- toll-not-seen-since-war-with-Denmarkin1814/2005/01/03/1104601300972. html>.

Taylor, Don (1990), *Days of Vision. Working with David Mercer: Television Drama Then and Now*, London: Methuen.

Thomas, K. (1992), 'Introduction', in J. B. Roodenburg (ed.), *A Cultural History of Gesture*, Ithaca, NY: Cornell University Press.

Thomas, Lyn (2002), *Fans, Feminisms and 'Quality' Media*, London and New York: Routledge.

Thompson, Robert J. (1996), *Television's Second Golden Age*, New York: Continuum.

Thornton, Sarah (1995), *Club Cultures: Music, Media and Subcultural Capital*, Cambridge: Polity Press.

Thumim, Janet (ed.) (2002), *Small Screens, Big Ideas: Television in the 1950s*, London and New York: I. B. Tauris.

Todorov, Tzvetan (1977), *The Poetics of Prose*, Oxford: Blackwell.

Tomlinson, John (1999), *Globalization and Culture*, Cambridge: Polity Press.

Tremblay, Gaëtan (2004), 'Canadian Television', in John Sinclair and Graeme Turner (eds), *Contemporary World Television*, London: BFI.

Tuchman, Gaye (ed.) (1978), *Hearth and Home: Images of Women in the Mass Media*, New York: Oxford University Press.

Tulloch, John (1990), *Television Drama: Agency, Audience and Myth*, London and New York: Routledge.

Tulloch, John (2000), *Watching Television Audiences: Cultural Theories and Methods*, London and New York: Arnold.

Tulloch, John and Alvarado, Manuel (1983), Doctor Who: *The Unfolding Text*, London: Macmillan.

Tulloch, John and Jenkins, Henry (1995), *Science Fiction Audiences: Watching* Doctor Who *and* Star Trek, London: Routledge.

Turner, Graeme (1990), *British Cultural Studies: An Introduction*, London and New York: Routledge.

Uricchio, William (2004), 'Technologies of Time', in Lynn Spigel and Jan Olsson (eds), *Television after TV: Essays on a Medium in Transition,* Durham, NC: Duke University Press. Online at: <www.let.uu.nl/~william.uricchio/personal/OLSSON2.html>.

Vahimagi, T. (1996), *British Television: An Illustrated Guide*, Oxford and New York: Oxford University Press.

Vartanova, Elna (2004), 'Television in Russia', in John Sinclair and Graeme Turner (eds), *Contemporary World Television*, London: BFI.

Verna, Tony (1993), *Global Television: How to Create Effective Television for the Future,* Boston, MA: Focal Press.

Vervliet, Hendrik D. L. (1972), *The Book through 5000 Years*, London: Phaidon/Brussels: Editions Arcade.

Volosinov, Valentin (1973), *Marxism and the Philosophy of Language*, New York: Seminar Press.

Wagg, Stephen (ed.) (1998), *Because I Tell a Joke or Two: Comedy, Politics and Social Difference*, London and New York: Routledge.

Warley, Stephen and Sheridan, James (2004), 'VOD: The Road to Mass Personalization', *TV Spy,*

Online at: <www.tvspy.com/nexttv/nexttvcolumn.cfm?t_nexttv_id=1904&page=1&t_content_cat_id=10>.

Wayne, Mike (2003), *Marxism and Media Studies: Key Concepts and Contemporary Trends*, London: Pluto Press.

Weight, R. (2002), *Patriots: National Identity in Britain 1940–2000,* London: Pan.

Weymouth, Tony and Lamizet (eds) (1996), *Markets and Myths: Forces for Change in the European Media*, London and New York: Longman.

Wheen, F. and Fiddick, P. (1985), *Television: A History*, London: Century.

Wikipedia: (atmosphere): <en.wikipedia.org/wiki/Earth%27s_atmosphere> (biosphere): <en.wikipedia.org/wiki/Biosphere> (noosphere): <en.wikipedia.org/wiki/Noosphere> (Vernadsky): <en.wikipedia.org/wiki/Vladimir_I._Vernadsky>.

Wilcox, Rhonda V. and Lavery, David (eds) (2002), *Fighting the Forces: What's at Stake in* Buffy the Vampire Slayer?, Boston, MA: Rowman & Littlefield.

Williams, Kevin (1998), *Get Me a Murder a Day: A History of Mass Communications in Britain,* London: Arnold.

Williams, Kevin (2003), *Understanding Media Theory*, London and New York: Arnold.

Williams, Raymond (1974), *Television, Technology and Cultural Form*, London and New York: Routledge.

Wimsatt, William K. and Beardsley, Monroe C. (1998), 'The Intentional Fallacy', in David Richter (ed.), *The Critical Tradition: Classic Texts and Critical Trends*, Boston, MA: Bedford.

Winston, Brian (2000), *Lies, Damn Lies and Documentaries,* London: BFI.

Winston, Brian (2003), 'The Development of Television', in M. Hilmes (ed.), *The Television History Book*, London: BFI.

Wortham, Erica (2002), 'Narratives of Location: Televisual Media and the Production of Indigenous Identities in Mexico', unpublished dissertation, Department of Anthropology, New York University.

Wright, Will (1975), *Sixguns and Society*, Berkeley:
    University of California Press.
    xtvworld.com at: <www.xtvworld.com/tv/bbc/
    tv_is_coming_back.htm>.
Zielinski, Siegfried (1999), *Audiovisions: Cinema and
    Television as Entr'actes in History*, Amsterdam:
    Amsterdam University Press.

Zoonen, Liesbet van (1994), *Feminist Media Studies*,
    London and New Delhi: Sage.

Note: All websites cited were last accessed by the editor
in spring 2005.

Index

LIST OF ILLUSTRATIONS

Whilst considerable effort has been made to correctly identify the copyright holders, this has not been possible in all cases. We apologise for any apparent negligence and any omissions or corrections brought to our attention will be remedied in any future editions.

The Avengers, ABC; *The Price is Right,* ABC/Mark Goodson–Bill Todman Productions/NBC; *The Cosby Show,* Bill Cosby/Carsey-Werner Company/NBC; *The Long Day Closes,* Film Four International/BFI Production; *Hill Street Blues,* MTM Enterprises Inc./NBC; *Cathy Come Home,* BBC; *Are You Being Served?,* BBC; *Star Trek,* Desilu Productions Inc./Norway Corporation/Paramount Television; *Sex and the City,* Darren Star Productions/HBO/Sex and the City Productions; *Kurt and Courtney,* Strength Ltd; *Big Brother,* Bazal/Brighter Pictures/Channel 4 Television Corporation/Endemol Entertainment UK; *Wife Swap,* Channel 4 Television Corporation; *Marty,* BBC; *24,* Imagine Entertainment/20th Century Fox Television; *The Sopranos,* HBO/Brad Grey Television/Chase Films/Soprano Productions Inc.; *The Prisoner,* Everyman Films/ITC; *Twin Peaks,* Lynch/Frost Productions/Spelling Entertainment/Twin Peaks Productions Inc.; *Buffy the Vampire Slayer,* 20th Century Fox Television/Mutant Enemy/Kuzui Enterprises/Sandollar Television/Mel Underwood Water Truck Inc.; *Doctor Who,* BBC; *Bonanza,* NBC; *The Black and White Minstrel Show,* BBC; *Dallas,* NBC; *Who Wants to be a Millionaire?,* Celador Productions.